Anglican Theology

Anglican Theology

Postcolonial Perspectives

Edited by
James Tengatenga
and
Stephen Burns

scm press

© James Tengatenga and Stephen Burns 2024

Published in 2024 by SCM Press
Editorial office
3rd Floor, Invicta House,
110 Golden Lane,
London EC1Y 0TG, UK

www.scmpress.co.uk

SCM Press is an imprint of Hymns Ancient & Modern Ltd
(a registered charity)

Hymns Ancient & Modern® is a registered trademark of
Hymns Ancient & Modern Ltd
13A Hellesdon Park Road, Norwich,
Norfolk NR6 5DR, UK

British Library Cataloguing in Publication data
A catalogue record for this book is available from the British Library

ISBN: 978-0-334-06623-1

Typeset by Regent Typesetting
Printed and bound by
CPI Group (UK) Ltd

Contents

Contributors

Patrick Bendera died in 2023. He was a priest in the Anglican Church of Tanzania. He recorded and edited the memoirs of Archbishop John Ramadhani, essential to the chapter on him in this book.

Herman Browne is former President of Cuttington University, Suacoco, Liberia, and was the 2023 visiting scholar at Virginia Theological Seminary (USA). His publications include *Grasshoppers No Longer: Critical Essays in Western Cultural History, Theology and Philosophy* (Sibiu: Sibiu Press, 2008) and *Know Your Church: The Many Ways to Serve the Episcopal Church of Liberia* (Monrovia: Graceland Publishers, 2021).

Stephen Burns is Professor of Liturgical and Practical Theology at Pilgrim Theological College, University of Divinity, Melbourne, Australia. His publications include *Postcolonial Practice of Ministry: Leadership, Liturgy, Interfaith Engagement*, co-edited with Kwok Pui-lan (Lanham: Lexington, 2016), *Feminist Theology: Interstices and Fractures*, co-edited with Rebekah Pryor (Lanham: Lexington, 2023), *From the Shores of Silence: Conversations in Feminist Practical Theology*, co-edited with Ashley Cocksworth and Rachel Starr (London: SCM Press, 2023), *Conversations about Divine Mystery*, co-edited with HyeRan Kim-Cragg (Minneapolis: Fortress Press, 2023) and three collections of Ann Loades's work: *Grace and Glory in One Another's Faces: Preaching and Worship*, ed. (Norwich: Canterbury Press, 2020), *Grace is Not Faceless: Reflections on Mary*, ed. (London: Darton, Longman and Todd, 2021) and *Explorations in Twentieth Century Theology and Philosophy: People Preoccupied with God*, ed. (London: Anthem Press, 2023). He edits the *International Journal for the Study of the Christian Church*.

Carlos Eduardo Calvani is Professor of Sciences of Religion: Phenomenology and Theology in the Federal University of Sergipe, Brazil. His publications include *Teologia and Brazilan Popular Music* (São Paulo: Loyola, 1998), *Teologia da Arte* (São Paulo: Paulinas/Fonte Editorial, 2010), *Religião: linguagens* (Curitiba: CRV, 2020), *Ite, missa est: tensões* *e conflitos na história do gênero musical missa* (São Cristóvão: Editora UFS, 2021) and articles in *Anglican Theological Review*, *Correlatio*, and *Numen*.

Julius Gathogo is a visiting distinguished Professor of Missiology and Historiography at the ANCCI University, Amarillo, Texas, USA, a senior lecturer at Kenyatta University, near Nairobi, Kenya, and a long-serving research fellow at the Research Institute of Theology and Religion, University of South Africa, Pretoria, South Africa. His publications number over 200, one being *Beyond Mount Kenya Region* (Nairobi: Evangel, 2017).

Michael Jagessar is a minister of the United Reformed Church, UK. He served as racial justice and intercultural ministry consultant and as national moderator. He was until recently Secretary for Europe and the Caribbean, Council for World Mission. His publications include *Black Theology in Britain: A Reader*, co-edited with Anthony G. Reddie (Sheffield: Equinox, 2007), *Christian Worship: Postcolonial Perspectives*, co-authored with Stephen Burns (Sheffield: Equinox, 2011) and *At Home with God and in the World: A Philip Potter Reader*, co-edited with Andrea Fröchtling et al. (Geneva: World Council of Churches Publications, 2013).

Stephen Kapinde is a post-doctoral scholar at Polin Institute, Abo Akademi University, Turku, Finland, and lecturer in religion and public life, Pwani University near Mombasa, Kenya. His publications include articles in the *Journal of Anglican Studies*.

Fergus J. King is lecturer in theology at Trinity College Theological School, University of Divinity, Melbourne, Australia. His publications include *Epicureanism and the Gospel of John: A Study of their Compatibility* (Tübingen: Mohr Siebeck, 2020), *A Missional Introduction to the New Testament* (North Augusta: Missional UP, 2021) and *Nuru na Uzima: Essays Celebrating the Golden Jubilee of the Anglican Church of Tanzania, 1970–2020*, co-edited with Emmanuel Mbennah et al. (North Augusta: Missional UP, 2021).

Cynthia Briggs Kittredge is Dean and President of the Seminary of the Southwest in Austin, Texas, USA. Her publications include *The Fortress Commentary on the New Testament*, co-edited with Margaret Aymer and David Sánchez (Minneapolis: Fortress Press, 2014), *A Lot of the Ways Trees Were Walking: Poems from the Gospel of Mark* (Eugene:

Wipf & Stock, 2015) and Wisdom Bible Commentary on *Philippians, Colossians, Philemon*, co-authored with Elsa Tamez et al. (Collegeville: Liturgical Press, 2017).

Henry Mbaya is Professor of Church History in the Faculty of Theology, Stellenbosch University, South Africa. His publications include *Resistance to and Acquiescence in Apartheid: St Paul's Anglican Theological College, Grahamstown, 1965–1992* (Stellenbosch: SunMedia Publications, 2018), and articles in the *Journal of Anglican Studies* and *Anglican and Episcopal History*.

Karen Meredith is Executive Director of EfM – Education for Ministry in the School of Theology, University of the South, Sewanee, Tennessee, USA.

Maimbo W. F. Mndolwa is Bishop of Tanga and Archbishop of the Anglican Church of Tanzania. His publications include articles in the *Journal of Anglican Studies* and *Mission Studies*.

Esther Mombo is Professor of Church History and Theology from women's perspectives at St Paul's University, Limuru, Kenya. Her publications include *Disability, Society and Theology: Voices from Africa*, co-edited with Samuel Kabue et al. (Nairobi: Zapf Chancellor, 2012), *The Postcolonial Church: Bible, Theology, Mission*, co-edited with R. S. Wufula (Alamanda: Borderless Press, 2016), *Mother Earth, Postcolonial and Liberation Theologies*, co-edited with Sophie Chirongoma (Minneapolis: Fortress Press, 2021).

Keun-joo Christine Pae is Associate Professor of Religion and Women's and Gender Studies as well as chair of the Religion Department at Denison University in Granville, Ohio, USA. Pae is also an Episcopal priest. Taking social ethics as a discipline, she has extensively published on the ethics of peace and war, transnational feminist theology and ethics, spiritual activism, and Asian/American feminist theology and ethics. Her recent publications include *Transpacific Imagination of Theology, Ethics, and Spiritual Activism: Doing Ethics Transnationally* (New York: Palgrave Macmillan, 2024), *Embodying Antiracist Christianity: Asian/American Theological Resource Book for Antiracism*, co-edited with Boyung Lee (New York: Palgrave Macmillan, 2024), and *Searching for the Future in the Past: Reclaiming Feminist Theological Visions*, co-edited with Kathleen Talvacchia (London: T&T Clark, 2024).

Peniel Rajkumar is Global Theologian with USPG and an adjunct lecturer at Ripon College Cuddesdon near Oxford, UK. His publications include *Dalit Theology and Dalit Liberation: Problems, Paradigms and Possibilities* (Farnham: Ashgate, 2010), *Asian Theology on the Way: Christianity, Culture and Context*, ed. (London: SPCK, 2012), *Mission At and From the Margins: Patterns, Protagonists and Perspectives*, co-edited with Joseph Prabhakar Dayam and I. P. Asheervadham (Oxford: Regnum, 2013) and *Many Yet One? Multiple Religious Belonging*, co-edited with Joseph Prabhakar Dayam (Geneva: World Council of Churches Publications, 2015).

Yazid Said is a senior lecturer in Islam in the Department of Theology, Philosophy and Religious Studies, Liverpool Hope University, Liverpool, UK. His publications include *Ghazali's Politics in Context* (Abingdon: Routledge, 2012) and *The Future of Interfaith Dialogue: Muslim–Christian Encounters through A Common Word*, co-edited with Lejla Dimiri (Cambridge: Cambridge University Press, 2018).

Frank Smith is Dean, Tikanga Polynesia, at St John's Theological College, Auckland, Aotearoa, New Zealand.

George Sumner is Bishop of Dallas, Episcopal Church, USA. Previously, he was Principal of Wycliffe College, University of Toronto, Canada.

Jenny Te Paa-Daniel is Te Rarawa, Te Māreikura and Interim Director of the National Centre for Conflict and Peace Studies at Otago University, Dunedin, Aotearoa, New Zealand. She was the first indigenous laywoman to lead an Anglican theological seminary anywhere in the world. Her publications include *Anglican Women on Church and Mission*, co-edited with Kwok Pui-lan et al. (Norwich: Canterbury Press, 2012).

James Tengatenga is Distinguished Professor in Global Anglicanism in the School of Theology, University of the South, Sewanee, Tennessee, USA. He was Bishop of Southern Malawi and served as chair of the Anglican Consultative Council. His publications include *Twentieth Century Anglican Theologians: From Evelyn Underhill to Esther Mombo*, co-edited with Stephen Burns and Bryan Cones (Chichester: Wiley, 2021).

Introduction | Worthy of God's Trust?

STEPHEN BURNS AND JAMES TENGATENGA

In their book *Love's Redeeming Work*, on 'the Anglican quest for holiness', three bishop-theologians make the point that 'the typical Anglican of the twenty-first century will be an African under thirty'. They add that 'statistically, this seems unchallengeable'. Their question that follows from this unchallengeable statistic is: 'What has the history of Anglican devotion and holiness to offer to this new model Anglican?'[1] In *Love's Redeeming Work*, Geoffrey Rowell, Kenneth Stevenson and Rowan Williams introduce and provide brief samples of writing from Anglicans dating from 1530 onwards, so as to induct the reader into an Anglican spirituality. The book comes towards its conclusion with extracts from the Church of England's *Alternative Service Book* of 1980 and, with the last author in their long list in the quest for holiness, an Australian, John Gaden (1938–90). Between their first subject, Hugh Latimer (1485–1555), and Gaden, their last, it is interesting to note the range of their inclusions. For instance, the second section of their large book, covering 1650–1830, features among others Henry Venn, the father of John (1759–1813), who was one of the founders of the Church Missionary Society (CMS) and who in turn was the father of another Henry (1796–1873) who in his own work with CMS 'secured the appointment of the first African Anglican Bishop in 1864'. That bishop, Samuel Ajayi Crowther (*c.* 1809–91), a Yoruba man from what is now Nigeria, is not named and does not have his own entry in the collection. The second section of *Love's Redeeming Work* also features, among others, Samuel Seabury (1729–96), the first Bishop of the Episcopal Church in America, something of whose eucharistic spirituality is represented in the sample from his writing. The same section closes with Reginald Heber (1783–1826), the Bishop of Calcutta in India, who from his role in Calcutta was the first episcopal overseer of the emerging Anglican Church in Australia, ahead of the first Bishop of Australia appointed in 1836. It is Heber who is depicted in the left-hand window of the photograph at the beginning of this chapter, who as Bishop of Calcutta has his hand on the head of a little Indian man, whose body is largely uncovered while the bishop towers above him wrapped in clerical haberdashery. On the adjacent window of the photo is that first bishop in the Great South Land itself, William Broughton; he is depicted with an unclad Aboriginal man, apparently tiny like the man from India, kneeling at his feet. The lamentable window 'adorns' a Melbourne parish building.[2]

There are many commendable and enjoyable things to appreciate about *Love's Redeeming Work*, one of which is the gradual incursion of women's voices – with Anne Askewe (1521–46) being the first represented. There is also a slowly increasing number of writers from beyond the Angles/Atlantic/British Isles. These include Krishna Moham Banerjea (1813–85) and Nilakantha Nehemial Goreh (1825–85), both of whom – under the influence of missionaries from Britain – came to Christian baptism from Brahminic Hindu backgrounds, and both of whom taught at Bishop's College, Calcutta, which had earlier been established by Heber. Their inclusion in a collection like *Love's Redeeming Work*, with representation of their own voices, suggests a different kind of status from the obeisance of Indians depicted in the window. Inevitably, such writers fall into *Love's Redeeming Work*'s third section, on 1830–2001, a period in which 'at the start ... Anglicanism still meant largely the Church of England and Ireland, whose Establishment included Wales, together with the small Episcopal Church of Scotland ...'[3] but which through the nineteenth century 'expanded into every part of the globe colonized by Britain, as well as in countries such as Korea and Japan'.[4]

Rowell, Stevenson and Williams's collection was published in 2001, the cusp of the twenty-first century in which the 'typical' or 'new model Anglican' would appear. No doubt the rich history of Anglican devotion – not to say doctrine – has much to yield to the imagined young African person to whom they refer, in response to their own question. However, our question in *Anglican Theology: Postcolonial Perspectives* is different from that of the three scholar-bishops in their work. Our question complements theirs, and is more to do with what those who may be steeped in a history of Anglican devotion might have to learn from the new model Anglican; *from* persons shaped by Anglican traditions that have formed them in contexts well beyond the British Isles, in times after which the British Empire had ostensibly crumbled – it lingers in insidious ways, as this collection makes plain – even as a 'Commonwealth' (at least, so-called) might limp along for a while. Another important question concerns what 'new' Anglicans like that young African might also have to learn from one another – and not only Africans, but also those from and in Asia, Oceania, the Americas, as well as Europe. In gathering up this postcolonial pastiche, we have sought to bring together a diversity of perspectives from around what came to be called the 'Anglican Communion'[5] in which Africa is well represented, but there are also soundings from other tri-continentals (with often-forgotten Pasifika, quad-continentals? Or is the sea of islands subsumed within 'Asia'?). Their voices in turn sit alongside a little insight from the 'second world' of Eastern Europe as well as representation of migrant experience to the North Atlantic environs – that is, to locations that continue to delineate the limits of attention in an awful lot of Anglican studies.

That point can be taken in by considering an article such as 'Anglican Theology' in *The Modern Theologians* (third edn, published in 2005) which introduces 'theology since 1918'. It concentrates on the work of six men from the UK and USA, most of whom are ordained, all of whom worked for at least some of their time in universities. They include scholar-bishops, who like the others served in a limited range of educational institutions – Oxbridge being most obvious.[6] Other texts also focus entirely on a limited range of figures, such as a book on *The Anglican Imagination*, which turns out to be a transatlantic affair,[7] and an anthology of Anglican 'spiritual counsel' which collects the wisdom of 50 admirable figures, all of whom are associated with either the UK or USA.[8] So although there are important exceptions – Kevin Ward's *A History of Global Anglicanism* and Bruce Kaye's *An Introduction to World Anglicanism* being two such examples,[9] and Ian Douglas and Kwok Pui-lan's *Beyond Colonial Anglicanism*[10] deserves special mention – it remains all-too-common for the Anglican Communion to be considered only in the last chapter of books in which many more chapters have been more narrowly focused on the UK. That is effectively what happens with the 'parts' of *Love's Redeeming Work*, and perhaps it may be inevitable in a historical approach. Larger views of the tradition do sometimes take in geographical surveys,[11] and as a result are more eclectic – and, valuably, more representative. But even when the tradition is mapped not historically but in other modes, Anglicanism may still be expounded in terms of 'churchmanship' or 'church styles' that are deeply rooted in the British scene, even if these styles then went on to be exported elsewhere by British colonialism around the globe.[12] That said, the development of local Books of Common Prayer (by whatever name) may be one of the best documented dimensions of Anglican diversity.[13] But overall it remains that 'the biggest gap is that because [so much of] the discussion has been essentially historical, there has been very little discussion of Anglican theology outside England'.[14] As Mark Chapman has noted, while the Church of England is now 'one church among many others' in the worldwide family of Anglican churches, 'the focus on England is obviously a deficiency that needs to be addressed'.[15]

We have our own sense of that deficiency, notwithstanding appreciation for other attempts to address it. Our awareness of difficulties arising from the limited optics of numerous studies lay behind an earlier collaboration by the current editors (and then with our colleague Bryan Cones) on the collection *Twentieth Century Anglican Theologians: From Evelyn Underhill to Esther Mombo*,[16] which in turn had its roots in the search for a textbook for a course in global Anglicanism that Kwok Pui-lan and Stephen Burns once taught together.[17] The sub-title of our own earlier collaboration was meant to signal intent to include women's contributions (in addition to Underhill and Mombo, whose names are in the sub-title: Dorothy L. Sayers (Britain, 1893–1957), Ann Loades (Britain, 1938–2022), Carter Heyward, USA, 1945–), and which placed alongside 'usual suspects' from North Atlantic regions more voices.[18] Various tri-continental representatives of the tradition found their place – T. C. Chao (China, 1888–1979), Sadhu Sundar Singh (India, 1889–1929), K. H. Ting (1915–2014), Desmond Tutu (South Africa, 1931–2021), John Pobee (Ghana, 1937–2020) and Esther Mombo (Kenya, 1957–). Chapters on these people sat among other chapters focused on more common inclusions in estimations of important Anglican theologians, such as William Temple (Britain, 1881–1944), Austin Farrer (Britain, 1904–68), Michael Ramsey (Britain, 1904–88) – lists that tend to extend earlier studies like that 'from Gore to Temple' with an even longer list of academically inclined men in ecclesial roles.[19]

While we did some recalibration of 'who counts', we were acutely aware that work begun in that book was unfinished, and so in the current collection we are keen to invite consideration of a larger range of global Anglican voices that came to some prominence in their own contexts – if not always in the UK – in the last century, and in this current one. As with *Twentieth Century Anglican Theologians*, women are included here, and there is a like-kind mix of the defiantly lay and those in one order or another of ministry.[20] The book also raises other important questions about what counts as Anglican theology. For example, Miroslav Volf wrote some of his work when identified with Pentecostalism, only later becoming Anglican (Episcopal) after moving to the USA; and some of Gale Yee's writing was published while she was Roman Catholic, before later becoming Anglican (Episcopal). Once acknowledged, the more expansive approach to what counts as Anglican theology taken here poses questions to narrower takes on the tradition. One thing that the diverse subjects of this book do have in common, however, is that none of the persons featured in what follows are as young as the 'new model' Anglican of which the three bishop-scholars speak in *Love's Redeeming Work*, with the youngest being nearer 60 than 30 years old. And just as with our earlier book, the work that this one attempts to carry forward is also unfinished, and there is much more still to be discovered about contemporary Anglican theology from around the world. Yet the hope is that the book beckons readers into what Jenny Te Paa-Daniel, a Māori theologian featured in what follows, evocatively speaks about as 'theological educational projects worthy of God's trust'.[21]

Towards the Indaba We Need

Twentieth Century Anglican Theologians closed with James Tengatenga's Afterword, which read in part:

> The Lambeth Conference of 1998 vividly demonstrated the passing of Anglican thinking from modernity to post-modernity. Despite the acrimonious fall out, it did usher in a new age of theological engagement that will continue to unfold. Many voices have yet to speak and those that have and are speaking are yet to be heard ... The silence of the absent, the unrecognized, tri-continentals and all those not yet in the discourse (theological *indaba*) is for us a loud *cri de coeur* for the fruition and coming into being of a more comprehensive Anglican theology.

James continued:

> The purist of the old school will surely worry about whether the resultant Anglican theology will still be recognizably Anglican. The progressive pan-Anglican will respond by pointing out that it is, just as it has been over the ages since the first Ecumenical Councils, if not since the beginning of creation.

Now, 'the journey has begun and I pray that, following this kind of lead, there will be a proliferation of bringing these hidden Anglican gems into the public so that more in-depth theological *indaba* can flourish'. And, 'I also hope that those who are now silent will speak without feeling judged for where they come from: location, linguistic, or worldview wise.' For, James said, 'Until *all* God's people speak, access the platforms and fora are heard, we have not finished doing theology. If we think we are there, we deceive ourselves and are caught in a "period captivity" from which stupor we need to be aroused. The eternal God will continue to reveal Godself to all and, indeed, Anglican theology will be one among many ecumenical attempts at articulating humanity's experience of the divine. It is tempting and even hubris to say, "Watch this space!" but we will say it.'[22]

Here, then, in *this space* are more gems no longer hidden, more steps in the direction of more comprehensive Anglican theology, further resources for *indaba* that is so essential to the future of the Communion. This volume on Anglican theologians little-known or neglected in the North and West, of our own and recent times, is meant for students and scholars of Anglicanism, and we hope it will find a place in courses in Anglican settings – not least seminaries and theological colleges – and among curious individual readers. We especially hope that it will speak to any who sense that something is wrong with what still so often passes as the Anglican 'norm'. Here we recall the lately-Anglican US theologian Stanley Hauerwas, who notes, and we concur, that 'the demand to be normal can be tyrannical unless we understand that the normal condition of our being together is that we are all different'.[23]

The following chapters focus on Denise Ackermann, Niam Ateek, Mukti Barton, Burgess Carr, Verna Dozier, Joseph Golgatho, Winston Halapua, Kwok Pui-lan, Jaci Marischin, John Mbiti, Jessie Mugambi, Jenny Te Paa-Daniel, Barney Pityana, John Ramadhani, Harry Sawyerr, Miroslav Volf, Gerard West and Gale Yee. Each chapter gives an outline of the theologian's social-political and cultural contexts, offers a brief biography, and explores the figure's theological scope and any shifts in their thinking, though it does not exclude attention to what they have made known of their personal lives, political commitments, prayer, ministry, and so on. Usually, two or three key themes in the work of the theologian are explored. Often, some indication is given of their present influence in the Anglican Communion and/or potential for engaging the contemporary Communion in negotiation of a current issue.

One challenge inherent in the celebration of diversity is how to resist a heavy overlay of a particular framework applied to people in all their difference, which could run the risk of 'flattening' distinctive voices. Our judgement has been that the best people to introduce the subjects are those who knew or know them or their work well, and to do so with considerable freedom. So each of the writers speaks in their own voice, and our editorial efforts have taken care not to quash. Writers in what follows have all responded to our invitation in their own way – and as the lion's share of them (but intentionally, not all) are Anglican, that itself is a portal into the diversity of contemporary Anglican theology. So some chapters are more personal, some more critical, some more focused on texts, some more attentive to contexts, than others. Yet each one is illuming.

One very notable observation about the work that writers have done is together to shed light that invites consideration of contrast with what transpired in the earlier *Twentieth Century Anglican Theologians*. In that book, representing some tri-continental theologians among others more familiar in North Atlantic regions, we wanted to test an assertion made about earlier generations of Anglican theology: that it is focused on the incarnation. So, Michael Ramsey suggested in *From Gore to Temple* that the tradition 'owes many of its characteristics to the central place held within it by the Incarnation'.[24] We did find many at least North Atlantic Anglicans evidently engaged directly with this doctrinal emphasis, even if in ways that diverged as well as converged with one another, so by no means uniformly. It is striking, therefore, to find incarnation apparently, on the surface, a lesser focus among the voices brought forward in the present collection, though this is not to say that the doctrine is unimportant to these theologians. Rather, it is to invite reflection on the fact that it is other themes, other concerns, that tend to predominate. If incarnation prevailed in the collective Anglican headspace of the twentieth-century figures in focus in *Twentieth Century Anglican Theologians*, here other matters seem to preoccupy thought. Inevitably, the legacy of colonialism – its long shadows – is in the foreground in more than a few pieces here, the workings of racism are painfully and repeatedly made present, and the quest for a liberative justice is perhaps the thing that grips these theologians most. Of course, all of that – and so much more – may be what an incarnational emphasis might encourage: attention to what is there to be found in actual lives, in particular contexts; whatever that needs to be loved and valued about human persons. God 'flesh-takes' as well as 'flesh-makes', as one theologian most memorably put it.[25] And God getting 'thrown in human waste' and mess, moreover to 'shine' when 'submerged', is one poet's striking take on what the doctrine involves – 'the whole irreducible point of the faith'.[26] So among all that there is to consider in the urgings of the theologians here, we invite the reader to notice how incarnation is treated, if sometimes seemingly obliquely among the complexities and struggles of human living, and how that may (or may not) differ from ways the doctrine comes into view in Anglican theologians who may be familiar from North Atlantic areas. We found in the last book an esteemed Anglican 'systematician', John Macquarrie, seeking and lauding 'God's gift in every voice', doing theology 'from a composition of a chorus of voices'.[27] If Macquarrie is right in that aspiration, we hope that this new book encourages others to bring their own sense and energy to that discovery.

Notes

1 *Love's Redeeming Work: The Anglican Quest for Holiness*, eds Geoffrey Rowell, Kenneth Stevenson and Rowan Williams (Oxford: Oxford University Press, 2001), xxvii.

2 I used this image in the journal *Liturgy*, 34.3 (2019), where the full image, taken by Nick White, is on the cover. Used with permission. One author in this collection, Michael N. Jagessar, also contributed to that volume.

3 Rowell, Stevenson and Williams, *Love's Redeeming Work*, 369.

4 Rowell, Stevenson and Williams, *Love's Redeeming Work*, 369. (The Melbourne parish with the window bearing witness to colonization, St George's Malvern, was not established until 1865.)

5 The term was first used at the Lambeth Conference in 1867.

6 Peter Sedgwick, 'Anglican Theology', in *The Modern Theologians: An Introduction to Christian Theology Since 1918*, eds David F. Ford with Rachel Muers (Oxford: Blackwell, 2005), 178–94. At the time of writing a fourth edition of *The Modern Theologians* is being prepared with a very different ordering of contents.

7 Robert Boak Slocum, *The Anglican Imagination: Portraits and Sketches of Modern Anglican Theologians* (Farnham: Ashgate, 2015).

8 *Spiritual Counsel in the Anglican Tradition*, eds David Hein and Charles R. Henery (Cambridge: James Clarke, 2010), with biographies, 161–72.

9 Kevin Ward, *A History of Global Anglicanism* (Cambridge: Cambridge University Press, 2007); Bruce Kaye, An *Introduction to World Anglicanism* (Cambridge: Cambridge University Press, 2008). So too is the work of William Sachs, for example, *The Transformation of Anglicanism: From State Church to Global Communion* (Cambridge: Cambridge University Press, 2002) and, with Robert Heaney, *The Promise of Anglicanism* (London: SCM Press, 2019). What is somewhat different about this postcolonial pastiche is that numerous tri-continental theologians are the major subject matter, while others get to speak for themselves.

10 *Beyond Colonial Anglicanism: The Anglican Communion in the Twenty-first Century*, eds Ian T. Douglas and Kwok Pui-lan (New York: Church Publishing, 2000).

11 So the *Oxford Handbook of Anglican Studies*, eds Mark Chapman, Martyn Percy and Sathinathan Clarke (Oxford: Oxford University Press, 2015), for example, after an opening section on 'historiography' and another on 'methods and styles', then has a large section (91 of 657 pages) on 'contextualization', with chapters on North America, Australasia, Sri Lanka, West Africa, Sudan, Hong Kong, and then Dan O'Connor on 'the geography of Anglicanism' (271–84).

12 Stephen Spencer, *Anglicanism* (SCM Studyguide) (London: SCM Press, 2012) is an example.

13 Colin Buchanan's work is exemplary, for example, *Anglican Eucharistic Liturgies, 1985–2010: The Authorized Rites of the Anglican Communion* (Norwich: Canterbury Press, 2012), the most recent in a series of such surveys.

14 Mark Chapman, *Anglican Theology* (Edinburgh: T&T Clark, 2012), 171.

15 Chapman, *Anglican Theology*, 172.

16 *Twentieth Century Anglican Theologians: From Evelyn Underhill to Esther Mombo*, eds Stephen Burns, Bryan Cones and James Tengatenga (Chichester: Wiley-Blackwell, 2021).

17 In addition to *Beyond Colonial Anglicanism*, Pui-lan's own work includes important contributions such as *Anglican Women on Church and Mission*, eds Kwok Pui-lan, Judith Berling and Jenny Plane Te Paa (Norwich: Canterbury Press, 2012), with a number of Anglican voices and persons in this current collection included in *Postcolonial Practice of Ministry: Leadership, Liturgy, Interfaith Engagement*, eds Kwok Pui-lan and Stephen Burns (Lanham: Lexington Press, 2016).

18 Stephen Burns and Bryan Cones, 'Un/usual Suspects', in *Twentieth Century Anglican Theologians*, x–xxi.

19 See Michael Ramsey, *From Gore to Temple: The Development of Anglican Theology Between Lux Mundi and the Second World War, 1889–1939* (London: Macmillan, 1960), and also Robert Page, *New Directions in Anglican Theology: A Survey from Temple to Robinson* (London: Mowbray, 1967).

20 We had planned for this book to include some representation of the United Churches, with chapters on Arvind Nirmal and Aruna Gnanadason. Unfortunately, neither emerged. Nirmal was part of the Church of North India (CNI) – which is part of the Anglican Communion while also part of the World Communion of Reformed Churches, Methodist World Council, and perhaps other bodies. The CNI was only formed in 1970, so the context in which Nirmal lived the last 25 years of his life was the time before union was not at all identified with Anglican tradition. Gnanadason is a member of the older Church of South India, formed in 1947. Vagaries that relate to the United Churches invite a large view of the contemporary ecumenical scene in which Anglican traditions are situated, and are not modelled on patterns of inter-church and united church relationship in the UK.

21 Jenny Te Paa-Daniel, 'To say my fate is not tied to your fate is like saying, "Your end of the boat is sinking"', 1–18, published online at https://progressivechristianitynzblog.files.wordpress.com/2014/03/jennytepaa-daniel-tikanga.pdf, 14 (accessed 23.5.2023).

22 James Tengatenga, 'Afterword: God's Gift in Every Voice', in *Twentieth Century Anglican Theologians*, 226–37 (237).

23 Stanley Hauerwas, *Suffering Presence: Theological Reflections on Medicine, the Mentally Handicapped, and the Church* (Notre Dame: University of Notre Dame Press, 1986), 214.

24 Ramsey, *From Gore to Temple*, 27.

25 Ann Loades, 'Why Worship?', in *Grace and Glory in One Another's Faces: Preaching and Worship*, ed. Stephen Burns (Norwich: Canterbury Press, 2020), 90.

26 Andrew Hudgkins, 'Piss Christ', in *Poems of Devotion: An Anthology of Recent Poets*, ed. Luke Hankins (Eugene: Wipf & Stock, 2012), 79.

27 Ryan Kuratko, 'John Macquarrie (1919–2007)', in *Twentieth Century Anglican Theologians*, 110–18 (111, 115).

Denise Ackermann

JENNY TE PAA-DANIEL

Elegant, articulate, fearless, beautiful ... these were both my first and my enduring impressions of Denise Ackermann, Anglican laywoman, Professor of Theology, staunch feminist advocate, indubitable academic, accomplished author.

In between times I consider myself blessed beyond imagining to add into this all too modest list of admired qualities, esteemed and beloved friend, mentor and colleague – qualities that have already been very readily attested by so many who have written either with or about Denise.

Twenty-five years ago, I travelled to Cambridge, Massachusetts, to attend a gathering of global Anglican scholars, teachers, thinkers, writers, leaders and activists. Hosted by the faculty from the iconic Episcopal Divinity School, it was incredibly encouraging to bear witness and to participate in what was perhaps the most significant gathering of its kind ever organized within the Anglican Communion. The focus was on postcoloniality and its implications for an historic ecclesial institution so deeply and largely uncritically mired in its colonial heritage. The gathering resulted in the book *Beyond Colonial Anglicanism*, edited by Ian Douglas and Kwok Pui-lan.[1] It gathers in some of the Anglican Communion's finest theological thinkers and scholars, among them Denise Ackermann.

At that time as a fledgling indigenous laywoman and still tentative academic, I felt so out of my depth as I observed those like Denise so confidently and passionately able to articulate their position on postcoloniality. I was in awe of the ease with which they spoke on how their work was impacting their province and, more especially, on how the transformative outworkings of postcoloniality were so sorely needed to begin impacting the fabric of the wider Anglican Communion. It was, however, also at that gathering that I had the first clue of how important my own work in the area of decolonizing Anglican theological education was set to be. It was in large part because of the gentle empathic encouragement and advocacy I received from Denise.

Coming alongside me to talk about my contribution to the gathering,

Denise offered both generous affirmation and wise advice on ways in which I ought to further develop my ideas. She already knew much about the context of Aotearoa New Zealand having followed with great interest the phenomenal indigenous response from Māori, in support of the struggles of the oppressed black majority in apartheid South Africa. Denise already knew how it is a self-evident gospel imperative to stand with those on the underside, those who are the least, the lost, the lonely. And in her I found a mentor, an experienced theological educator, an experienced and globally recognized laywoman leader – and I found a friend, a wise and generous-hearted friend, one who would continue to support and encourage, to correct and challenge, to listen and to laugh alongside!

The Sound of Her Voice

In thinking about what I could best contribute to this collection my first thought was naturally to look at what has already been written not only by Denise but also about her. In both instances the literature is voluminous.[2] Professor Ackermann is indeed an extraordinary academic theologian. Her own writings traverse the personal to the political and all are imbued with her trademark impeccable theologically grounded insistence for justice to prevail. It is no wonder that during my experience of working on various representative commissions and committees of the Anglican Communion I found time and again that hers was a name at once feared by the more conservative/punitive episcopal leaders with whom I interacted. Conversely, among those whose understanding of God's mission is premised on a firmly theologically grounded unequivocal acceptance and inclusion of all, she is so deservedly respected as the exemplary practical theologian she has always been.

For Denise, theology is always grounded in the *intersecting* of humanity with God. As she asserts, 'Theology is sustained reflection about what we worry about, what *we believe*, and what *we do* about what we believe ... we seek words about God and about all things and all actions in relation to God.'[3] So theology is a human activity done in contemplation of God by reflecting through one's own context and particularities.[4] 'Theology, thinking about God through our human condition, then necessarily begins with the incarnation because it is the intersection between divinity and human particularity. What God is like, how God relates to us, and we relate to God begins with the mystery of the incarnation, "God with us".'[5]

Perhaps one of Denise's most oft-quoted observations comes from her book *Surprised by the Man on the Borrowed Donkey*. A poignant blend of both wise theological and astute political analysis, this compelling title was inspired when Denise was in the UK observing a typically extravagant Church of England processional, replete with church leaders resplendent in formal robes adorned with gold. Where in all of this, she puzzled, might Jesus be found? 'Jesus, whom Christians attest is the incarnation of the living God, had nowhere to lay his head, washed the feet of his disciples, and had to borrow a donkey for a bittersweet ride that ended on a cross.'[6]

Closer to home, Denise's theology was profoundly critically reflective of the apartheid context of her homeland South Africa. Her incredibly courageous publication *After the Locusts: Letters from a Landscape of Faith* attests to her faith-filled moral courage during the darkest apartheid period. Her letters, while intensely personal, are a testimony to her understanding of praxis, as 'the inseparable relationship between reflecting and acting, between what I think I believe and what I do to achieve my beliefs'.[7] Her long-term membership of Black Sash, an anti-apartheid group of white women, is one witness to actions aligned to such beliefs. It was this activism that enabled her to quickly establish a natural and easy affinity with the struggles of indigenous Māori to which I introduced her in our various encounters. She was especially interested in the role of the Anglican Church in Aotearoa New Zealand and its endeavours to redeem some of the inglorious colonial history in which the Church played no small part.

There is, however, one piece of Denise's own writing that has so impressed me that I cannot but reflect that while she was paying the most fulsome and loving tribute to her dear friend and colleague Steve de Gruchy,[8] all that she said was so profoundly emblematic of her own ministry of teaching, of witnessing, of advocacy and of compassion. I want therefore, by way of similarly offering tribute to Denise, to use many of her own words but to reframe them to reflect the depth of admiration, appreciation and awe with which she is so widely held:

> The task before us cannot be underestimated. But we believe that God is ceaselessly engaged with this world and with us. We are not alone as we respond to God's call to make a difference and to continue the work of redemption.[9]

Fundamental to Denise's consummate faith understanding, and her practice of it, is her unerring sense of God with us. Time and again in all her writings is the reminder that our priority project as people of faith is to 'make what we believe, and what we do about what we believe, congruent'.[10] The inherent riskiness personal and political of discipleship is not lost on Denise as she rightly identifies the imperative to act: 'Awareness of the irreparable damage of structural evil, and hearing the cries of the needy, necessitate actions that are risky, imaginative and courageous.'[11]

Over and again in her life journey Denise has modelled precisely what she writes of here. Whether against institutionalized racism, sexism, homophobia, clericalism or political corruption she remains fearless in calling out any and all of these evils in society, the nation, in the Church and in the world.

It is the biblical imperative towards both doing justice and loving justice that compels her activism, as she herself so eloquently explains:

> God seeks to deliver those who suffer and who have been wronged. This is the redemptive story line of our scriptures. The biblical tradition regards concern for the least privileged persons and groups as essential for a just community; and the exploitation of people is a primary injustice that must be resisted and corrected. Action for justice is directed towards the creation of the common good, something that all who are oppressed and on the margins of society deserve.[12]

At no point does Denise disavow the costliness of discipleship. In this regard she is especially conscious of the disproportionate costliness to women – in particular women of colour. It was her very early recognition of just how white power in apartheid South Africa was accumulated and wielded that led her into a lifetime of solidarity with black activism. By her own 'admission' she justifies the theological quest for answers to human suffering:

> A mature theologian questions, is open to the unexpected, probes, and seeks new ways of relieving our human plight. She knows that outcomes are fragile, often fraught with contradiction and sometimes unseen. Change is at best partial. The work of justice requires a kind of moral and theological stubbornness that refuses to give up, is never naïve, and believes that every little effort is worthwhile ...[13]

Denise is now well into her eighth decade and yet her unflagging energy for speaking of, writing about – and doing – the work of God's justice is testimony to the relentlessness of which she speaks, her refusal to ever give up; that unshakeable belief that even the tiniest level of effort, sincerely held, is always worthwhile. As she says:

> So we believe that a healed world is God's intention. It is not only possible but a given, and we have a part to play in bringing it about.

We hope for an existence that is transformed and redeemed within the just reign of God. Christian hope is not blind optimism – a sort of 'alles sal regkom' attitude. To hope is to live with expectation, under-girded by patience, in a creative manner that commits us to actions for justice. Hope, unlike wishful thinking, is realistic and open to the unforeseen because we cannot predict tomorrow. But it does demand that we become creatively involved in making that which we hope for come about.[14]

And:

Holding on to the promises of God, means placing our hope in God's love for humanity and God's ongoing, just and merciful acts in mending this world. God is a lover of life. God is a God of life.[15]

It is the women of the Church, and in particular women in the Anglican Church in Southern Africa but also beyond into the Anglican Communion, for whom Denise has always held infinite hope. Again and again, though, she is clear concerning the responsibility of women also to seize the moments of opportunity for leadership that, while still too rare, are nonetheless occasionally presented.

Denise is a theologian who takes the 'doing *of the word*' seriously as the measure by which its integrity and its authority would be judged in the public square. The witness of the Anglican Church, its mission to the world, needs wise women and men whose actions are marked by critical consciousness, imagination, a concern for justice, courage to put their bodies on the line, and fidelity to the teachings of the One who showed us the way.

These are all of the exemplary qualities found in the legacy that Denise has gifted to countless others through her extraordinary public witness of speaking and teaching, of urging and challenging, of preaching and praying that together we would all continue the struggle to 'reconstitute the world' as one in which all may belong and flourish and none would ever again either be unjustly dominated or excluded.

There was one piece of advice that Denise gave me and it is one that I did not immediately heed. However, knowing Denise will likely read this I want to reassure her that I did not leave it too late to take her urging of me seriously! Denise was concerned that my demanding work-load was unsustainable; she said, 'Women in Anglican Church leadership are precious, they are also all too rare and so it is of vital importance that we help one another to take good care of ourselves physically as well as spiritually and emotionally.' She urged me to consider that while in my forties, even my fifties, I may have strength and energy in abundance, I needed also to begin conserving some of that for my seventies and beyond.

I am so pleased to report that I did heed Denise's advice and that no one is more grateful to her for that sage advice than my darling husband, my wider *whanau* and friends, my beloved *mokopuna*, my grandchildren with whom I too now get to spend that quality time they both need and so richly deserve. And so it seems to me to be fitting to return to Denise the words of one of her peers, another extraordinary woman leader of deep and abiding faith-filled dignity, of abundant compassion, of outstanding integrity. Ruth Bader Ginsburg's words speak to me of Denise Ackermann who I and so many others thank for the tracks she has crafted so carefully and lovingly for us to follow: 'Whatever you choose to do, leave tracks. That means don't do it just for yourself. You will want to leave the world a little better for your having lived.'[16]

Notes

1 *Beyond Colonial Anglicanism: The Anglican Communion in the Twenty-First Century*, eds Ian Douglas and Kwok Pui-lan (New York: Church Publishing, 2000).

2 *Ragbag Theologies: Essays in Honour of Denise M. Ackermann, a Feminist Theologian of Praxis*, eds M. Pillay, S. Nader, S. and C. Le Bruyns (Stellenbosch: Sun Press, 2009) is perhaps the most comprehensive and intimate of publications in which those closest to Denise provide a dazzling array of essays in her honour. It is also a rich literary resource filled with theological wisdom, insight, critique and challenge all inspired by the association with Denise of its many authors over many years.

3 Denise Ackermann, *After the Locusts: Letters from a Landscape of Faith* (Grand Rapids/Glosderry, Republic of South Africa: Eerdmans/D. Philip Publishers, 2003), 27.

4 Ackermann, *After the Locusts*, 35.

5 Denise Ackermann, *Surprised by the Man on the Borrowed Donkey: Ordinary Blessings* (Cape Town: Lux Verbi, 2014), 101.

6 Ackermann, *Borrowed Donkey*, 23.

7 Ackermann, *After the Locusts*, 35.

8 https://kairossouthernafrica.wordpress.com/2013/03/27/2nd-steve-de-gruchy-memorial-lecture-denise-m-ackermann/ (accessed 29.1.2024).

9 https://kairossouthernafrica.wordpress.com/2013/03/27/2nd-steve-de-gruchy-memorial-lecture-denise-m-ackermann/, 2 (accessed 29.1.2024).

10 https://kairossouthernafrica.wordpress.com/2013/03/27/2nd-steve-de-gruchy-memorial-lecture-denise-m-ackermann/, 2 (accessed 29.1.2024).

11 https://kairossouthernafrica.wordpress.com/2013/03/27/2nd-steve-de-gruchy-memorial-lecture-denise-m-ackermann/, 3 (accessed 29.1.2024).

12 https://kairossouthernafrica.wordpress.com/2013/03/27/2nd-steve-de-gruchy-memorial-lecture-denise-m-ackermann/, 4 (accessed 29.1.2024).

13 https://kairossouthernafrica.wordpress.com/2013/03/27/2nd-steve-de-gruchy-memorial-lecture-denise-m-ackermann/, 6 (accessed 29.1.2024).

14 https://kairossouthernafrica.wordpress.com/2013/03/27/2nd-steve-de-gruchy-memorial-lecture-denise-m-ackermann/, 6 (accessed 29.1.2024).

15 https://kairossouthernafrica.wordpress.com/2013/03/27/2nd-steve-de-gruchy-memorial-lecture-denise-m-ackermann/, 8 (accessed 29.1.2024).

16 Ruth Bader Ginsburg, cited in the *Smithsonian Magazine*, 6 April 2022, see https://www.smithsonianmag.com/smithsonian-institution/new-artifacts-document-the-soaring-popularity-of-ruth-bader-ginsburg-180979873/ (accessed 29.1.2024).

2

Naim Ateek

YAZID SAID

Naim Stefan Ateek, born on 2 February 1937, is an Anglican priest, activist and writer who led the movement that became known as Palestinian liberation theology. In the turbulent political and ecclesiastical climate of Palestine and Israel, such a claim was bound to be controversial in its meaning and theological implication. Assis Naim, as many fondly called him (colloquial Arabic for *qassis*, priest), espoused liberationist ideas, but broke out of the normative categories of reading the Bible. With the cataclysmic impact on the Church's history in Palestine prior to and after 1948, his activism, in turn, had an important impact on the Western Church's perception of Palestinian Christianity. The Palestinian Christian political climate was one of increasing awareness of the need to relate to the biblical narrative of Israel afresh in light of the challenges of the ancient Palestinian Christian communities with the new loyalty that evolved in the Holy Land – the modern political reality of the state of Israel.

To understand properly the development of Ateek's thought, it is important to be aware of the constant motion of his family's story as they responded to the fast-changing political history around them.[1] His family is part of the ancient Palestinian Christian community, and his father's household was shaped by both Eastern Orthodoxy and Anglican evangelical Christianity. Despite the family roots in Eastern Orthodoxy, they were among the many local Christians who became involved with the Church Missionary Society (CMS) in Palestine, which was behind the development of Anglican identity in the Middle East more broadly – and one of the main strands in the missionary movement through which the Anglican Communion eventually came into being.[2] His father, Stefan Ateek, was originally from Nablus. CMS founded what is now St Luke's hospital in Nablus with whom Stefan Ateek worked. He married a young woman from nearby Tul Karem and the wedding was at the local Anglican church. Naim Ateek's mother had a Turkish Armenian father but was orphaned at the age of six and married early. The connection to CMS strengthened among locals, such as the Ateek family, fostering an experiential sense of justification by faith and a more overt dependence on scripture, together with an emphasis on sanctification. The Ateek family combined this with abiding knowledge of Orthodox liturgies.

Well before facing Zionist encroachment on their territories, movement for the family across the country and the region was easy – although not always for happy reasons. Stefan Ateek had to reckon with military service for the Ottomans during World War One. However, after an illness in Istanbul, he returned to Nablus and managed to escape military service while being guarded by local Bedouins under a different name. With the passing of Naim Ateek's grandmother, the father moved with the family to Bisan in the north of Palestine (today's Bet She'an near the Sea of Galilee). Being trained as a goldsmith, he sought to develop a business in jewellery-making and selling in Bisan where goldsmiths were not available.

Naim Ateek was born in Bisan after the family moved, though two of his older siblings were born in Nablus. While in Bisan, and as a keen preacher, Ateek the father invited CMS missionaries to build a house in the town and establish a mission post there. The people who responded to the call included a Mrs Fisher, thought to be the sister of the late Archbishop of Canterbury, Geoffrey Fisher. This would eventually develop into a local Anglican church in Bisan, thanks to the cooperation between CMS and the Ateek family. That church was abandoned in 1948.

The following years brought with them the challenges of World War Two when Palestine was under the British Mandate. At this stage, Palestinians were facing the growth of Zionist influence and expansion in Palestine as the world was responding to the evils of Nazism. One of the historical tragedies in the light of that history was the fate of the Palestinian Arabs that included the Ateek family, a tragedy whose consequences the world is still trying to reckon with. In 1948, the family was expelled by force from Bisan by Zionist militias and evicted to Nazareth, where Naim attended the local Baptist high school. The Anglican clergy in Nazareth at the time, Farid Odeh and Khalil Jamal, helped the Ateek family to settle into their new environment.

These political challenges became the catalyst for the development of Ateek's calling and thought. Understanding his break from traditional engagement with the Bible, as explained below, and even his own struggles with the Church hierarchy, itself shaped his theological existence, to the extent that liberation theology, based on his Western education, and his own story go hand in hand. This is reflected in his various writings, which took the form of a narrative reflection on the context in which he grew.[3] This narrative form of writing, however, is common among other local Palestinian Christian leaders.[4]

Ateek believed from a very young age that he had a clear call for ordination in the Anglican Church. The common practice was to study theology abroad. However, on his completing high school, the Church was not forthcoming in deciding where to send him for theological training. Given the inaccessibility of training in Beirut for political reasons, and the lack of other regional theological colleges at the time, he worked for three years while waiting to get the answer regarding his training. At that point, the Baptists in Nazareth offered him a full scholarship to study at Hardin-Simmons University in Texas to complete his BA, which he accepted in 1959. He remained an unrepentant Episcopalian, however, and was able to further his education with a Master of Divinity at the Church Divinity School of the Pacific in Berkeley, California, with the support of Bishop James Pike of California. Pike himself was considered a controversial figure at the time, as he had participated in an investigative trip to Israel to report on Arab refugees.[5]

With this ecumenical Protestant theological training, Ateek was accepted for ordination back in the Anglican province of Jerusalem; he was ordained a deacon on 16 May 1966, and a priest on 21 May 1967 at St John's Church in Haifa by Archbishop Campbell MacInnes. His priestly ordination took place two weeks before the eruption of the 1967 Six-Day War. His first official title was at St Paul's Church in Shefa Amr in Galilee, where he served for about five years. He was then asked to move to Haifa, while serving at the same time the parish in the historic Crusader town of Acre to the north, as well as Ramleh to the south near Jaffa on the Mediterranean coast.

During Ateek's time in Haifa, he completed his doctorate at the San Francisco Theological Seminary which is part of the Graduate Theological Union in Berkeley. The original title of the dissertation was 'Toward a Strategy for the Episcopal Church in Israel with special focus on the political situation: Analysis and Prospects'. With these qualifications, Ateek was invited to join the bourgeois citadels of the Anglican Church in Jerusalem when he was appointed the parish priest of the Arabic-speaking congregation and canon of St George's Cathedral in Jerusalem in 1985.

After moving to Jerusalem, Ateek began work on his first book, *Justice and Only Justice*. Most of the material for the book came from his doctoral work; however, the focus of the book was not on the Episcopal Church in Israel per se, but on the work of justice and peace-making and the broader scope of a Palestinian liberation theology. This marked the beginning of what would become the significant development of Palestinian liberation theology, and later the centre he founded called Sabeel (the Way, or the stream of water in Arabic). Sabeel today defines its mission as an ecumenical grassroots movement that 'strives towards theological liberation through instilling the Christian faith in the daily lives of those who suffer under occupation, violence, injustice and discrimination'.[6] His first book was published in 1989. Since then, Ateek has published two other books, *A Palestinian Christian Cry for Reconciliation* (2008) and *A Palestinian Theology of Liberation: The Bible, Justice, and the Israel–Palestine Conflict* (2017). He has also edited and co-edited various other books that came out of various Sabeel international conferences.

Ateek lived through the period of the restructuring of the Anglican province of the Middle East during the time of Archbishop George Appleton, which culminated in 1976 with giving the local church its own native leadership. Nonetheless, this native church's sanctuaries proved to be less than sedate or cooperative and a more tense relationship developed between him and the ecclesiastical authority of the diocese. He was one of two candidates to succeed Samir Kafity as the diocesan bishop. After the election of Riah Abu el-Assal as co-adjutor bishop, the two bishops asked him to move to Nablus to be the parish priest. In response to this request, and contrary to what Samuel Kuruvilla reports in his study,[7] Ateek asked the bishops to place him in Ramallah instead, as it would allow his daughter to continue her studies at the Anglican International School in Jerusalem in a full English-speaking curriculum. He would not have been hesitant to affirm his willingness to serve in Nablus, the home town of his father, had it not been difficult for his daughter to continue her studies in Jerusalem. When the two bishops refused, Ateek resigned, bringing a sad ending to his work in the diocese. He is now retired and lives with his family in Texas but continues to guide and help with the ongoing work of Sabeel in Jerusalem.

Ateek's Liberation Theology in Context

Almost one year after the publication of his first book, Ateek led the first international conference to be held at the Tantur Ecumenical Institute near Bethlehem during the First Palestinian Intifada. The event included various local Christian political leaders, religious intellectuals, as well as international scholars – including the notable feminist Roman Catholic theologian Rosemary Radford Ruether, and the Jewish liberation theologian Marc Ellis. Ellis and Ruether became co-editors with Ateek of the conference proceedings under the title *Faith and the Intifada: Palestinian Christian Voices*. This make-up of the participants suggests that Naim Ateek's thought needs to be assessed in relationship to two developments that shaped the broader context of the time: firstly, the development of a local Palestinian Christian theology, and secondly the development of liberation theology more globally.

When considering the first point, it is important to remember that the participation and activity of Palestinian Christian figures in national political life took place long before any of his books were published. Ateek himself refers to the Melkite Archbishop of Galilee Joseph Raya (1916–2005), who was thought to be one of the first church officials to speak for the Christian victims of the *Nakba* (catastrophe).[8] Others included political figures such as George Habash, Emile Habibi and Hanan Ashrawi. The list of names is not exhausted here. The development of religious political movements both in Israel and Palestine provided the impetus for a clearer Christian Palestinian reflection on the historical challenges of the 1948 war (remembered as the *Nakba*) and the 1967 Six-Day War (remembered as the *Naksa*, setback).[9] Ateek frames his second book between the rise of Hamas (the Islamic resistance movement) and Hamam (the movement for Christian resistance) on the one hand,[10] and the religious Jewish settler movement after the Six-Day War in Israel, on the other.[11]

The key historical moments in witnessing a more visible Christian engagement with politics are associated with the 1970s and 1980s.[12] In 1971 The Justice and Peace Committee of the Assembly of Catholic Ordinaries of the Holy Land was established.[13] It published its first document in 1980 on the political commitment of Palestinian Christians.[14] The 1970s saw the rise of church intellectuals, notably Rafiq Khoury, a Roman Catholic priest in Jerusalem, who completed his doctoral work in Rome,[15] and later Mitri Raheb, a Lutheran pastor based in Bethlehem who trained in Germany. Lay intellectuals, such as the late Greek Catholic Melkite Geries Khoury from Galilee, founded Al-Liqa Center in Bethlehem in 1982, an important local institution for Palestinian theology with its own press.[16] The appointment of Michel Sabbah as the first native Palestinian Latin Patriarch of Jerusalem also had significant reverberating effects on the development of a local Palestinian Christian voice; his first three pastoral letters that were issued in the 1980s and 1990s show a clear direct willingness to engage with the political context by the Church leadership.[17]

The emergence of various Palestinian writers and thinkers resulted in some writers suggesting a diversity of approaches. Kuruvilla, for instance, makes a distinction between Ateek's liberation theology and the 'contextual theology' of Raheb and Khoury.[18] However, this distinction is not convincing enough; to begin with, liberation theology originally applied to a contextual theology; when it originated in Latin America, the word 'liberation' was generated from the contexts of struggle.[19] Likewise, all the emerging Palestinian Christian thinkers have had similar concerns. They all describe political theological concerns in the context of Palestine, and all have engaged with questions of biblical interpretation, the relationship of religion and state, the meaning of justice, forgiveness and reconciliation.[20] They tried to present a Christian voice that is less marred by certain forms of nationalism or religious fundamentalism.

So what are the distinctive features of Ateek's work? This leads us to think of his relationship with the second issue – namely, wider liberation theology movements. When Ateek was completing his theological education in the 1960s, the work of Gustavo Gutiérrez on liberation theology in South America was only beginning to emerge. But, as Ruether noted in her contribution to the first conference, 'Most Western liberation theologians are not prepared to put the Palestinian issue on their agenda.'[21] This absence suggests a closer link between Palestinian liberation theology and feminist theology. One might say that Palestinian liberation theology developed out of the conviction that wider Christian liberationists excluded the Palestinian experience, to the same extent that feminists argued that Christian thought and practice radically excludes women's experience.[22] At the same time, while feminist thought itself was heavily influenced by the liberation theology of Latin America,[23] Palestinian liberation theology had its own features: it was ecumenical and had a different approach to the Bible.

Like other liberationists, Ateek argues that Christian allegiance necessitates political involvement and work for the oppressed groups in which the Palestinians formed a forgotten part.[24] Therefore, in all his books, he presents a succinct and powerful summary of the history of the conflict and of the Palestinian situation, stemming from the author's own life experience, as has been noted above. He provides an important critique of current Israeli policies and of the theological claims used to justify them.[25] Central to his writings, therefore, is a counter critique of Christian Zionism, especially as it evolved in the USA.[26] Therefore, how to read biblical texts becomes an essential aspect of Ateek's writings. In all of his books we do not find so much a development in his thought as a reinforcement of his earlier claims. As David Neuhaus has noted, Ateek's first book, *Justice and Only Justice*, was translated into Arabic 13 years later, with very little change from the original English text.[27]

While Ateek's activism and engagement with the Bible show a clear commitment to non-violence,[28] it was his critique of the classical Christian approach to the scriptures that makes him closer to some feminist approaches to the Bible than to fellow Palestinian Christian writers. Ateek is confronted with sacred texts that are easily used today to justify the expulsion of Palestinians from their lands. He notices the various passages that may convey a belief in the inferiority of Palestinians under Israel's control. Isaiah 43 and Isaiah 61 are considered by Ateek to carry racist overtones.[29] The Exodus story, beloved of liberation theology, does not appear to be promising for Ateek in the Palestinian context, when Palestinians see themselves as the modern-day nations who were driven out to make way for the people of Israel.[30] Like feminist biblical scholars,[31] not content with certain biblical verses, he makes bold assertions; for instance, he suggests that a number of Old Testament texts are propaganda and adds: 'the reader should sometimes say, "this is not the word of the Lord"'.[32] As Elisabeth Schüssler Fiorenza has said: 'Intellectual neutrality is not possible in a historical world of exploitation and oppression',[33] and Ateek applies this non-neutrality literally to the biblical text, which allows him to negate certain passages at will.

For Ateek, Palestinian Christians cannot affirm Old Testament promises, most notably the promise of the land, as exclusive to the Jews. There is also a clear distinction between the God of Jesus, as universal, loving and compassionate, and how the God of the Old Testament is portrayed in certain parts of the Bible, which emphasizes exclusive loyalty on the part of the people of Israel.[34] The promises of the Old Testament, for Ateek, have been superseded in Jesus Christ with the Church as the New Israel, giving no significance to the land as a territorial fixity.[35] He also makes a clear distinction within the Old Testament between the covenant with the Davidic royal family (2 Samuel 7.8–13; Psalm 89) and the covenant with Jonah. Jonah's covenant appears to be more promissory, a covenant that engages wider humanity.[36]

While one can find similar supersessionism among some other Arab Christians,[37] other Palestinian thinkers are a bit more nuanced in their approach.[38] Western reviewers of Ateek's books tend to point to an uncomfortable supersessionism that could have devastating anti-Jewish claims.[39] The attitude has resonances with Marcion's teaching that the God of the Hebrew scriptures was not the God of Jesus, which eventually resulted in a sense of Christian superiority and arrogance that proved fateful for the Jewish community.[40] As such, even those who are sympathetic to the cause point out a failure to understand the theological basis of covenant in Israel.[41] They also point to an oversimplified contrast between law and gospel.[42]

However, considering the comparison with Fiorenza's feminist methodology above, Ateek emphasizes from the start the importance of his activism. He states clearly in his first book that he was not writing 'for scholars or theologians, but for people from all professions and walks of life'.[43] In this sense, and like other liberation theologians, his emphasis is on activism and *praxis*. It is often forgotten that as a parish priest Ateek always engaged his congregation in discussion and was keen to hear their views on his Sunday disquisitions on a weekly basis. He was concerned about the pastoral needs of the Palestinian Christian community as he himself notes.[44] Also, his work, unlike that of others in South American contexts, was ecumenical. Those who engaged with him came from many Christian communities in Jerusalem. A popular part of engaging visitors with this activism was the issuing of a pamphlet, a 'Contemporary Way of the Cross: A Liturgical Journey along the Palestinian Via Dolorosa' – that is, a liturgy that aimed to transform the views of the visitors with the hope of transforming the condition of the context.

Ateek's emphasis on activism suggests that the beginning of reflection in his work is in making explicit the Palestinian experiences together with his political standpoint and, as such, declaring his presuppositions first. He does not start with a classical reflection on the nature of God. The reflection is based first on the experience of the author and the context. His books generally begin by analysing the context, socially and politically, with reference to economic and other hardships. In this way, he points to the roots of oppression as he sees them displayed. If his writing is 'theological', it works with the help of sociology, statistics and politics. Palestinian liberation theology begins with the ways in which living as a Palestinian today allows Christians to reconstruct their biblical theology. Ateek says: 'In reading [the Bible] with my Palestinian eyes, I see its meaning and its relevance for my social and political context.'[45]

Consequently, 'justice' for Ateek stands in judgement on the existing order of relations between Israel and Palestine and on which parts of the Bible to read or not read; hence his first book, *Justice and Only Justice*. Across his works, he demands radical change both in the structure of political power and what is due to the Palestinian historic hurt through what he calls 'repentance'. There is an emphasis on the structural aspects of sin that perpetuate political injustices. Although his second book is titled *A Palestinian Christian Cry for Reconciliation*, liberation based on justice must come first.[46] He recalls a biblical basis for justice, confirming that it is not about revenge.[47] But, as with other Palestinian Christian writers, reconciliation is taken seriously when the oppressor first shows signs of genuine repentance. Colin Chapman, in his unpublished response to Ateek's second book, pointed to this ultimate emphasis on justice alone as a possible obstacle to reconciliation, simply because there is a danger that reconciliation is also relegated to an unrealizable future in which 'justice' is fully attained.[48]

Chapman's critique here suggests that despite Ateek's closeness to Desmond Tutu's political activism and his own engagement with the South African context,[49] it is arguable as to what extent he mirrors Tutu's vision. If reconciliation without liberation can be an empty pretence at bringing faith into the political forum, the quest for liberation without reconciliation is no more realistic – and indeed no more Christian. Even if we recognize that in certain circumstances the one or the other requires a pragmatic priority, and while the struggle for liberation and justice must often come first in point of time, reconciliation for Tutu remained prior in point of purpose and moral significance.[50]

In addition, central to Ateek's liberation theology has been the contention that classical Orthodox Christianity is 'theologically loaded'. He adds that Christ's divinity may be so emphasized that his humanity gets sidelined. Instead, Ateek confirms: 'Palestinian theology of liberation has re-established the balance between Christ's two natures ... [and] focuses on the humanity of Jesus of Nazareth, who was also a Palestinian living under an occupation.'[51] The assumption here is that classical approaches to Christology suggest that it is better to exercise power over people than to work with them for justice. Jesus, however, still stands in Ateek's writings for divine immanence in sufferings, even though that suffering does not seem to offer more than an 'ethic'.[52] Although the language of Christ's sacrifice for salvation is briefly mentioned,[53] the universalism of Christ's act does not sit lightly with the importance and particularity of Christ's own land where it happened, to the same extent that the significance of place and land in the Old Testament is not favoured either. The significance of 'place' and time for Christian revelation may seem to give way to a form of Gnosticism.[54]

Conclusion

Palestinian liberation theology as articulated by Ateek comes in reaction to the catastrophe and the historic hurt that the Palestinian people have experienced. It reminds us of a moment that still needs the world's attention. The significance of this project for the pastoral needs of the Palestinian Christian community, let alone the challenge to Western views of Palestine, is beyond questioning. Since the publication of Ateek's first book, some significant political changes have occurred. These include what looks like the triumph of unrestrained settler land-grab in Palestine. The option for the 'poor' has become the option for those who have no voice and no land to claim. Some questions remain unanswered, however.

Ateek's theology, while politically activist, lacks a clearer incarnational understanding of how our accountability before the events of the life, death and resurrection of Christ engages with that same context on various levels. His emphasis on the universalism of Christ makes him lose touch with the importance of the particularity of Christians in Palestine across history, let alone accepting the Church's understanding of the canon of scripture; this makes it difficult to engage with the nuances of the historical relationship between Judaism and Christianity in context. One is left asking 'what is the basis of dialogue with Judaism in this case?' Indeed, what is distinctive of the Palestinian Christian role in inter-religious dialogue? Contrary to the assumption of a 'loaded Orthodox theology', the church fathers would have enriched the conversation beyond measure, some of whom of course wrote in Arabic.

Secondly, as Ateek's own struggles with the local church suggest, changes within the structures of the leadership of the Anglican Church as it became native meant that the concept of a church leadership has frozen in a defensive postcolonial stance, allowing power struggles to flourish with damaging effect. These were valid criticisms on his part at the time. The question remains, therefore, 'how can the Church be good news for all people in the land?' If Ateek has the answer to this, he has not provided it clearly in his writings.

Notes

1 It is possible to pick up central moments in the biography of Naim Ateek from his writings. What is presented here is the fruit of a personal interview with him; in this interview, he confirmed that fuller details of his biography will be given in a forthcoming memoir.

2 Yazid Said, 'Anglicans', in *Christianity in North Africa and West Asia*, eds Kenneth R. Ross, Mariz Tadros and Todd M. Johnson (Edinburgh: Edinburgh University Press, 2018), 219–20.

3 Naim Ateek, *Justice and Only Justice: A Palestinian Theology of Liberation* (Maryknoll: Orbis Books, 1989), 164.

4 Rafiq Khoury, *al-Lahut al-Mahalli al-falastini (1967–2019): ru'ya shamila* (Jerusalem: al-liqa' publications, 2019), 173–4.

5 https://library.syracuse.edu/digital/guides/p/pike_ja.htm (accessed 29.1.2024).

6 https://sabeel.org/ (accessed 29.1.2024).

7 Samuel Kuruvilla, *Radical Christianity in Palestine and Israel: Liberation and Theology in the Middle East* (London: Tauris, 2013), 92.

8 Naim Ateek, *A Palestinian Theology of Liberation: The Bible, Justice and the Palestine-Israel Conflict* (Maryknoll: Orbis Books, 2017), 124. He refers to him as well in his first book, *Justice and Only Justice*, 57.

9 A. Omer and J. A. Springs, *Religious Nationalism: A Reference Handbook* (Santa Barbara: Abc-clio, 2013).

10 Ateek, *Liberation*, 7, 9.

11 Ateek, *Liberation*, 171–2.

12 Elizabeth S. Mareijn, 'The Revival of Palestinian Christianity: Developments in Palestinian Theology', *Exchange*, 49 (2020): 257–77. See also D. Christiansen, 'Palestinian Christians: Recent Developments', in *The Vatican-Israel Accords:*

Political, Legal and Theological Concerns, ed. Marshal Berger (Notre Dame: University of Notre Dame Press, 2004), 309.

13 Khoury, *al-Lahut al-Mahalli al-falastini*, 128.

14 https://www.lpj.org/posts/statements-of-justice-and-peace-commission (accessed 29.1.2024).

15 Khoury, *al-Lahut al-Mahalli al-falastini*, 15.

16 http://al-liqacenter.org.ps/ (accessed 1.9.2022).

17 Khoury, *al-Lahut al-Mahalli al-falastini*, 133–5.

18 Kuruvilla, *Radical Christianity*, 72, 80.

19 Gustavo Gutiérrez, 'The Task and Content of Liberation Theology', in *The Cambridge Companion to Liberation Theology*, ed. Christopher Rowland (Cambridge: Cambridge University Press, 1999), 19–38.

20 Mitri Raheb, *I Am a Palestinian Christian: God and Politics in the Holy Land – A Personal Testimony* (Minneapolis: Fortress Press, 1995); Mitri Rahab, *Faith in the face of Empire: The Bible through Palestinian Eyes* (Maryknoll, Orbis Books, 2014); Munther Isaac, *The Other Side of the Wall: A Palestinian Christian Narrative of Lament and Hope* (Downers Grove: InterVarsity Press, 2020); Elias Chacour and David Hazard, *Blood Brothers: The Dramatic Story of a Palestinian Christian Working for Peace in Israel* (Grand Rapids: Baker Books, 1984).

21 *Faith and the Intifada: Palestinian Christian Voices*, eds Naim S. Ateek, Mark H. Ellis and Rosemary Radford Ruether (Maryknoll: Orbis Books, 1992), xi.

22 Elisabeth Schüssler Fiorenza, *Bread Not Stone: The Challenge of Feminist Biblical Interpretation* (Edinburgh: T&T Clark, 1990), 44.

23 Fiorenza, *Bread Not Stone*, chapter 3. See also Mary Grey, 'Feminist Theology: A Critical Theology of Liberation', in *The Cambridge Companion to Liberation Theology*, ed. Christopher Rowland (Cambridge: Cambridge University Press, 1999), 105–22.

24 Naim Ateek, *A Palestinian Cry for Reconciliation* (Maryknoll: Orbis Books, 2008), 8–10.

25 Ateek, *A Palestinian Cry*, 15–48.

26 Ateek, *A Palestinian Cry*, 81–91. Christian Zionism here means 'the belief that the Jewish people were destined by God to have a national homeland in Palestine and that Christians were obliged to use means to enable this to take place'. See Donald M. Lewis, *The Origins of Christian Zionism: Lord Shaftesbury and Evangelical Support for a Jewish Homeland* (Cambridge: Cambridge University Press, 2013), 5.

27 David Neuhaus, 'Muraja'at kutub: *As-Sira' min ajil al-'adala* (Book Review: The Struggle for Justice)', *Al-Liqa'* 1–2.17 (2002): 218–30.

28 Ateek, *A Palestinian Cry*, 180–3.

29 Ateek, *A Palestinian Cry*, 53–6.

30 Ateek, *A Palestinian Cry*, 110.

31 As a contrast, see Fiorenza, *Bread Not Stone*, 60: 'A feminist theological interpretation of the Bible that has as its canon the liberation of women from oppressive sexist structures, institutions, and internalized values must maintain, therefore, that only the nonsexist and nonpatriarchal traditions of the Bible and the non-oppressive traditions of traditional interpretation have the theological authority of revelation if the Bible is not to continue as a tool for the oppression of women.'

32 Ateek, *Liberation*, 141.

33 Fiorenza, *Bread Not Stone*, 45. See also Fiorenza's book *Changing Horizons:*

Explorations in Feminist Interpretation (Minneapolis: Fortress Press, 2012), chapter 1.

34 Ateek, *A Palestinian Cry*, 58.

35 Naim Ateek, Cedar Duaybis and Maurine Tobin, *Challenging Christian Zionism: Theology, Politics and the Israel-Palestine Conflict* (London: Melisende, 2005).

36 Ateek, *A Palestinian Cry*, chapters 5, 7 and 10.

37 Paul Charles Merkley, *Christian Attitudes Towards the State of Israel* (Montreal: McGill University Press, 2001), 187; Gavin D'Costa, *Catholic Doctrine on the Jewish People after Vatican II* (Oxford: Oxford University Press, 2019), 125.

38 Jamal Khader, former academic Dean of Bethlehem University, does not quite cancel out the biblical narrative; he suggests that God's faithfulness to Israel can be understood as a faithfulness to the particular and to the Church without cancelling out the importance of the text itself. See his Arabic chapter, 'nahwa qira'atin masihiyya falastiniyya li-'l'ahd al-qadim', in *madkhal ila al-lahut al-falastini*, ed. Munther Isaac (Bethlehem: Diyar Press, 2017), 113–23.

39 Amy-Jill Levine, *The Misunderstood Jew: The Church and the Scandal of the Jewish Jesus* (New York: HarperOne, 2006), 183.

40 Joseph B. Tyson, 'Anti-Judaism in Marcion and his Opponents', *Studies in Christian-Jewish Relations*, 1:2 (2006): 196–208.

41 Todd Walatka, 'Naim Stifan Ateek, A Palestinian Theology of Liberation: The Bible, Justice, and the Palestinian Conflict', *Studies in Christian–Jewish Relations*, 14.1 (2019): 1–3. Also, Peter Waddell's review in *Religion and Theology*, 25.4 (2018): 620–2.

42 Colin Chapman, an unpublished response to Naim Ateek's book *A Palestinian Cry for Reconciliation*.

43 Ateek, *Justice and Only Justice*, 1.

44 Ateek, *A Palestinian Cry*, 8–9.

45 Ateek, *A Palestinian Cry*, 54.

46 Ateek, *A Palestinian Cry*, 184.

47 Ateek, *A Palestinian Cry*, 180.

48 Chapman, unpublished response.

49 Ateek, *Justice and Only Justice*, 137–8.

50 Desmond Tutu, *God Has a Dream* (London: Rider, 2004), 43–58.

51 Ateek, *A Palestinian Cry*, 11.

52 Ateek, *A Palestinian Cry*, 111, 124–5, 136.

53 Ateek, *A Palestinian Cry*, 124.

54 Ateek, *A Palestinian Cry*, 146.

3

Mukti Barton

MICHAEL N. JAGESSAR

Here Comes Trouble

This chapter on the contributions of Mukti Barton to theological discourse in the UK is intended to offer readers an overview of the larger body of Barton's work. This 'offering' to a volume focused on 'unjustly neglected Anglican theologians of the twentieth century' is in order to correct the Western bias, which could not be timelier. Neglect or amnesia, though, is not only a matter for the 'white' establishment. It is the case that except by a very few black and Asian voices in the UK, Barton's contributions to black theology in Britain, Asian feminist hermeneutics and Bible and liberation remain largely unengaged. I will demonstrate that Barton's contributions to British theological discourse reach beyond the insularities of 'colours' attached to theological discourse in Britain. Yet Mukti Barton's work and contributions to black theology in the UK are in danger of being overlooked, undervalued and lost. This can especially be seen in newer articulation theorized as black theological discourse in the UK. With the exception of colleagues such as Anthony Reddie,[1] British theological discourse on racism and in solidarity with black and Asian theologies has barely considered referencing Mukti Barton.

There may be reasons for this. One is that Mukti is a woman and an Asian feminist biblical theologian, with the latter leading to a possible second reason for the overlooking. She is an Indian-Asian woman resident in the UK. She used to be 'black' when the term was deployed as a political descriptor to identify those not 'white' British. It is understandable why and how 'black' in black theology has now become the domain of colleagues of African ancestry and of the African diaspora in the UK, ranging from a variety of neo-conservative theological perspectives to the more radical tradition of black theology. Besides the 'politics of identity', another possible reason may be that in spite of the rhetoric from minoritized colleagues in the UK about giving our own more and greater agency and from moving away from Eurocentric modes of written theology, we have ended up in our own writing taking a lazy attitude to that by referencing only a very few voices.

Eurocentric mode has locked us in. Whiteness, particularly white feminism, which Mukti Barton is one of very few among the early black British theologians to have taken on and continues to trenchantly critique, may be having a laugh at how it has effectively dismantled the much more dangerous collective and political approach of 'black'. As different ethnic groups now fight for positions, white structure is still dominant in regulating who is invited into a so-called converted space where 'Black Lives' seem to matter to 'whiteness'. In the context of having the wool drawn over our eyes and ears, revisiting the contributions of Mukti Barton is critical. From womanist scholars we learn that as long as we perpetuate the domination of only a few voices in theological discourse, we hinder movement towards liberation for all voices. Giving agency to and listening to only a limited number of voices crowds out other voices and other perspectives, preventing us from hearing them fully – including our own.

My contribution is not intended to be an exhaustive take on Barton's life, work and writings. I will attempt to pull some of the key threads meandering across her contributions as I make a case for Barton as a key postcolonial voice that Anglicans would do well to read, listen to, and engage with. Her advocacy work and writings have all been talking back to Anglicanism, especially in the UK. Whether it was her re-reading of scripture, crafting of liturgy, mentoring of young black and Asian theologians, anti-racism advocacy, teaching Bible and liberation or black, Asian and feminist theologies, Mukti Barton has continuously spoken truth to power. The recently formed Archbishops' Commission on Racial Justice, with its fascinating remit of 'setting out a compelling agenda for change, in careful gospel-driven discernment, balancing the needs of individuals, communities, and society, maximizing opportunities, and ensuring fairness for all', would have been unnecessary had the Church of England paid closer attention to Mukti Barton, among others. Barton, though, will not offer much comfort to the Church of England – therefore listening to her remains a challenge.

From the inception of her work and across all of her writings Barton has been asking and probing the 'why' of oppression of marginalized people. As Barton wrote in a reflective piece looking back on her contributions as a racial justice advocate:

Once again, we are at a historical moment when after the murder of George Floyd at the hands of the US police, our collective human spirit is rising through Black Lives Matter movements. Through these campaigns, people's vision has been confronted with a core problem, the

Western imperialistic worldview, which constantly begets structural ills such as racism and causes oppression. I share this vision. I am also aware that human abuse and Western Christianity have been coexisting for hundreds of years. For many years I have been asking, 'why?'[2]

Always wishing to get to underlying systemic causes for injustices, Barton's input may be summed up in the words of Rastafarian singer Chronixx: 'Here comes trouble, here comes the danger'.[3] Barton troubles the establishment.

Embodying Liberation

Mukti Barton (nee Mukhopadhyay) locates herself as Indian, Bengali and British. Her baptismal name (Mukti) means liberation, freedom or emancipation, and Mukti has noted that when her mother named her at baptism, she understood her name to mean salvation. With and in the spirit of her Bengali and Christian heritages it is not surprising that Mukti Barton locates herself as a feminist biblical theologian championing the cause of the oppressed and marginalized. Barton's whole undertaking has been, and continues to be, the reclaiming of the fuller meaning of the biblical understanding of salvation as she engages across the various sites of contention related to the injustices of sexism, racism and classism.

A lay canon of Birmingham cathedral, Barton served as the bishop's adviser for black and Asian ministries in the diocese and a lecturer at The Queen's Foundation for Ecumenical Theological Education. She was brought up in a clergy family in west Bengal. In her childhood, her church was Anglican until the churches were united into the Church of North India (CNI) in 1970. After meeting and marrying Stephen Barton, an English Anglican ordinand in India, she came to live in the UK, where their two sons were born. In the UK (during these early years) her experience as a woman of colour, starting at Heathrow Airport on her arrival,[4] and later, proved psychologically harmful. Recounting stories of how she was viewed from the perspective of her 'otherness', Barton notes how church people saw her 'Indian-ness' and refused to accept her as a fellow Christian. In their perception, 'India is inferior, and Britain is superior.'[5] So when an invitation came from the Church of Bangladesh, via the United Society for the Propagation of the Gospel (USPG), the family moved to Bangladesh.

Barton's experience in Bangladesh was enriching, creative and fruitful. This was a period when women in countries such as Bangladesh were part of the global revolution of the 1980s as the poor and the oppressed were rising up and reclaiming their scriptures for human liberation. Barton's encounters through various ecumenical international conferences allowed her active engagement with other Asian feminist hermeneuts, especially on how to bring their questions about oppression to the Bible, displacing the largely Western hermeneutic framework with liberative interpretations and galvanizing Asian women to work for justice and peace. It was in Bangladesh that Barton was asked by the women to become the founder-director of an ecumenical women's centre for reading the Bible from women's perspective. Her key aim in this critical role was to nurture, develop and deepen feminist consciousness in the struggle for justice for women in the family, Church and society. Her work also had an interfaith focus.

After 11 years in Bangladesh the Barton family moved back to the UK where Mukti gained her PhD degree from Bristol University. It was published as *Scripture as Empowerment for Liberation and Justice: The Experience of Christian and Muslim Women in Bangladesh*.[6] In her PhD thesis, Barton reclaimed the black Egyptian Hagar and did Bible workshops with church people to challenge sexism and racism. Soon after obtaining her PhD, the family moved to Birmingham. From 1998 to 2010, she worked with the clergy and laity as Adviser for Black and Asian Ministries. It was also during this period that she developed resources, ran training sessions, and advocated for racial justice within churches. She developed courses on racial justice and taught at the Queen's Foundation from 1998 to 2015. On retirement, she has remained a lay canon of Birmingham Cathedral and an honorary research fellow at Queen's while continuing her writing, leading workshops and lecturing. So her biblical and theological work against racism and other forms of injustices continues.

Influences on Mukti Barton include her Indian Bengali context and heritage and the interfaith activism of Muslim feminist women of Bangladesh. Barton's passion for scripture, liberation and social justice that was kindled in Bangladesh took intentional shape and depth in the UK; here she found the same global biblical revolution and solidarity in the caucus groups of the marginalized from various postcolonial nations. While staying in contact with Asian women's theology through the Asian Women's Resource Centre for Culture and Theology (then in Taiwan), Barton also found a home in – and solidarity with – the emerging black and Asian people's theology in the UK through the Black Theology Forum and the Asian Theology Forum. Further influences include the work and writings of African American scholar Renita J. Weems, with their call for 'hermeneutical insubordination'. As Barton notes, Weems asks scholars to continue to search the Bible 'for something available in this canon(s)

– something hidden, something familiar, but something eternal – that will inspire us to fight on and sing *new-er* song. It is our stubborn faith that even our small, uncelebrated, but persistent acts of hermeneutical insubordination will eventually topple kingdoms.'[7] Another key influence is Paulo Freire, especially drawing on Freire's methodology as a way of teaching the Bible for conscientization (awareness-building). I suggest that Barton's distinctive contribution in the British landscape is her deploying of the Bible towards colour consciousness to provincialize Eurocentric biblical interpretations and readings. As she observed:

> I find Western Christianity guilty of using the Bible to divide the world into colour lines. When I am attacked both covertly and overtly during my teaching and workshops, I know that I am approaching the central problem. I continue my work in the belief that hermeneutical insubordination will eventually topple racist kingdoms.[8]

Racism's reach, however, is long and entrenched. It is a long-haul and costly undertaking. The sort of engagement that Barton invested in and directed at injustice has been 'emotionally battering', having to search for 'safe spaces' where she was not the lone voice. One such space was the then constituted Black Theology Forum in Birmingham. Later, Barton ascribed her survival and thriving at Queen's to the support of her BAME teaching colleagues and the diocesan Black and Asian Network.[9] Reflecting on this and her 'solidarity' approach, Barton suggested:

> I have not worked in isolation, knowing that as a part of the body of Christ I could not and that I should not even try to do so. I have tried to work jointly and therefore the credit for our achievements is shared with all with whom I have worked.[10]

For her work and contributions in the UK, Barton has been named and honoured by the Churches Together in Britain and Ireland (CTBI) as a significant Racial Justice Champion. While her initial work was in the context of Bangladeshi women across faiths and focused on sexism and poverty, in the UK the experience of racism saw her engagement intersecting across sexism, class/caste and race. Whether it was Bangladesh or Birmingham, Barton's life, work, advocacy and writings remain impressively consistent around the issues of justice for the oppressed; rejection of narrow constructions of single-group or single-issue strategies; and the deploying of an intersectional approach to the issues while continually naming whiteness, patriarchy and capitalism as core props of the system that needs to be overthrown. Mukti Barton has been both a cathartic voice challenging 'white theological constructs' and one that was ahead of its time.

Key Insights

What, then, are some of the key contributions and insights of Mukti Barton that current theological discourse on the British landscape should remember, revisit and engage? What should postcolonial Anglicanism pay attention to among the contributions of Barton? What is Barton's continuing relevance for Anglicanism? In answer, I will identify some of Barton's key thrusts. In my selected reading of her writings, what is crucially significant is how her God-talk evolved in the context of working with marginalized groups. Orthopraxis and activist theology may best describe her approach. This is important in order to locate the communal nature of Barton's contributions, largely situated in ecclesial contexts – especially marginal spaces in these contexts – and the many who have been part of her journey. Barton quickly became aware that her freedom is also a calling – to work for the freedom of others: 'As I felt more and more free to be the person God created me to be, I realized that my freedom is for freeing others.'

Interrogating systemic injustice

Mukti Barton is a product of the influence of the Bengal 'renewal', a movement by the Bengalis that saw a social awakening in the fields of art, culture, science, religions, intellect and society as a whole. This movement took shape from the nineteenth century to the early twentieth century, during the period of British colonial rule in India. Interrogating the prevailing state of affairs, the movement took on religious practices, British colonial rule, the dowry system, the caste system, the practice of sati, Brahmin supremacy, and more. Barton walks in this tradition while also interrogating its male and heteronormative tendencies. At the heart of this is Barton's advocacy of moving from the 'what?' question of lived realities to the tougher demand of the 'why?' question, which leads to tackling the systemic reasons behind the marginalization of oppressed peoples. This is where her encounter with theologies of liberation took intentional shape and pushed her to explore larger systemic issues. Barton wrote: 'I could see how our faith can work in our lives, freeing us from all that keeps us in bondage from within and without.' So, 'liberation optics' taught Barton to stand tall, raise the deeper questions, and 'challenge all that is unjust, so that God's kingdom may be established on earth'.[11]

In a 2013 interview with Lizzie Gawen, Barton notes: 'Liberation and justice are beneficial for the underprivileged but not for the overprivileged.' She goes on to assert that justice will only be realized when 'the over-privileged give up privileges that they have usurped'.[12] Such emptying is the sort of systemic challenge that Barton calls for, mindful that reality on the ground suggests that the privileged will not easily give up their privileges.[13] To this end, Barton interrogates whiteness, patriarchy, sexism, racist habits and entrenched racist practices by deploying her skilful re-reading of the Bible. For Barton, when the Bible is read from the perspectives of the powerless, its liberative aspects are activated to help bring release from social injustices. I cite two examples from Barton's work.

Firstly, in the context of the sexual exploitation of women in Bangladesh, Barton notes: 'Society all over the world labels its prostitutes as "sinners" and not the men who visit them.' Barton proceeds to do the maths around how many men (in a town as an example) would have visited in comparison to the number of women having to sell their bodies. For in order to earn a living, such a woman needs several clients each night, making the number of guilty men much higher than the number of prostitutes. Barton then asks: '*Where* are these culprits? *Who* hides them? Who gives them the right to live in normal society as "good" men while the prostitutes are totally cut off and abhorred by the same society? *Why* this hypocrisy?'[14] Deploying scriptures, Barton poses this question in the context of the woman who was labelled adulterous and hauled before Jesus (John 8.1–11). Pushing the systemic question, Barton asks what has happened to 'the adulterous man in the gospel story', why the men were picking up stones to throw, and what scriptures are justifying this?[15] A second example is her use of a play, the script of which she wrote around Luke 13.10–17. What is significant is the way she located and interpreted a familiar text (drawing on rabbinical interpretations and Bob Marley) to interrogate and expose patriarchal and religious barriers while drawing readers and audience into the context in order to grasp the layers of subversion in the text.[16] The underlying 'why?' question remains a constant.

Hermeneutical insubordination – humble lifted up, mighty tumbled down

As a South Asian biblical scholar and theologian working largely within ecclesial spaces, Mukti Barton draws on scriptures towards her habit of hermeneutical disobedience, insubordination and subversion. A liberation method-habit-optic is evident from the courses she crafted/taught, including black theology and Bible and liberation, in her approach to diocesan racial justice and anti-racism work, in her advocacy work,[17] and in mentoring BAME theologians and activists. Long before 'intersectionality' was on the radar of male black theologians in the UK, in writing from a black and Asian feminist perspective Barton was flagging up how various forms of oppression intersected. She was championing intersectional awareness to point out how black and Asian women were experiencing multiple oppressions.

Noting that the primary source for most church doctrines is the Bible, Barton wondered why for some ecclesial traditions 'women may be ordained', while for others they cannot. Or why, for some, equity in terms of roles occurs across gender while for others 'only secondary roles are allocated to women'. The question for Barton is how ecclesial communities can read the same scriptures with 'such serious discrepancies'? While sympathetic to a variety of readings, her problem is when such readings 'become oppressive for some people'.[18] The fact that the Bible has been and continues to be deployed to oppress groups of people, and that 'Christians are unwilling to blame the Bible itself for their oppression', is where Barton perceives that the 'question of hermeneutics' is critical.[19]

Working on the premise that interpreting scriptures favours either 'the perspective of the powerful or that of the powerless people', Barton sees the work of the hermeneut as 'a political activity'. Thus, the re-reading of Christian scriptures 'is not only a religious activity, but an important task towards creating a just society'.[20] Any 'absence of the voice of the powerless', often from 'traditional hermeneutics' of dominant male and white patriarchal perspectives, continues to 'legitimize structures of oppression' and silence marginalized voices. Barton perceives her task as unearthing these silenced voices.[21] She likens them to the 'stubborn faith of women whose persistent acts of hermeneutical insubordination will eventually topple kingdoms'.[22]

Barton's writings are replete with examples of her habit and method of hermeneutical insubordination. For the purposes of this short chapter, I cite a few examples. Reflecting on the story of Tamar, Barton observes how a victim becomes victor and how power located in the male (Judah) works to 'drive the powerless Tamar to the edge of life'. While it is often the case that the oppressed die unnoticed and the sins of the powerful remain hidden, 'the Tamar of the Hebrew scripture refuses to die silently'. The entrenched dominant hold of interpreters tends to invite readers to gravitate towards the 'what?' question in their response to Tamar's story. For Barton, though, 'Tamar is the woman who compels us to ask the "why?" question before the spiral of injustice pushes the whole of humanity to the edge of life.'[23]

Another daring intervention from Barton is to re-read the Hagar story with Christian and Muslim women in Bangladesh as a way for the women to reclaim their scriptures as a source of empowerment.[24] Her re-reading is situated by focusing on three strong women (Hagar, Susannah and the Samaritan woman) whose stories feature water and springs.[25] In Hagar, Barton works the angle that 'as the mother of Jews, Christians and Muslims', Hagar 'might become the first feminist role model for women of the Book'.[26] And, more:

> Hagar is a black Egyptian woman who, according to the Muslim tradition, was given asylum in Arabia. She can be seen symbolically as a black feminine figure with one foot in Africa and the other in Asia; the two continents where most of the world's poor live. Like Hagar, the black women of today's world still have to resist life denying forces in order to protect the lives of their children.[27]

Barton proceeds to advocate for 'a theology of the Hagars of today' and a more holistic and broader approach to Jesus as liberator of the marginalized than white feminist theology tended to take.[28] An unfinished piece of work that Barton has hinted at is about possible connection between 'the black feminine figure, Hagar' and '*Shakti* of the Tantric tradition in Bengal'. As she says, '*Shakti* is also symbolized by a black woman in the Tantric traditions that have inspired resistance movements in India, constantly subverting patriarchal religious culture.'[29]

Mukti Barton also took on the task of re-reading the biblical stories of creation and fall from the perspective of marginalized women.[30] Her original re-reading in the context of Bangladeshi women was later developed in the UK. Barton holds that oppression of women still gets justified through these stories of creation and fall. So, tackling these narratives and their interpretations is critical to both liberation and justice for all women. Biblical stories of creation need to be liberated from male and patriarchal interpretative captivity.[31] So Barton deploys a series of 'why?' and 'how?' questions: why are these narratives so formative in Christian theology and practice (with Eve still in the dock) even though Jesus only once referred to the texts, and in a positive and creative way? How and why do we 'keep quiet, when some people want to prove that "the word of God" is an instrument of torture?' Is this the God 'who is just and the liberator of all oppressed people, a God by whom all people are created equally' in the divine image?[32] Why are Christian men unable to 'find any stories, passages or verses in the Bible which makes them feel humiliated or inferior, just because they are created as men'?[33] A very important insight from Barton with implications for liturgy is her critique of vows of obedience (women to men) especially in marriage ceremonies, which continue to 'perpetuate women's oppression and subordination'.[34]

Mukti Barton's work on re-reading, reinterpreting and reclaiming scriptures from years of patriarchal, sexist, racist and heteronormative interpretations has been a major contribution to black theology in the UK. It has been a costly undertaking in the classroom and in the Church of England.

Feminism, solidarity and whiteness

Taking on patriarchy and whiteness, Barton challenged Christians in Bangladesh on their gullibility to European biblical interpretation and theological frames especially since such patriarchal and gender binary frameworks worked out even worse in Bangladesh.[35] In the UK, her experience of sexism was compounded by the added oppression of racism. Barton has documented her arrival in Britain in 1975 and the humiliation she faced at immigration. Her return from Bangladesh did not mean that the situation had improved. What was different for Barton was her greater awareness and engagement with feminism as a result of her active involvement in the United Nations Decade for Women (1976–85) and the World Council of Churches' Ecumenical Decade in Solidarity with Women (1989–98).[36]

Barton's engagement with feminism revealed the deficiency of white feminist solidarity in the UK. In spite of its rhetoric, white feminism 'was deficient in providing [Asian and black women] with resources that could fight imperial patriarchy'.[37] Thus, solidarity with white feminists in Britain continued to be a struggle for Barton, which she documents as 'painful'. Drawing insights from Hagar, Barton writes that in her estimation 'white women unconsciously collude with imperial patriarchy', making it challenging for the Hagars to form solidarity and sisterhood with the Sarahs. Sisterhood is compromised because of 'power imbalance'. It became clear to Barton that '[g]ender analysis without thorough race analysis keeps white feminists in a state of unknowing regarding their racism' and privilege.[38] This became ever more evident to Barton in academia. Felt called to teach after completing her PhD, she observed that while some of her white peers found lectureships in feminist theology on completing their doctorates, it was not the case for her. She soon realized that 'Feminist Theology meant *white* Feminist Theology, and no one can picture an Asian woman teaching this subject.'[39] As an invited 'token' side-show to teach occasional sessions, Barton could always predict what invited topics would be: suttee, Muslim veiling, Chinese foot binding, and African female genital mutilation.[40]

Barton's way into teaching was through black and Asian theology and theologies of liberation, linking to her diocesan role specifically geared at black and Asian ministries. In this context, Barton found solidarity in – and with – postcolonial feminist and womanist theologies, rather than with white feminist theology. The insidious reach and aliveness of whiteness meant that Barton found collective consciousness with people of colour, whether men or women.[41] Because white feminist theologians were still working within an imperial colonial framework, she reasoned: 'It must be extremely difficult for white feminists to be critical of the imperialism/colonialism that has bestowed on them the immeasurable privileges that they enjoy in today's world.'[42]

Barton takes on Mary Daly's *Gyn/Ecology: The Metaethics of Radical Feminism* to show how Daly operated within Western epistemology as the only one available. This is seen in the way Daly represented Asian women in stereotypes of docility. Barton's contention is that the idea of Western superiority runs through white feminist theology. Daly's optic was not the colonial context of Western feminism.[43] Noting the ease with which Daly wrote on Chinese foot binding and such like, Barton wondered why she did not then proceed to interrogate 'the oppressiveness of the Victorian corset or tight lacing'. This 'would have exposed the hypocrisy of the Victorian patriarchy which was criticizing Chinese foot-binding at a time when the Victorian woman's torso was bound', revealing 'how sexism, racism, classism functioned in unison', and it would have demonstrated 'the connection between torso binding, prolapsed uterus, hysterectomy and the rise of gynaecology in the West'.[44]

Barton pleads for 'an awareness of the part that imperial patriarchy has been playing in the lives of women of colour' and the collective need 'to be more vocal when imperial patriarchy uses feminist language in order to perpetuate Western hegemony in the world'. She challenges white feminists 'to be extra vigilant so that they do not inadvertently use imperial patriarchal language'. And all people of colour must especially invest in constantly growing their own knowledge production 'so that we are not solely dependent on western epistemology'.[45] In my view, the work of Barton in her teaching at Queen's has been critical in reversing the Euro/Western epistemology in ministerial formation in the UK.

Bible, black theology, racism

To reiterate: for Barton, a biblical scholar re-reading texts from an Asian feminist optic and through theologies of liberation, the Bible remains her key text. Barton's analysis has been intersectional as she deployed gender, colour and class lenses.[46] While feminists who followed Rosemary Radford Ruether have asked whether 'a male saviour can save women',[47] white theologians are yet to contemplate whether 'a black saviour can save white people'.[48] Barton suggests that part of the avoidance tactic of Western theology has been to make the Jewish Jesus 'into a blue-eyed blond-haired European' all within 'the parameters of a theology that is seen as an objective science of faith'.[49]

In her essay on 'The Bible in Black Theology'[50] Barton underscores that while the Bible was used to cause much suffering for black people, it remains pivotal in their lives and towards liberation. Among Barton's contributions is the case she makes about reclaiming the Bible's African and Asian roots. In this undertaking, Barton also points out how the very scriptures came back packaged to black and Asian peoples through distorted colonial missionary optics.[51] Drawing on black, womanist and contextual hermeneutics Barton's interpretative journey gives agency to subjective experiences and realities in which minorities are located. For Barton, this relates to Jesus' methodology: 'what is written in the law? What do *you* read here?' (Luke 10.26).[52]

Barton's main aim has been to wrest away biblical interpretation from dominant white and patriarchal classes: 'History shows that unless the powerful are constantly checked, they will manipulate the Bible for their own gain.' This is why liberation theologies remain a threat, for they have 'drawn the readers' attention to the socio-political-economic-cultural contexts of the Bible to understand their own contexts better'. Given the massive task of decolonizing, including minds, the tasks of black re-reading of the Bible and black theology remain urgent. For:

> Black Theology has shown how the spiritualization of the Bible, instead of enriching people spiritually, impoverishes them. By moving the sole focus from the individual sins, Black Theology has exposed the seriousness of structural sins and has consolidated corporate goodness to challenge corporate evil. Whenever injustice has been perpetuated in the name of the Bible, Black Theology has raised the alarm and proclaimed good news from the Bible to counteract evil.[53]

The reach of this distortion is so deep that Barton observes that if 'Jesus walked the streets of Britain today, most probably he would either be racially abused, or some good Christians would try to convert him to Christianity'. The inherited deposits from our ecclesial traditions have reached so far into psyches that people cannot even see truth when it stares them in the face. Hence Barton insists on a methodology 'of *unlearning everything* that our oppressors ever taught us'. To this end, 'recognition that the Bible is actually a book of the African-Asiatic people is immensely empowering for people who are oppressed just because of their skin colour'.[54] At the same time, the resulting cognitive dissonance of such teaching is challenging: 'If Christians have been indoctrinated to believe "all other species" to be naturally inferior to the whites', Barton notes, then it is not surprising that 'the African-Asiatic Jesus poses a huge challenge to that belief.' The result can be greater energy being invested by the white status quo into ensuring that Jesus remains a white male, and 'The myth of the White Jesus continues to be perpetuated through many things such as stained-glass windows, biblical films, theological book covers, Christmas and other religious cards.'[55]

In two significant essays, 'I Am Black and Beautiful' (2004)[56] and 'The Skin of Miriam Became as White as Snow' (2001),[57] Barton explores key issues around racism and anti-racist practice, interrogating the negative representation of 'black'. She challenges students, teaching colleagues and church leaders to become more aware of ways in which 'black' has been, and continues to be, used in negative ways that contribute to racism. While some might suggest that 'light and darkness, black and white are biblical metaphors', Barton disagrees. Her conclusion is that 'colours do not feature a great deal in the Bible'. However, she notes that there are occasions when 'European interpreters have read black and white colours into the texts when they are not present'. In fact, 'black hair and black human skin colours are praised in the Bible' in which the colour 'hardly ever has any negative significance'. Negative connections come with interpretations, the English language, and a clear link to the European colonial project.[58] In Barton's view, black and Asian scholars need to suspend and ignore 'European interpretations in order to understand the Bible in the context of the Black and Asian cultures from which the Bible originated'.[59] Rather, 'Black people [need] to rediscover their highly civilized heritage from the pages of the Bible.' And then demand that 'white people ... challenge their racist stereotyping especially of Black people'.[60] In this undertaking, Barton challenges her white feminist colleagues to work in solidarity with black and Asian women to rediscover this history. For 'unless the White feminists consciously reaffirm the non-white skin colour of the biblical people, their writings continue to perpetuate the myth that the Bible is about White people'.[61] Barton goes on to challenge:

White feminists have achieved much in challenging white patriarchy; but if their success in gaining leadership roles is won while Black people, especially Black women, remain excluded, then they collude with society's racism. Women genuinely struggling for justice for women in male societies will not need to have their power at the expense of anybody more vulnerable than them.[62]

There will be no justice in a society if racism continues. Solidarity is dead (from white feminists) if agency is given to Miriam at the expense of Zipporah.

Lest it be missed, Barton's critique and challenge was also directed to dominant male voices in black theology in Britain. While the afterlives of colonialism 'automatically group us as communities of black people, men and women together in our sufferings', Barton highlights a dangerous tendency. Similar to the ways white feminist theologians might claim to speak for all women, black male theologians unwittingly might suppose to do so for all black people. This is why Barton is clear that she is doing theology from black and Asian women's perspective.

What Mukti Barton observed in 2005 is still the case today: in (re)telling their stories, black and Asian peoples continue to open 'their resurrected wounds', inviting listeners and readers to 'Come see, come touch; don't run away from the pain; see if you too can know something of the joy of resurrection.'[63] Barton's 2015 assessment sums up both her journey and undertaking:

> I have come to recognize that the White superiority complex has seriously distorted the truth about humanity, the Bible and Jesus and divided the world on colour/ethnic lines. If we really want to deal with this serious world issue, a lot of time has to be given to systematic awareness-building processes ... It is a great pity that most theological colleges are not teaching theology from ethnic and colour perspectives in a systemic way.[64]

Spirituality for the Long Haul

Barton's engagement across theological education, ministerial and lay formation, minority ethnic matters and racism awareness work in the Church of England has sometimes been personally costly for her. On numerous occasions she has written about the physical, mental, emotional and intellectual demands placed on her that cannot be remotely compared to that of her white colleagues in their roles. At all levels of ecclesial life and their associated bodies, church systems in the UK are geared for whiteness and against black and Asian peoples. This fact does not need footnotes. For one to thrive in such circumstances there is a need for a sustaining spirituality for the long haul. This is one reason why Barton has worked continuously in partnership with others.

What Mukti Barton wrote in *Rejection, Resistance and Resurrection* includes her own wrestlings towards a sustaining spirituality. She facilitated a collection of stories from black and Asian Anglicans about the festering wounds of racism they experienced in the Church of England. Barton notes how 'through their storytelling Black people have opened up their wounds', not knowing 'whether there will be any chance of cleansing them' and pouring on ointment. But at least 'wounds will be aired', in hope of repentance on the part of the Church and some beginnings of a process of healing.[65] That process is only now taking some serious and intentional shape – many years later – hence the qualifier 'sustaining'. For Barton, 'the opening of wounds is a courageous act and so it is to view the wound'. But resurrection begins with these acts.

Barton, though, is not naïve about the cost. This is why she advocates the need for minority ethnic people to withdraw periodically into and among their own groups for their own health and well-being to avoid being crushed. This 'spirituality of space(s)' is critical for her work and that of the Black and Asian Network. To be able to pronounce and say a loud 'no' to dehumanization Barton recognizes the huge importance of creating a space for a spirituality to sustain both body and mind.[66] Barton's understanding of spirituality is communal as this is always a matter of being in relation to one's neighbour and in community. For Barton, signs of transcendence are 'to be found in death-defying hope, the hope of transforming the world for human betterment *together*, with acts of courage and self-sacrifice'. What feeds her spirituality is the strong liberating consciousness arising from common experiences 'leading to common hope of a transformed society'.[67] And key to Barton's sustaining spirituality is that of drawing strongly on the Bible through liberation and justice lenses with the overarching perspective being that of full and flourishing life for all. This becomes evident from the ways Barton models locating herself in a disposition necessary to interrogate the scriptures. Spirituality must be incarnational, communal and liberating.

It is crucially important to note that while Barton is critical of ecclesial practices and its oppressive theologies, she does so within her ecclesial family. It may be the case that Barton's spirituality for the long haul of presence and engagement in the Church of England also has a poetic element to it (through liturgy) which may have also been a source of energy and encouragement. Space does not allow me to reflect on how Barton deploys drama and short liturgical plays as part of her larger project of conscientization around re-reading the Bible.[68] But I note that drama and poetry are suggested as a communal act to give the Bible back to the people, as they inhabit the characters and the stories.[69] So in an Advent play, Barton intentionally begins and ends the play with words from Rabindranath Tagore both as a tribute and to talk back to coloniality which puts down Asian cultural forms. At the same time, in reclaiming cultural practices, Barton flags the need for extreme vigilance about oppressive elements in what might be taken to be cultural. Spirituality has to be vigilant.[70]

Postcolonial and Decolonial Impulses

Mukti Barton's contributions will always remain a challenge to both ecclesial communities and academic rhetoric. Like the Zapatistas and their approach of 'walking, we ask questions', Barton's work and articulation happen on the frontline of everyday realities: witness, solidarity, struggle, realism, dreaming and actions. Often perceived as 'the other' in the UK, Barton's God-talk blossomed 'from a will to resist and challenge destructive stereotypes' about herself and all people perceived similarly. She has conscientized and empowered a wide cross-section of people in ministries across the ecumenical family. Her work is always about justice for others.

Unlike what currently passes as decolonial work which is not necessarily of much benefit for a more just world, Barton's work and relevance sits elsewhere. It is directed towards a more just view of community and the world. The relevance of Barton's contributions will continue to be necessary given the urgent and ongoing work around whiteness and coloniality in the Church of England, wider Anglicanism, and elsewhere. The work of epistemic subordination and disobedience has only just started.

Reading all her contributions as a whole I sense Barton leading us through a thick undergrowth of theological and biblical distortions, witnessing to her fullest of what was taken from us, what was lost to us, what has been concealed from us, and what we have let slip into forgetfulness. In so doing, Barton challenges us to join the project of seeing, unearthing, mourning and of recovering for the victims of colonial violence and for ourselves the possibility of waking up in another book and on a kinder and more flourishing page.

Notes

1 This will be evident from his numerous books, citing and references, and at https://www.theosthinktank.co.uk/comment/2020/08/12/black-theology-an-intro duction (accessed 29.1.2024).

2 Mukti Barton, 'Reflections on being a Racial Justice Champion', in *Racial Justice Champions*, ed. Richard Reddie (CTBI, 2021), 6, https://ctbi.org.uk/racial-justice-champions/ (accessed 29.1.2024).

3 See Chronixx, https://www.youtube.com/watch?v=LfeIfiiBTfY (accessed 29.1.2024).

4 'Immediately at arrival, without any explanation, very swiftly I was separated from my husband and was taken to a room where I was ordered to strip the top half of my body. I tried desperately to cover myself as I had to walk through a corridor to another room to have my chest x-rayed. I noticed that all the others going through the same process were women of colour. After the x-ray, I was allowed to go, as no sign of tuberculosis was found. Because of the heavy-handedness and the abusing nature, I felt violated as a woman of colour. I also wondered why my white husband was exempt from this treatment. Has he not been living in a "TB-ridden India" with his wife? I understood well that while tuberculosis is not racially biased, the nation I was entering definitely was' (Barton, 'Reflections', 6). It is important to remember that Barton's experience would not have been different from the 'virgin-ity tests' carried out by immigration at Heathrow on South Asian women in the late 1970s. See https://www.runnymedetrust.org/histories/race-equality/73/virginity-tests-at-heathrow.html/ (accessed 29.1.2024).

5 'Mukti's Story', in *Ethnicity*, ed. Michael Jagessar (London: Darton, Long-man and Todd, 2015), 35–44 (36).

6 Mukti Barton, *Scripture as Empowerment for Liberation and Justice: The Experience of Christian and Muslim Women in Bangladesh* (Bristol: University of Bristol, 1999).

7 Barton, 'Reflections', 7.

8 Barton, 'Reflections', 7.

9 Barton, 'Reflections', 8.

10 Mukti Barton, *Freedom Is for Freeing* (Birmingham: Birmingham Diocese, 2010), 2.

11 Barton, *Freedom*, 2.

12 Mukti Barton, 'Sowing the Seeds: Liberation, Emancipation and Freedom', Interview by Lizzie Gawen (15 February 2013). Unnumbered pages. This was a blog that is no longer available, but a printed copy of the blog was shared with the author.

13 Here Barton pointed to Matthew 23.13, 'For you lock people out of the king-dom of heaven. For you do not go in yourselves, and when others are going in, you stop them', to underscore her point.

14 Mukti Barton, 'Jesus Christ and the Sexual Exploitation of Women', *In God's Image*, 26 (1990): 24–6 (25).

15 Barton, 'Sexual Exploitation': 26.

16 Mukti Barton, 'Get Up, Stand Up, Stand Up for Your Rights' (A Play based on Luke 13:10–17)', *In God's Image*, 28 (2009): 3–6.

17 Barton writes that her work may be described as 'advocacy theology'. See Barton, *Scripture as Empowerment*, 154.

18 Mukti Barton, 'Hermeneutical Insubordination: Toppling Worldly Kingdom', in *Black Theology in Britain: A Reader*, eds Michael N. Jagessar and Anthony G. Reddie (London: Equinox Publishing, 2007), 166–74 (167).

19 Barton, 'Hermeneutical Insubordination', 168.

20 Barton, *Scripture as Empowerment*, 153.

21 Barton, 'Hermeneutical Insubordination', 168.

22 Barton, 'Hermeneutical Insubordination', 173.

23 Mukti Barton, 'From Victim to Victor: A Black Feminist Re-reading of Genesis 38', in *The Women's Christian Yearbook 2003*, eds Natalie K. Watson, Brigitte Enzner-Probst and Hanna Strack (Norwich: Canterbury Press, 2003), unnumbered pages.

24 Barton, *Scripture as Empowerment*, 1.

25 Barton, *Scripture as Empowerment*, 152.

26 Barton, *Scripture as Empowerment*, 151.

27 Barton, *Scripture as Empowerment*, 151.

28 Barton, *Scripture as Empowerment*, 152.

29 Barton, *Scripture as Empowerment*, 152.

30 Mukti Barton, *Creation and Fall and the Women of Bangladesh* (Dhaka: Netritto Proshikkhon Kendro, 1992); also, 'Woman and Man in Creation', in *Women of Courage: Asian Women Reading the Bible*, ed. the Asian Women's Resource Centre for Culture and Theology (Seoul: AWRC, 1992), 35–51.

31 Barton, *Creation and Fall*, 6.

32 Barton, *Creation and Fall*, 14.

33 Barton, *Creation and Fall*, 15.

34 Barton, *Creation and Fall*, 30.

35 Barton, *Creation and Fall*, 16.

36 Mukti Barton, 'Wrestling with Imperial Patriarchy', *Feminist Theology*, 21.1 (2012): 7–25 (9).

37 Barton, 'Wrestling': 9.

38 Barton, 'Wrestling': 11.

39 Barton, 'Wrestling': 12.

40 Barton, 'Wrestling': 11

41 Barton, 'Wrestling': 12

42 Barton, 'Wrestling': 14.

43 Barton, 'Wrestling': 17.

44 Barton, 'Wrestling': 21.

45 Barton, 'Wrestling': 25.

46 Mukti Barton, 'Race, Gender, Class and the Theology of Empowerment: an Indian Perspective', in *Gender, Religion and Diversity: Cross Cultural Perspectives*, eds Ursula King and Tina Beattie (London: Continuum, 2004), 225–37 (226).

47 Rosemary Radford Ruether, *Sexism and God-talk: Towards a Feminist Theology* (London: SCM Press), 98–116.

48 See, for example, Anthony G. Reddie, *Introducing James H. Cone: A Personal Exploration* (London: SCM Press, 2023), 33, note 8.

49 Barton, 'Race, Gender, Class', 234.

50 Mukti Barton, 'The Bible in Black Theology', *Black Theology: An International Journal*, 9.1 (2011): 57–76.

51 Barton, 'Bible': 59.

52 Barton, 'Bible': 61.

53 Barton, 'Bible': 74.

54 Barton, 'Race, Gender, Class', 234.

55 'Mukti's Story', 41.

56 Mukti Barton, 'I Am Black and Beautiful', *Black Theology: An International Journal*, 2.2 (2004): 167–87.

57 Mukti Barton, 'The Skin of Miriam Became as White as Snow: The Bible, Western Feminism and Colour Politics', *Feminist Theology* 9 (2001): 68–80. Reprinted in *The Bible, Gender and Sexuality: Critical Readings*, eds Rhiannon Graybill and Lynn R. Huber (London: T&T Clark, 2021), 291–300. My references from the latter.

58 Barton, 'Beautiful': 185.

59 Barton, 'Beautiful': 186.

60 Barton, 'Skin of Miriam': 293.

61 Barton, 'Skin of Miriam': 293.

62 Barton, 'Skin of Miriam': 297.

63 Mukti Barton, *Rejection, Resistance and Resurrection: Speaking out on Racism in the Church* (London: Darton, Longman and Todd, 2005), 135.

64 'Mukti's Story', 42.

65 Barton, *Rejection*, 10.

66 Barton, 'Race, Gender, Class', 229.

67 Mukti Barton, *Liberation Spirituality as a Signal of Transcendence: Christian and Muslim Women in Bangladesh* (Oxford: Westminster College, 1988), 1, 22.

68 Mukti Barton, 'An Advent Play', *Black Theology: An International Journal*, 12.1 (2014): 33–43 (33).

69 Barton, 'Advent': 37.

70 Barton, 'Advent': 39.

4

Burgess Carr

HERMAN BROWNE

Burgess Carr, who was born on 8 July 1935 and died on 14 May 2012, was the third child of his father, George S. Best,[1] and the first of his mother, Cerue Henderson.[2] Burgess had several siblings,[3] and spent his early childhood in Crozierville,[4] a peri-urban town about 30 miles outside Monrovia. His early education was at the St Patrick's High School in Monrovia, and the boarding school of St John's High in Robertsport for his secondary education. He then did undergraduate studies at Cuttington College and Divinity School,[5] where in 1955–8 he studied for a BSc in Agriculture,[6] and in 1959–61 a Bachelor of Divinity. Shortly after becoming a priest in 1962, he obtained in 1964 a Master of Theology degree in Old Testament from Harvard Divinity School.[7] Between his time at Cuttington and Harvard, Carr married Francesca Verdier[8] whom he had met while at Cuttington.

Carr was a committed priest, a fiery preacher and a sensitive pastor. His first major posting was at the World Council of Churches (WCC) in Geneva as the Africa Secretary; and soon after he became Executive Secretary for the Commission of Churches on International Affairs. The Biafran War in Nigeria had begun, and he was travelling back and forth to deliver food aid while doing WCC business from Geneva. He made his mark on the WCC, and in 1972 Carr was asked to take up the post of Secretary General of the All Africa Conference of Churches (AACC), a position he held from 1972 to 1978.

In 1972, Carr moderated the Addis Ababa Agreement[9] which ended the first Sudanese civil war. He was awarded the distinction of Grand Corodon in the Order of the Two Niles by Sudanese president Gaafar Nimiery for this mediating role. For this as well as his work for relief and reconciliation work during Nigeria's civil war, he was awarded the Commander in the Order of the Star of Africa by Liberian president William V. S. Tubman.[10] It was from this vantage point at the AACC that much of the scope of Carr's interests and the depth of his passion for the Church's mission and ministry came to the fore. Yet, as Harold Miller relates:

despite being the site of his finest achievements, Burgess' tenure at AACC ended in turmoil. He had made powerful enemies within the Kenyan government and many in the AACC organization had grown weary of its politicization. He was suspended from his position at an emergency meeting in Lome, Togo and soon after stepped down. Like the people he would learn to serve in later appointments, in 1978, Burgess and his family became refugees, hastily leaving Kenya for the USA. He held lectureships at Harvard Divinity School, Andover Newton, Boston Theological School, Episcopal Divinity School (Boston), and was Associate Professor at Yale Divinity School. From 1987 to 1994 Burgess worked as the Partnership Officer for Africa and Executive Director of Episcopal Migration ministries.[11]

Despite this very unsettled experience, his 'reputation as a scholar and advocate for peace and justice lent credibility to his work, and allowed him to influence Africa's trajectory', especially in the 1980s.[12] He did so again (perhaps even more so) in the 1990s while in Geneva with the World Bank, the United Nations Development Program, UNICEF, and the Economic Commission for Africa through which he influenced responses to problems ranging from refugees, children involved in armed conflict, post-conflict reconstruction and peace-building. In 2000, he moved to the Atlanta area of Georgia, USA, taking up the role of vicar of St Timothy Episcopal Church, while also teaching at the Candler School of Theology in Emory University. But in 2004 he became ill with Lewy body disease, had a stroke in 2007, and died peacefully in his sleep on 14 May 2012.

Context

Burgess Carr rose to prominence at a time when several major society-altering events were coming to public attention in Liberia and elsewhere. They came together to form clearly in his mind a sense of what must be the issues of the day and therefore what the theologian must face, the churchperson who cares must address, and what leaders who shepherd people well must heed. His legacy is shaped by several biographical, political and theological factors converging.

Biography

Carr grew up with an uncle who was a political activist constantly on the national scene and in the print media. This uncle was extremely popular because he took up the causes of underprivileged people. Carr's very articulate uncle would later – in the 1980s – be hailed as the 'father of the revolution' that overthrew a 133-year one-party political hegemony. Carr's father was also an erudite churchman, agriculturalist and rhetorician, using print media to advance his views and change the attitude of Liberians towards nation-building. He urged Liberians to pride themselves in self-governance and self-reliance, and reduce the deep divisions nurtured and fostered by denominations. Perhaps like his father, Carr's enthusiasm for leadership, grip on the politics of change, and pursuit of eloquence manifested itself in his ministry early on; and all of this was re-enforced by Carr's theological training which left him deeply suspicious of a crude separation between Church and state. Having acquainted himself somewhat with rumours of a new way of doing theology that was emerging from the slums of Latin America (later to be characterized as liberation theology), it is as if Carr felt himself to be on a personal mission – like his vocal male role models before him – not to keep quiet while injustice prevailed in the land.

Politics

Carr's upbringing and education placed him squarely in the elite class of the infamous government of the True Whig Party. The sentiment against a one-party state, and the overwhelming push for multi-party democracy, was palpable in the circles in which he moved. In the West African region, liberation struggles in countries like Ghana, Togo, Nigeria and Côte d'Ivoire had recently resulted in new democracies and new national fervour, with secessionist strife like the Biafran War. The justice issues surrounding the Vietnam war, apartheid South Africa, the liberation struggles of Angola, Mozambique, Guinea-Bissau, and Cape Verde were in all the news media, and Carr's theological filter would soon crystallize into a sense of who would fall into the category of the 'oppressors' as distinct from the victims.

Socio-economics

While the 1960s and early 1970s saw a rise in GDP growth and industry in Liberia, the acute feeling was that a small portion of the population, generally assumed to be the Americo-Liberians, disproportionately benefited. Farther afield, the newly independent countries were already beginning to discover the tenuousness of political freedom without economic security.

There was a strong sense of an ever-widening divide between the Americo-Liberians (descendants of freed formerly enslaved African settlers) and the indigenous Liberians (descendants of those who the settlers met on the soil). The economic disparities stretched the socio-economic divide along these ethnic lines. Social inequities became stark, such that economically deprived communities were predominantly those with indigenous backgrounds and the societal prejudices re-enforced their low status. People were aware through the 1960s of intensification of racism elsewhere too, especially in the social inequity of segregation in America, the civil rights movement that led to the assassination of President John F. Kennedy, Robert Kennedy and Martin Luther King Jr, and eventual amendments to the American Constitution affirming liberties hitherto denied to African Americans.

Ecclesially

The American Episcopal Church had reached a point where it felt that it was inevitable that indigenous personnel should take on the leadership, and in 1970 the first indigenous bishop was elected by Liberians. This was not just signalling that Liberians should take the lead, but that Liberians should take pride in a 'truly Liberian' church. This change required a healthy dialogue with, and an adaptation to, the indigenous culture and milieu. The drive for indigenization or inculturation would later show itself on two fronts: our liturgy that needed to take on the colour or ethos of the culture; and our theological language that soon took on the logic of indigenous beliefs consonant with our Christian faith.

At this point, one can almost predict the dominant themes that would eventually emerge in Carr's ministry, yet it would take a further four decades to develop in nationally and globally significant ways. But it is from this biographical, political, socio-economic and ecclesial milieu that Carr released his passion for justice through prophetic advocacy. He knocked on doors, and shouted from the rooftops announcing his sense that God's people deserved better. Public advocacy was his means, while the pen was an ancillary tactic. His passion for justice and his work towards unity in both national life and church life are enduring legacies.

One way of looking at Carr's contribution is through his lens of (what at the time was called 'self-determination') autonomy or independence. He sought economic, cultural and political independence both for churches and states of Africa; and this came out clearly both in his writing and in what he said. In what follows, I highlight his penchant for justice and unity in political and ecclesial fields, his shaping of national and church life, and I do so in relation to four of his key areas of interest: (1) justice; (2) inculturation; (3) moratorium on funding; and (4) churches standing together.

Justice

Burgess Carr's legacy is that he lifted up justice as a non-negotiable value, and unity as its resultant corollary. He was vociferous in pursuit of both. The complexity of Carr's passion is reflected in the twists and turns of his ministry. Though critical of the Liberian 26-year regime under William Tubman, it was Tubman who gave him a national distinction for his sterling role in the ending of the Biafran War.[13] Tubman would later be banished from Kenya, for having confronted the dictator Idi Amin of Uganda (whose government had assassinated the Anglican Archbishop Janani Luwum),[14] and branded a 'meddler' by the Kenyan attorney general Charles Njonjo was also decorated by Sudan for his key role in ending the civil war between the south and north of that country.

Justice for Carr was the fundamental insight of the Christian faith, and it could only find expression in reality through the taking of sides.[15] There could be no real and actual, tangible, more just, state of affairs unless and until a position or a stance with the oppressed was both adopted and pursued. This inevitably means being reviled, hated, avoided and disregarded by some, while accepted and championed by others. The Christian has the option to choose which side to take. The preference that should be made by the Christian theologian, in Carr's unswerving view, is that they must align with the interests of the poor, the exploited, disadvantaged and marginal groups. Carr's advocacy in his home country, Liberia, is well documented, as is his work on the African continent in Sudan, Nigeria and Kenya. Yet his little-known period spent working in the refugee and migrant sector in his later years illustrates his undying commitment to justice for the poor.

Carr was well aware that those on whose behalf he advocated for freedom and liberation had a responsibility to maintain and keep themselves 'free' and 'unshackled'. The churches could be crucial to this effort.[16] Churches needed to promote freedom in real space and real time. At a time when patriotism and nationalism were watchwords, especially for new African democracies, Carr believed that the churches should also be equally independent culturally, financially and politically. They were invited by him to take pride in their own indigenous culture, be less dependent on their 'mother churches' for their daily bread, and urged to resist any foreign leadership of their churches on their continent. In other words, he was clearly of the mind that the churches of Africa had come of age.[17]

Inculturation

Part of the struggle for independence was a fight for a people's self-determination. This demanded that others recognize their potential and ability to be a sovereign nation, to take their own place in the comity of nations. They must struggle for their dignity, worth and value as a people to be recognized. But the struggle, for Carr, was not just about being free to do what we want with our resources, but being free to be ourselves – in other words, not to have to duplicate what others do. In one most memorable statement he said: 'As long as the churches in Africa remain "potted plants", nurtured by ideas, funds and personnel from churches in Europe and North America, their real relevance to the urgent questions facing Africa and its people will continue to be distorted.'[18] While we are all of the one human race, we have different values, cultural milieux, and social and political restraints. The Church must be itself where it finds itself.

His call to indigenize, enculturate and acclimatize to the ethnicity of our continent became very loud and clear in Carr's work. He was one of the earliest popularizers of what has now become a common feature of our churches: to review worship (music, drama, language, images, etc.), laws and theology, and to reflect better and more deeply our African identity as Church. He also advocated that by adopting local theological and culturally grounded concepts, the Church could better communicate the gospel to local people and more effectively minister to them.[19] In the Liberian Anglican setting, Carr was the key pioneer in advocating a Christian theology that was authentically African.[20]

Moratorium on funding

In many of his sermons and speeches, Carr urged the churches in Africa to strive towards financial self-reliance, warning of the day when their respective churches whose headquarters were based in Geneva, Hamburg, London, New York or elsewhere would no longer be willing or able to support their 'satellite' churches in Africa. So, he called for a moratorium on all funding from overseas to churches in Africa and on all mission-aries being sent to Africa. Money and missionaries should both cease.[21] His rationale was clearly to thrust on to the churches the predicament of sustaining themselves and governing themselves. Carr felt the time was long overdue to end the missionary sentiment that the unconverted on the continent were incapable of being converted by the churches on the continent.[22]

Many agreed that the churches in Africa had come of age, but Carr's call for a moratorium was controversial. His moratorium call felt like a stab in the back to some churches in Africa. It 'caused a huge rift among African churches, with many unwilling to let go the lucrative purse strings flowing from the Western churches'.[23] And while it took many churches a great deal of time to adjust to the reality for which Carr hoped, it hit home very quickly for the Lutheran Church in Liberia.[24] But whether they supported the moratorium or not, many churches stood firmly behind a 'three-self' approach: self-reliance, self-governance, and self-propagation, all principles first articulated by Anglican elders Henry Venn and Rufus Anderson.[25]

Churches standing together

Carr quickly became aware from his work at the AACC that ecumenical diversity had the corollary of foreign allegiances. Some churches could not cooperate with one another without first getting approvals from their foreign headquarters. This made ecumenical work on the continent frustrating and difficult. The Western churches were already dialoguing among themselves in search of a unified structure of authority that would give the greatest expression to what it means to be fully and visibly united.

In this context, Carr advocated that what churches needed in Africa was not the structural, institutional unity that Western churches were seeking, but something else. He did not want to downplay effort towards full visible unity among churches. But he was against others getting involved in the building of sovereign nations. As institutionally divided as they were, churches could still express the mystical unity of the body of Christ in their love expressed for one another locally. Their ecumenical cooperation in relief work and their collaboration in advocacy should never be overlooked.[26] For the local churches, this was not just about being free, but about being felt – being felt as collective actors on their own country's politically charged stage.[27] This was his message from the AACC. Gradually, churches heeded his call to cooperate and collaborate within local ecumenical bodies, and this brought much renewed fervour and a transforming aspect to the African ecumenical landscape.[28]

Incarnation

Given his work over the years in pursuing a more equitable and just society, his work towards the self-reliance of churches, their cultural renewal, and their having a united local voice, one can surmise Burgess Carr's view of the incarnation. That 'the word was made flesh' was not enough to generate the level of passion and compulsion within Carr to have driven him to become as involved in socio-political matters as he did. Any god can come and go. To understand Carr's convictions about incarnation it is necessary also to feel the weight of the additional insight: '... and dwelt among us' (John 1.14). This is what drove Carr's enthusiastic fight for justice. It was the engagement of God himself with our world, and with the powers that be, that holds the key to Carr's beliefs. If God was sufficiently moved by love for the world (John 3.16) that he visited it, and this same God in his wholly other-ness and pure radiance visited us *as us*, engaging the most difficult of human affairs, then this leaves Carr with no excuse to be either absent or silent in the midst of the problems wrought by injustice and heaped on to the faithful and the unfaithful alike. Carr's conviction of the incarnation as event was his theological warrant to engage the political sphere, and to fight against the inequities that resulted from the ferocious injustice of political institutions, policies and actions.

Carr's Relevance

As a theologian, Burgess Carr is a role model, an inspiration for others to follow, and an example of what it is possible to achieve in highly pressured political environments. He demonstrated the value of Christian theologians in peace-building efforts. Carr was theologically pioneering, ecumenically vocal, and politically impactful.

He is one of the earliest African theologians to sit rather loosely to ideas that separated the domain of the state from the domain of the Church. He believed that the 'people of God' were void of nationalities, ethnicities, colour or gender. The wholesome flourishing of the human person was what mattered most to him, and injustice was a way of speaking of anything that frustrated or quenched that flourishing, its potential, and benefit to future generations.

Carr's genius also lies in his striving to bring out the better side of both oppressor and victim. His focus on public actors and institutions was matched only by his insistence that those adversely affected must also demonstrate greater responsibility for a more just world. He gave much-needed confidence to churches to take seriously their responsibility for their own sustainability (or self-reliance efforts), their own liturgical renewal, and indigenous leadership.

Notes

1 Best emigrated to Liberia from Trinidad in 1926. Having graduated from Howard University in 1913 in theology, he was conscripted in World War One as a British subject and sent to many parts of Africa, the Middle East and Europe. He was both tiller of the soil, and quite a public-speaking linguist, speaking six European languages, including Arabic, French and Spanish. He moved to Crozierville, Montserrado County, and ardently attached himself to Christ Episcopal Church there, breaking grounds for the present edifice in 1929. He died on 13 April 1945 (Kenneth Y. Best, *Albert Porte: A Lifetime Trying to Save Liberia* (Monrovia: Observer Publishing House, 2007), 28).

2 After her firstborn, she later had Mala and Carmena. This matriarch also mothered Anthony Deline (Most Worshipful Grand Master, F&AM, RL) and Charles Gyude Bryant, who at one time was Head of State of the Republic of Liberia (2003–5); and brought up Albert Porte of great renown in Liberia as a free-thinking political activist, constitutional analyst and crusader for human rights opposing a one-party democracy, then led by Presidents Tubman and William R. Tolbert Jr. The more than a century-old political hegemony was overturned in 1980 in a bloody coup d'etat, which brought the infamous Samuel K. Doe to power.

3 Muriel Best, Sybil Best, Beryl Best, Kenneth Best, Guinevere, Anthony Deline, C. Gyude Bryant, Mala and Carmena.

4 A rather small town known as an enclave for Americo-Liberian settlers was also home to the Weeks, Portes, Goodridges, Coxes, Crawfords, Padmores, Thorpes, Eastmans, Holders, and many elite families.

5 Cuttington, founded in 1889, was the first four-year degree-granting, co-educational, liberal arts college in Sub-Saharan Africa. Some of his classmates became equally well known, such as Kate Bryant (a Cabinet minister), Dr Varney Freeman (Liberia's first paediatrician), Dr Joseph Diggs, George Browne (first indigenous Anglican diocesan bishop), Dr Vuyu Golakai (first radiologist), Arthur Kulah, Roland Diggs (first indigenous Methodist and Lutheran bishops, respectively), etc.

6 An odd choice of one whose calling was the priesthood, one would think, but his brother does not think so. 'He wanted to be a priest and felt he needed to help his people and his family by showing them how to grow crops and become self-reliant in food production' (Best, *Albert Porte*, 32).

7 Although Bishop Bravid Harris at the time preferred Virginia Theological Seminary, Carr's choice put him on an academic track, and left his pursuit of a doctorate from Harvard Divinity School to take up a job in Geneva as the Africa Secretary of the World Council of Churches, 1964–7.

8 Married for more than 50 years, they were blessed with five children, Audrey (1963), Kedrick (1964), Oyeshiku (1970), Yao (1975) and Mleh (1977). See Harold Miller, 'Burgess Carr (A Life)', in John Ashworth and South Sudan Info (Nairobi, Kenya, 2021).

9 Also known as the Addis Ababa Accord, this was a set of compromises within a 1972 treaty that ended the first all-out war between residents in the South of

Sudan (1955–72). It was incorporated into the constitution of Sudan, granting greater autonomy to the Southern region. At the time, it diffused the steam from a Southern secessionist movement.

10 'Burgess Carr', Wikipedia (accessed 17.5.2022).

11 See Miller, 'A Life'.

12 Miller, 'A Life'.

13 He accepted this recognition, though rumoured not himself to be a fan of Tubman owing to his own sympathy with the integrity and justice issues incessantly raised against Tubman's government by his uncle Albert Porte. His uncle would later (in 1980) be owned and proclaimed 'Father' of the Liberian revolution by the Peoples Redemption Council (Best, *Albert Porte*, 169).

14 Janani Luwum, the Anglican Archbishop of Uganda, Rwanda, Burundi and Boga-Zaire, was executed along with two other Cabinet ministers accused of treason. Their bodies were found riddled with bullet holes in early February 1977. Luwum's amazing courage and calm in the face of clear danger is celebrated worldwide. He protested against Idi Amin's arbitrary killings and unexplained disappearance of people. He is commemorated around the Anglican Communion as a martyr of the Christian faith.

15 He was a firebrand preacher and supported anti-colonial resistance politically and militarily. His justification was sharp and short, 'In accepting the violence of the cross, God in Jesus Christ, sanctified violence into a redemptive instrument'. As a freedom fighter, in the words of a Kenyan carpenter, 'he roared like a jumbo jet, and his words were like bullets'. See 'Religion: Ousting the Pope of Africa', *Time Magazine* (March 1978).

16 While some agreed with the general principle here of the critical role of churches, others still questioned whether the argument had been fully made. One participant, Tom Wright, accused the WCC of taking an ideological position of liberation/action that was still in search of a thorough-going philosophical and theological basis and argumentation. Since a methodology was simply adopted and the rationale for doing so was not made clear, then far from simply being a critique of WCC's position the real import of Wright's critique was to make the WCC, and with it the AACC, more self-aware of the starkly different methodology employed in their position and theological reflections which careful thinkers like himself could quickly identify. See N. T. Wright, *Nairobi: Action in Search of Reflection*, https://biblicalstudies.org.uk/pdf/churchman/090-02_110.pdf, 24 pages (accessed 29.1.2024).

17 Carr's precise language was equally tactful. 'Leave us alone for a while, so that we may be able to discover ourselves, and you, in Jesus Christ' (Burgess Carr, 'The Mission of the Moratorium', *Occasional Bulletin of the Missionary Research Library*, 25.2 (1975), 1–9 (9)).

18 Burgess Carr, 'African Churches in Conflict', *The Harvard Crimson* (April 1978).

19 See Carr, 'Moratorium'.

20 Carr, 'African Churches in Conflict': 4. 'The moratorium strategy also calls upon the churches to become more authentically African by incorporating into their theological, liturgical and administrative life style Africa's own religious traditions. Much of this is already happening in the so-called Independent churches of Africa. It is the missionary established churches that are being urged to change.'

21 Carr was not the first to call for a moratorium on funding and personnel from

foreigners. That fame goes to John Gatu, then Secretary General of the Presbyterian Church of East Africa, who had raised the suggestion back in 1971, and only formally proposed it in 1972. However, Carr's position at the AACC gave him the platform to be the face behind the idea. It was only following Carr's presentation to the Lusaka Conference in 1974 that it got the attention it deserved up to this day. For Carr, it was essentially ... a strategy designed to promote the self-reliance of the churches and, by implication, greater freedom to speak out and act on African issues ...' See Carr, 'Moratorium'. For background and debates in the 1970s on this issue, see Robert Reese, 'John Gatu and the Moratorium on Missionaries', *Missiology: An International Review*, 42.3 (2014): 245–56.

22 By 1972, his native church in Liberia had taken up that challenge with its first indigenous bishop, George D. Browne, to renew or replant the church in the African soil, and from being a satellite of the American Episcopal Church in 1981 joined the African Church of the Anglican Province of West Africa. See G. D. Browne, *The Episcopal Church Under Indigenous Leadership* (Chicago: Third World Publishers, 1994); Reese, 'John Gatu': 31.

23 Best, *Albert Porte*, 39.

24 Best, *Albert Porte*, 39: 'In 1973, for example, the American Lutherans, who had for decades been supporting the Lutheran Church in Liberia, announced that owing to the shortage of funds, they could no longer continue to finance the ultra-modern hospital, Phebe, which they had built in the rural Liberian town of Suacoco. The church in America said it was now devoting its attention to "the heathen at home", rather than "the heathen abroad".'

25 Henry Venn was Secretary General of the Church Missionary Society, and Rufus Anderson was Foreign Secretary of the American Board of Commissioners for Foreign Missions in the mid-nineteenth century. John Livingstone Nevius (a missionary to China and Korea) developed the three self principles of Venn and Anderson into a plan for establishing indigenous churches, known as the Nevius Method. In the twentieth century, Roland Allen (Anglican missionary to China) promoted this principle in establishing indigenous churches; and the Three Self Patriotic Movement is now the officially sanctioned form of Protestant Christianity in mainland China.

26 At a young age, Carr had a passion for synergies and knew the real impact that standing together can bring about. He was still an undergraduate at Cuttington College and Divinity School in 1957 when he organized a group of young Liberians into the National Student Christian Council (NSCC), now an affiliate of the World Student Christian Federation. Carr was elected the NSCC's first chairman.

27 In his native Liberia, it was not until 1982 that a Liberian Council of Churches was formed, primarily in order to raise a common voice on issues of national concern during a military regime when freedom of speech was effectively banned with the promulgation of Decree 88A. Its first President was a contemporary of Carr, a former member of the NSCC, and the first indigenous Liberian Diocesan Bishop, George Browne.

28 Ecumenical synergies (national councils, sub-regional fellowships) across the continent have accompanied decolonization and nation-building on the African continent, and played their part in the dismantling of apartheid in South Africa. Both as a platform for a collective voice and collective action, local churches standing together continue to have an impact on issues affecting social and economic justice, health and wholeness, the environment, governance, and international trade and relations.

5

Verna J. Dozier

KAREN MEREDITH

Verna Josephine Dozier was born on 9 October 1917, in Washington DC, the city in which she lived her entire life (except for a year teaching in Baltimore).[1] The family lived in a black working-class neighbourhood in north-east Washington. Her father Lonna, whose education in rural Georgia had ended at eighth grade, worked as a labourer at the government printing office, adding a second job to support the family and allow his wife Lucie, a graduate of Armstrong High School, to leave her job to stay at home with their children, Verna and her younger sister Lois.

Despite his limited formal education, Lonna Dozier had a passion for learning which he instilled in Verna. She describes him as one with 'a searching mind' and expressed belief that racism had prevented him from opportunities to exercise his intellectual potential. He read every book his daughters brought home from school and discussed with them what they learned. Her mother shared with the girls her love of Shakespeare and the Bible, and she was determined that both girls would be college educated. Verna recalled spending evenings with her mother and sister, taking different parts in a play or reading dramatically from the Bible – the prophet Amos being her favourite. She claimed that her talent was in 'oration', a love she carried into her teaching of English literature and her preaching and Bible study. She was known throughout her life for her beautiful speaking voice.

An avid student, Verna Dozier graduated from Dunbar High School at 15, having skipped two grades, and went on to Howard University in Washington where she was greatly influenced by the sermons of the dean of the chapel, Howard Thurman. She was awarded a BA in English in 1937 and an MA in English Literature in 1938.

Dozier taught English Literature for 27 years in the Washington DC public school system (state school system in the UK), mostly in segregated high schools. When the new integrated Ballou High School opened in 1959 she was hired as chair of the English Department. After leaving Ballou in 1972 she became a department head in the Division of Instruction for the

Washington DC Schools, from which she retired in 1975. She was known for her innovative approach to developing the curriculum.

Dozier's family were members of the Nineteenth Street Baptist Church. Her sister and mother remained Baptists, but the young Verna was, she said, a child who asked too many questions to be comfortable with the constrictions she felt in Baptist teaching. By the time she graduated from high school, she had left the Baptist Church, yet remained a seeking Christian. She regularly attended chapel on Sundays at Howard University, accompanied by her father with whom she would have deep conversations about the new things they were hearing from Howard Thurman and other preachers. At university she also read from the writings of liberal Baptist theologian Harry Emerson Fosdick. She explored the Unitarian and Quaker traditions before she encountered Gordon Cosby through the ecumenical Washington Federation of Churches. She was drawn to Cosby as a clergyman who took seriously gospel teaching about the poor and oppressed, and so she joined the Church of the Saviour, a multi-denominational and economically diverse community known for its disciplined practices of devotion, study and social action.

From the 1950s on, Verna also became known for her approach to Bible study. She began to teach at conferences, retreats and classes in the Episcopal Diocese of Washington. In 1955, while teaching at the Diocesan School for Christian Living, Dozier was invited to join St Mark's Episcopal Church on Capitol Hill. The Revd Bill Baxter, who had been encouraging the traditional Episcopal congregation to become more focused on social justice, told Dozier that the parish was ready for its first black member. The reality was not quite that straightforward. Despite initial obstacles to formal membership in the parish, she persevered, drawn to the liturgical language and intellectual freedom of the Episcopal Church. She was confirmed, entered into teaching and leadership roles with enthusiasm, and served as the parish vestry's first woman senior warden. She remained a member of St Mark's for the rest of her life. Her memory is celebrated there, memorialized in a stained-glass window depicting Amos preaching in the marketplace, starting a fund that awards college scholarships to senior students at Dunbar High School, and establishing a parish library in support of lifelong learning. She is interred in the St Mark's Columbarium.[2]

Living Differently

Over the years Dozier was a much sought-after teacher in a variety of settings across the Church. *The Dream of God: A Call to Return* has been published in several editions and is widely read across many denominations.[3] Dozier valued her role as a lay theologian and became widely known as a passionate advocate for the authority of the ministry of the laity. Dozier served as a consultant on leadership education for organizations and individuals and as a trainer of consultants, led workshops and retreats across the country, and was a regular participant in the Alban Institute, an ecumenical group focused on strengthening congregations. She travelled twice to Kenya to teach her approach to Bible study. She also taught courses on the Bible as an adjunct instructor at Virginia Theological Seminary, an Episcopal Church institution in the environs of Washington. Although she never formally studied theology in an academic institution, two Episcopal seminaries awarded her honorary doctorates; and despite her small stature, Verna Dozier has had an outsized influence on Christian formation across the Church.

Dozier was a courageous preacher, one of only a few Episcopal laywomen to be invited to preach at the consecration of an Episcopal bishop. In her sermon at the consecration of Jane Holmes Dixon as Suffragan Bishop of the Diocese of Washington, she reminded the new bishop that the people of God are called to minister to the world in the midst of their daily lives, and that clergy are called to support that work outside the walls of the church building:

> The Church of God is all the people of God, lay and ordained, each order with its own unique vocation, the lay order to be the people of God in the world, to witness by their choices and their values, in the kingdoms of the world, in the systems of commerce and government, education and medicine, law and human relations, science and exploration, art and vision, to witness to all these worlds that there is another possibility for human life than the way of exploitation and domination; and the vocation of the ordained order is to serve the lay order, to refresh and restore the weary souls with the Body and the Blood, to maintain those islands, the institutional church, where life is lived differently but always in order that life may be lived differently everywhere.[4]

Her desire 'that life may be lived differently everywhere' grows not just from her deep faith that the call of God was a call to freedom but also out of her experience as a black woman in the USA. Living in the tension of the struggle for civil rights in society and in the Church colours her theology as well as her pedagogical method, whether teaching about English poetry or about the Bible.

As mentioned previously, Dozier grew up in, and lived most of her life in, a black neighbourhood in segregated north-east Washington DC. Grateful to be given educational opportunities denied her parents, she immersed herself in her studies at Howard University where she wrote her MA thesis on a composer of African American hymns. Having taught in segregated schools early on, she was then invited to an administrative post in Washington's first integrated high school, going on from there to become a respected public schools administrator.

In her work with the Church, Dozier continued to witness to her belief that God's dream was for a world where life is lived differently. Her time at the Church of the Saviour showed Dozier the possibilities for a diverse Christian community of prayer, study and practice. She described herself as 'radical', and noted that the prophetic nature of her message as a black laywoman was often undercut by racism and sexism in a church that was more attentive to the voices of white clergymen:

> I probably am one of the most radical voices in this church today but people respond to me with great affection and love because I look like Aunt Jemima. I sound like Sojourner Truth, but they don't pay any attention. I think that is a manifestation of racism ... [And] I think a lot of men don't hear what women have to say. I don't think there is a woman operating in any of our church systems who hasn't experienced that special kind of condescension.[5]

This awareness of who is heard and who is not heard was at the heart of her way of teaching, whether in the high school classroom or the church hall. While the institutional Church has privileged the voice of the ordained, the learned, Verna Dozier flips that standard. The voice of the laity, she asserts, has authority. For her, 'All learning begins not with the answers of the teacher, but with the questions of the learner.'[6] Like liberation theologians, she gives the marginalized a voice in her Bible study method – as she did in classroom teaching where she says she felt the most important learning came through the students' own observations and responses. Her teaching was often Socratic, and she enjoyed being provocative in her questions. She was known for pushing the hearer to think beyond platitudes. 'Do you want to follow Jesus? Or are you content just to worship him and postpone for just a little longer the fulfillment of the dream of God?'[7]

Three themes on the authority of the laity run through Dozier's works, from the early workshops to *The Dream of God*: Bible study is the key to understanding and claiming the authority of the laity; there are no second-class citizens in the household of God; and God's Church is not an institution but a people.

Knowing the Story of the People of God

'First, lay people have to become informed about what the faith actually is.'[8] For Dozier the study of the Bible is foundational to understanding and living into God's call to the whole people of God. Further, the Bible is not a rule book but a faith response to being in relationship with God, 'a book of wrestlings, not a book of answers'.[9] She rejects a fundamentalist or literal reading of the text, instead approaching the Bible as story in the service of meaning-making:

> What we have in the Bible is the record of hundreds of years in which the two communities of faith looked at the experiences of their lives and asked what these experiences meant ... The question we must put to the records they have left is not 'Which is right?' but questions like 'What does it mean?' and 'What did it mean for them?' and 'What does it mean for us?'[10]

It is not surprising that her first published work was a method of Bible study focused on questions.

In *Equipping the Saints: A Method of Self-directed Bible Study for Lay Groups*, Dozier taught that lay persons need to study the Bible, not simply read it. Further, they could employ scholarly resources as tools of interpretation to enhance that study, just as the clergy did, to bring different voices into the conversation.

Her method assumes a community of learners and encourages the use of several translations of the Bible, along with commentaries, dictionaries and suchlike. Beginning with several different voices reading the passage aloud from more than one translation, the design moves to questions of meaning for the whole group:

- Clarify what the passage is saying: What do the words mean? What are the key concepts?
- Clarify why the passage was preserved: What did it mean to the early Christian community? What issues were they dealing with? How did the passage help them make sense of their lives?
- Reflect on what the passage means to you and to the Church today.

The object of Dozier's method is not to strive for a single understanding for the entire group. Each student will bring different information to the clarifying questions. Each student will have a different reflection. While there may be right answers and wrong answers offered in the course of the first two steps as students learn from one another, in step three every individual reflection has value and contributes to deepening the reflections of all the others in the group.

Dozier believes that we cannot understand who we are as the people of God unless we know the story of the people of God. 'We are the people of a story, a story that is told in the pages of the Bible, in many forms of literature. No part of it stands by itself.'[11]

No Second-class Citizens in the Household of God

'There are no second-class citizens in the household of God. Religious authority comes with baptism, and it is nurtured by prayer, worship, bible study, life together.'[12]

Early on, Dozier pushed back against ministerial hierarchy in the Church, which was likely influenced by her father's scepticism about religious institutions in general and what he had been taught in the Baptist Church in particular. He especially deplored what he saw as the hypocrisy of wealthy and privileged clergy. Dozier talks about her own approach to faith as lying in the tension between her devout mother teaching the faith once delivered, and her agnostic father teaching the need to be sceptical of the delivery.[13]

Dozier notes that too often we see the institutional Church as the place we need to go to in order to be with God. She describes a moment at a conference when the attendees were moved to another room to create a sacred space for the Eucharist and reflects on the implications of that move for our understanding of the authority of the laity as ministers:

I believe the 'sacred space' is where the institutionally ordained preside. I believe it is also where mothers tend their children, teachers guide their students, doctors care for their patients, police officers patrol the streets, executives make decisions, laborers ply their trades – laity everywhere doing the work they are called to do.

The ground on which we stand is holy ground.

God is where we are. What space could be more sacred than where God is? As long as we intentionally or unintentionally believe or act out that we have to go somewhere special to meet God or do something special to be close to God, lay people will see themselves as second class citizens in the household of faith and the work they do as second-class activity, their work not a calling, themselves not called.[14]

She continued to fervently believe that all of the people of God are called to ministry in the course of their daily lives in the world. Their work in the world is their ministry, not something they must tack on to churchy acts of ministry. Her ministry was education:

> Back when I first started talking about ministry, it was seen as something the ordained did. Lay people had no ministry at all except as they participated in the work of the institution. If you taught in the Christian education program, you had a ministry. If you taught in the public schools, you 'did time' five days a week until you could get to your ministry. When I began my second career, people would say, 'You taught school for thirty-two years; then you began your ministry.' In my unredeemed way, I would steel myself and reply through clenched teeth, 'No, I continued my ministry.'[15]

Dozier expresses scepticism about lay persons who focus their ministry solely within the structures of the institutional Church and don't understand that their work in the world is the higher calling. In her mind this comes from a failure to know the story and can be addressed through Bible study.

The Church Is the People of God

'A funny thing happened on the way to the Kingdom. The Church, the people of God, became the Church, the institution.'[16]

As we have seen, Dozier asserted from early on that the Church is not actually the institution. The Church is the whole people of God. She also draws a distinction between the work of the institution and the work of God's people in their everyday lives. The primary work of the Church is to witness to the world through their work, their behaviour, their very lives, that there is a better way to live, that domination and oppression are not God's dream for creation.

Pushing back against a Church she saw teaching the laity that their role is to support the work of the institution through attendance and giving, Dozier insists instead that the role of the institution is to support the work of the laity in the world. 'What happens on Sunday morning is not half so important as what happens on Monday morning ... If the people who gather for word and sacrament go back to that world unchanged and unchanging, they have participated in empty ritual.'[17] The institution too often showcases stories of ministry to those whose lives are negatively affected by unjust structures – feeding the poor, volunteering in shelters, clothing the naked, and many other acts of generosity and compassion – while it ignores the Church's calling to dismantle the very structures that make those ministries necessary.

The dream of God is freedom. The call to ministry is a call to effect transformation where injustice prevents that freedom. An institution, Dozier says, is risk averse – and faith calls for taking a risk. Dozier's criticism of the institutional Church is a prophetic call for the Church to remember and return to God's dream for it – wholeness, freedom. She does not call for abolishing the institution but for reordering our understanding of its relationship to the people of God doing God's work in the world.

The ministries of the laity and the clergy are bound up with each other, but the primary location of the work for clergy is in the institution while the primary location of the work of the laity is in the world. On the one hand, Dozier takes the institutional Church to task for not living up to the dream of God, for placing power and hierarchy above serving the world, for privileging ordained ministry over the ministry of the laity. That Church, she says, is replaceable. On the other hand, she calls the institutional Church to live into its true function by providing a place where the whole people of God are nourished and equipped to live into the call to transform the world, to offer it the example of a different way to live:

> The people of God are called to a possibility other than the kingdoms of this world. They must be ambassadors – again, St Paul's word – in every part of life. They witness to another way that governments can relate to one another, that money can be earned and spent, that doctors and caregivers and engineers and lawyers and teachers can serve their constituencies, that wordsmiths and musicians and artists and philosophers can give us new visions of the human condition. That is the ministry of the laity.
>
> All of them need the support system of the institutional church. There must be those resting places where the story is treasured and passed on in liturgy and education. There must be those islands of refuge where the wounded find healing; the confused, light; the fearful, courage; the lonely, community; the alienated, acceptance; the strong, gratitude. Maintaining such institutions is the ministry of the clergy.[18]

In *The Dream of God*, Dozier makes a clear distinction between the ministry of the Church gathered and the ministry of the Church scattered, between the institutional Church and the Church as the people of God out in the world. Both are needed, but each has a different role. In her view, the institutional Church's role is to nurture those whose call is to witness to the kingdom of God beyond the institution. It is an important and necessary task:

> It is in communal worship that we get our 'beat', Verna told her listeners. At the end of the service we are sent back into the world in peace to love and serve the Lord. And so, she said, we march out together, sharing the same beat that calls us to rejoice in the power of the Spirit.
>
> But when the cares of the world assail us, we begin to stumble as we try to keep to the cadence. Somewhere along the way, she said softly, most of us lose that beat. The [institutional] church creates a place for us every week to get our beat back, allowing us once again to go forth in the name of Christ to be in the world.[19]

The Church gathers to restore and remind us that the people of God are needed to be about God's business in all the structures of the world – to bring the vision of the divine reign into financial and economic structures; into political structures, into structures that serve social well-being, into structures in the humanities, the structures of meaning-making. 'There is no place,' Dozier says, 'where the people of God should not be, and wherever they are they are called to witness to another possibility for life.'[20]

Notes

1 A fuller account of Dozier's life, work and influence in the field of Christian education, along with a comprehensive bibliography, may be found in *Christian Educators of the 20th Century*, https://www.biola.edu/talbot/ce20/database/verna-josephine-dozier (accessed 29.1.2024).

2 A photo of the window is on the St Mark's webpage: https://www.stmarks.net/learning/dozierlibrary/dozierlife/ (accessed 29.1.2024). The two women listening to Amos represent Verna Dozier and her sister Lois.

3 Verna J. Dozier, *The Dream of God: A Call to Return* (New York: Seabury, 2006).

4 Verna J. Dozier, sermon preached at the consecration of Jane Holmes Dixon as Suffragan Bishop of Washington on 19 November 1992, published in *Virginia Seminary Journal* (April 1993): 33–4.

5 *Confronted by God: The Essential Verna Dozier*, eds Cynthia L. Shattuck and Fredrica Harris Thompsett, (New York: Church Publishing, 2006), 31.

6 'Praying the Lord's Prayer', commencement address given at the Episcopal Theological Seminary of the Southwest in May 1997, published in *Ratherview* (Fall 1997): 8.

7 Dozier, *The Dream of God*, 109.

8 Verna J. Dozier with Celia A. Hahn, *The Authority of the Laity* (Washington DC: The Alban Institute, 1982), 32.

9 Dozier, *The Dream of God*, 18.

10 Dozier, *The Dream of God*, 19.

11 Shattuck and Thompsett, *Confronted by God*, 85.

12 Verna J. Dozier, 'Toward a Theology of the Laity', in *The Calling of the Laity: Verna Dozier's Anthology* (Washington DC: The Alban Institute, 1988), 115.

13 Shattuck and Thompsett, *Confronted by God*, 14.

14 Verna J. Dozier, 'A Sacred Space', in *The Calling of the Laity: Verna Dozier's Anthology* (Washington DC: The Alban Institute, 1988), 111.

15 Dozier, *The Dream of God*, 107.

16 Dozier, *The Authority of the Laity*, 3.

17 Dozier, *The Calling of the Laity*, 115.

18 Dozier, *The Dream of God*, 114.

19 Dorothy Linthicum, 'Verna Dozier', *Episcopal Teacher Special Edition: The Center for the Ministry of Teaching*, Winter 2019 (Virginia Theological Seminary), 10.

20 Dozier, *The Dream of God*, 109.

6

Julius Gathogo

STEPHEN KAPINDE

As a prolific African Anglican theologian, Julius Gathogo addresses diverse themes in line with the holistic nature of African Christian theology and goes on to address oral and ecclesiastical histories with gusto. This drives him to embrace human and social sciences – such as history, sociology, anthropology and sociology – so as to work out his multidisciplinary academic enterprise. In turn, his all-embracing approach to African heritage leads him to address many critical themes relating to precolonial, colonial and postcolonial Africa – hence he embraces a multidisciplinary approach in order to meet the needs and concerns of his broad socio-academic constituency. In sampling some of these themes that range from the coronavirus disease (Covid-19), HIV and AIDS, oral and mission histories, the nature of theological education in Africa, liberation and reconstruction, gospel and culture, domestic violence, gender and God, and liturgy in Africa, among other themes, he displays his optimism about African Christianity solving the myriad challenges facing tropical Africa.

In sampling one of his cherished themes on liturgy *of* Africa, as opposed to the foreign-influenced liturgy *for* Africa, Gathogo argues that there are concrete areas that need 'liturgical inculturation'.[1] He suggests:

> In addressing the concrete areas where the twenty-first-century church is in dire need of inculturation, I suggest that it will need to have a positive attitude to African Religion so as to use the same or similar concepts in order to eliminate dualism. Such concepts include: a shrine for church and a medium for priest, among others. The beauty of the local language, the use of Proverbs and local expressions must clearly appear. The prayers as found in the Roman Missal must be adapted to the African reality. Composition of new prayers, structured on African spirituality and concerns is long overdue. Africa can produce its Psalms to complement the Biblical Psalms. I also suggest that family, as the domestic church, should be made the centre of inculturation. The role

of the father and mother as the parents and priests of the family; their ability to bless, pray over the children, to initiate, to share roles with all members of the family, to involve everyone, to express worries and joys – such should be emphasized.[2]

In historicizing theological education in African Christianity, and in employing multidisciplinary approaches, he extols the value of greater dialogue among cultures and religions of Africa. He also urges caution, and suggests:

As early as 1888, Mojola Agbedi (1860–1917), a Nigerian Yoruba Baptist minister, had already defected from his Baptist church and founded the Native Baptist Church. In demonstrating his Afro-optimist perspective, he defended the creation of African Churches with the words: 'To render Christianity indigenous to Africa, it must be watered by native hands, pruned with the native hatchet, and tendered with native earth … It is a curse if we intend for ever to hold on to the apron strings of foreign teachers doing the baby for aye.' Although he may have taken an extreme position, his African instituted Baptist church fared well, for by 1914, it had more than twice as many adherents as the American Baptist Mission where he was previously serving. Like James Johnson (1832–1917), his senior, he had great faith in Africans and feared that the European missionary tutelage had the potential of hindering the full development of the Africans. In the same spirit, as with Agbedi, Johnson attributed the success of Islam in the then Nigeria of 1880s to its use of African customs and institutions. Around this time (1888), Agbedi had changed his westernized baptismal name (David Brown Vincent) as a measure of asserting his Afro-optimist dignity and identity, though remaining an evangelical Christian. Was this his way of decolonizing the mind, in using Ngũgĩ wa Thiong'o's words? In his book *Decolonising the Mind* Thiong'o expresses his Afro-optimist identity when he offers a distinctly anti-imperialist perspective on the destiny of Africa, as he demonstrates the role of names and languages in combating imperialism and neo-colonialism in our minds and in our general social practice. It is in this book where he bids farewell to the English language and its resultant names, hence his dropping of his 'Christian' name, 'James' is clearly justified along these Afro-optimist identity lines. Beyond this, wa Thiong'o dedicates his book to 'all those who write in African languages, and to all those who over the years have maintained the dignity of the literature, culture, philosophy, and other treasures carried by African languages'. Was wa Thiong'o an ideo-philosophical student of the Baptist, Mojola Agbedi, albeit unconsciously? Was he the originator of 'decolonizing the mind' concept in African scholarship?[3]

Consider also his commendation of hybridity in African indigenous knowledge and Western science and technology as the way to address the many medical challenges in Africa. He insists that 'western science and technology did not erase African indigenous knowledge and/or knowledge relationally based on African world view and culture'; rather, it complemented it.[4] He goes on to say:

This indigenous knowledge that is basically relational includes community, ethos of wholeness, harmony with the stranger (Ubuntu) and appreciation of knowledge and/or technology that promotes humanity for all. This drives us to build on the premise that postcolonial Africa has paradoxically embraced hybridity of western science and the indigenous heritage by design or by default ... Jomo Kenyatta analyses the various industries that were prevalent in African indigenous society as including 'ironwork, hut building, pottery, basket making, skin tanning, musical instruments, and agricultural activities'.[5] ... Other activities that required technical knowledge included: 'the building and repair of houses, land cultivation and clearance of bushy areas, hunting, and fishing among others'.[6] ... This further confirms our hypothesis on hybridity and continuity of African indigenous knowledge systems with Western science, as was presented by the European missionary societies and the colonial authorities. Instead, African knowledge systems, with their resultant 'science' of survival, did not suffer from a radical discontinuity, even though the Western science stamped its 'superiority' elaborately, as missionaries and the colonial authorities were largely seen as viewing the matter from the same lenses.[7]

With regard to indigenous resources in light of the recent Covid-19 pandemic, Gathogo again sees logic in hybridity, a phenomenon where Western science, especially in the practice of medicine, and African indigenous knowledge become critical partners in fighting such pandemics or any other ailment for that matter. Use of indigenous resources to combat the pandemic also has its place in Kenya's medical history. He notes that:

African-Christians make concoctions that seek to treat COVID-19 [and other ailments]. Clearly, the use of ginger, a natural antioxidant, lemon, and honey as *Dawa* (medicine) has gained a momentum ... in the [Kenyan context], and is seen as one that provides COVID-19 healing properties among other creative ways rooted in African indigenous society. While ginger is found to be critical in boosting people's health as it protects against colorectal cancer, lemon is, on the other hand, seen as rich in vitamin C and critically important for detoxification. Other herbal methods of treating COVID-19 in [the Kenyan context] ... include steam therapy or steam inhalation to fight respiratory tract infections, use of hot steam mistily wafts from a pan, use of culinary herbs and Neem trees [*Azadirachta indica*], among other medicinal plants.[8]

Besides ginger, culinary herbs and Neem trees, among other medicinal plants, Gathogo has noted that other indigenous medicinal plants are also critical in addressing related challenges:

Wanjiru-wa-rurii [*Ajuga remota*], a plant in central Kenya [recommended by 66 per cent of Kenyan herbalists in the treatment of Malaria] that is best known for treating diseases such as Malaria and Typhoid, also came in as a cure for Covid-19 as well. From time immemorial, the plant has been known to treat the above ailments, as well as the sexually transmitted diseases. It also treats livestock and chicken alike. Unlike when it is used with animals and birds, this plant is never boiled. Rather, it is crushed and mixed with water, the juice is taken at intervals of several hours and the results are promising ... Today the plant continues to be precious especially for people living in the rural setup. It is the plant used in Madagascar to prepare Malagasy organic [medicine] which came to limelight during this Corona virus pandemic season. A larger population relies on it for treatment and cure of different complications.[9]

With more than 80 per cent of Africans relying on African indigenous knowledge and its practice in medicine, Gathogo advocates strongly for hybridity in addressing human well-being, just as he insists on dialogue between gospel and culture as a crucial dialogue partner within African Christianity. He bemoans the tendency to reduce inculturation (dialogue between culture and the gospel) to syncretism (unscientific mixture of religious traditions). This gets out of hand when African scholars promote Euro-American scholarships by bashing local African initiatives, and eventually employ Western jargon unapologetically. He is critical of those African scholars who call the dialogue between African heritage and the gospel as syncretic rather than inculturation, or who call African religion 'African traditional religion' as the latter connotes archaic-ancient religion, tribalism rather than negative ethnicity, conversion rather than proselytization (false conversion) in cases where genuine dialogue has not taken place, and other related concepts.[10] Could this be a case of conceptual misunderstanding, or is the confusion seen in the above jargon and phrases a by-product of the identity crisis that exists in postcolonial Africa? If it is the case of he who pays the piper calling the tune, then African scholars have sold their intellectual souls, Gathogo hints.[11]

Roots

Julius M. Gathogo (born 23 July 1967) is a leading scholar in oral history and ecclesiastical history, theology, missiology and other related disciplines. This is demonstrated clearly in his multidisciplinary scholarship. He was ordained by Archbishop David Gitari as a cleric of the Anglican Church in 1995. Since then, he has metamorphosed into a leading African scholar, comparable to Jesse Mugambi, Musa Dube, Tinyiko Sam Maluleke and Ezra Chitando, among other scholars of African descent, in terms of his prolific writing and researching. He brings out many fresh insights to both church and academia via his multidisciplinary perspectives. Among his many publications, he is most widely known for his much-cited publication 'African Philosophy as Expressed in the Concepts of Hospitality and Ubuntu', which was published in the *Journal of Theology for Southern Africa* in 2008.[12]

Gathogo comes from a tiny Kiamai village, about 150 metres from the famous Njumbi-Mutira centre (Kirinyaga County).[13] This was the precursor centre of the early twentieth-century European missionaries, the Church Missionary Society (CMS), who first entered the area in 1908, but settled fully from 15 November 1912 onwards.[14] Etymologically, Njumbi comes from the word *Gacumbirira*, meaning the hilly place; hence Njumbi-Mutira refers to the hilly Mutira area.[15] In his book *The Imprints of NITD-Kabete in Mutira Mission, Kenya*, where he chronicles the life of his father Josphat Kathogo Kamoni (1918–78), Gathogo endeavours to demonstrate how Western science was introduced in the Njumbi-Mutira area as early as 1902, and sought to 'conquer' the African indigenous knowledge systems, by default or by design.[16] He explains that the first British administrative station in this area went hand-in-hand with the Anglican missions, even though the British soldiers had briefly stayed at Kiathigani, near the present-day Kagumo Town, as early as 1902.[17] The first colonial administrative centre in his home area (Njumbi-Mutira) was set up in 1908. It was specifically established in the area where we now have the Kagumo coffee factory (otherwise called Mutira Farmers' Cooperative Society), which was established in 1954.[18]

In addition to the Western medicine that was introduced in Njumbi-

Mutira locality and the larger central Kenya region, Gathogo has also noted that there were indigenous medicine practitioners, diviners and seers, who handled both physical ailments and metaphysical issues such as undoing witchcraft and sorcery.[19] Further, there was a Mutira-Kirinyaga seer/prophet by the name of Kigombe wa Andiru who prophesied about the coming of the European missionaries and the colonial establishment.[20]

Kigombe also cautioned about an incoming generation that would never listen to anyone ('*Andu matari mbuguiro*', meaning people who have no sense of hearing, and who will be largely irresponsible, not care, and be permissive in their daily activities, hence they would not stick to the norms of society).[21] According to him, the prophesied people would ironically be deaf to their care-givers, parents, elders, guardians and mentors among other people who matter most in their own lives.[22] The lives of the prophesied people would be characterized by self-destructive tendencies. Kigombe's prophecy of *Andu Matari Mbuguiro* (a non-listening generation or a know-it-all society) looked like a perennial joke, as he spoke in the late 1800s when the morality of the locals was strong, and youths would stringently obey their respective elders.[23] Indigenous medicine was a whole-person approach that addressed physical and spiritual health.[24] But the full settlement of both the 'London' missionaries at the Njumbi-Mutira (1908–12 when they finally settled) and the establishment of colonial structures (from 1902 to 1908 when they established a centre at the Mutira Farmers' Cooperative Society, near Gathogo's Kiamai home) confirmed the seer's prophecy, though it had initially appeared to be an impossible mission.[25] As Westernization and the breakdown of indigenous moral codes crept in, by the 1930s most of what Kigombe the Seer had prophesied had come to pass, and his counsel could be recalled 100 years later.[26] In other words, stories about the African seer (Kigombe) that had been passed orally could be retold with gusto.

Out of these encounters with the European missionaries who opened up the first school (Mutira primary) in January 1913 under the Revd Brandon Laight, and later with a Mr Clacker who in 1915 joined him with a black missionary from the present-day Taita-Taveta county, Thomas Meero. The Taita-Taveta area has retained the nickname 'London', as it has long hosted the 'people from London'.[27] The first class at Mutira primary school had the Revd Brandon Laight teaching his first students, 'Gideon Kabugi, Philip Karanja, Joshua Nguba, Stephano Kathuki and another eight',[28] but by January 1915 when Mr Clacker and Mr Meero joined the Revd Laight, classes now attracted 60 students who included Johana Njumbi wa Kamuku (who later became the pioneer African Anglican cleric of 1934), 'Philip Karanja Ngungi,

Petero Kanjobe, Hezekiah Ngigi Ngari' (the second African medical practitioner in Njumbi-Mutira area and its surroundings), Zakariah Gakure
(the first African medical practitioner in the area), Gideon Kibugi (father
to Njumbi's wife, Wangari), Musa Nguri and Stefano Kabuitu (father to
a pioneer accountant in the locality, Leonard Kunga), among others.[29]
Indeed, the first European missionaries, mainly from London, in the UK,
settled in the Njumbi-Mutira locality and slowly changed the lifestyles of
people in the area where Gathogo grew up.[30]

The hilly Mutira centre is within the Kirinyaga West area of Kenya.[31]
As Gathogo grew older, he witnessed his locality taking on the mantle of
being the leading beacon of 'modernity' as a result of the availability of
Western education that was introduced through the local Mutira primary
school. Further, local graduates from the then prestigious Makerere University College of London University had completed their education as
early as 1955. He explained that the sons and daughters of the old Mutira
pastorate, in Makerere University College, Uganda in the 1950s, were
'Robert Ndegwa, Gerald Mugera, Madam Wanjiku Kabuitu, John Ngata
Kariuki, Philip Ndegwa, Daniel Muriithi, Murage Kagunga, John Matere
Keriri, and Josphat Mutugi among others.'[32] Gathogo goes on to speak
about the inspirational role of pioneer graduates in the locality, thus:

> Of interest to note is that while Mathenge specialized in mathematics,
> Matere specialized in economics and political science; Philip Ndegwa,
> from Kiini, in economics; Josphat Mutugi, also from Kiini south of
> Mutira, became the first African Labour Commissioner in Kenya after
> independence, Daniel Muriithi, who came from Kerugoya area, became
> a leading veterinary doctor; while Gerald Mugera, another veterinary
> doctor, from Karaini near Mutira went on to become the first person in
> the locality to become a university professor. However, the first person
> in the old Mutira pastorate to be awarded a university degree is the
> late Robert Ndegwa who hailed from Kagio area, Mwirua location
> of Ndia Division. This was certainly a climactic moment for the Ndia
> people and the entire Embu District of the late 1950s, as none had been
> awarded such a high academic honour in the entire [old Embu] District
> [which had the current Embu and Kirinyaga counties, 1933–63].[33]

The return of the Makerere University College graduates of the 1950s
was critical in inspiring diverse professional dexterities in the locality. Through the by-products of the missionary labours, the Anglican
Church in particular, they strengthened the social influence of both
Roman Catholics and Protestants in the locality. Seeing how they now
lived 'quality' lives was a huge inspirational moment for the youths

who were looking forward to some guidance on life prospects, hence Gathogo grew in such a rich religio-social environment that impacted greatly on his theo-scholarly discourses.[34] Additionally, it was an added pleasure for Gathogo who came from this Mutira Pastorate, an area that was fertile and had a good climate that enabled the growing of coffee and tea, and was also good for dairy and horticultural farming. With a habitable climate, the area was attractive, and it flourished holistically.[35] Julius Gathogo's father (Josphat Kinyua aka wakamoni) was himself a well-informed man who had gone through the then 'Africans Only' Native Industrial Training Depot, Kabete (NITD-Kabete) College, now the Kabete National Polytechnic, in the late 1930s, had studied for work in the construction industry, and was at home in this place.[36]

The area in which Gathogo grew up was also favoured as a tourist destination owing to its serenity. In particular, it features the Gikumbo dam which is one of the largest human-made dams; the fringes of Mount Kenya at Karandi-Gatwe; President Idi Amin camp at Kamuruana hill; St Peter's Kamuiru gate where General Chui the freedom fighter was bizarrely burnt to death in May 1956 by the colonial authorities; the River Sagana rapids; the magic stone (*Ithiga Ithae*) of Muragara, Mau-Mau (1950s freedom fighters) caves; and so on. Gathogo's passion and commitment to academia is much informed by this intriguing background and environment. He was also shaped by the sense that there were illustrious people who had made huge contributions in their respective professional fields. Gathogo has unearthed and published deep history regarding the locality and surroundings in which he was formed, including his father's biography.[37]

Reach

With over 200 publications in journals, book chapters, individually authored books, edited books, co-edited books, and collaborative works, Gathogo has been highly productive. He has long held a position as a senior lecturer in the Department of Philosophy and Religious Studies, and in the School of Law, Arts and Humanities, Kenyatta University, since 2008. It is significant, though, that he is also a long-serving research fellow at the University of South Africa. His first doctoral studies on African theology (the interface between Christianity and African culture and its historicity) were at the University of KwaZulu-Natal, Pietermaritzburg, South Africa, from which he graduated with a PhD in 2007 (and after a MA at the then University of Natal, also in South Africa). His second PhD was in History, with a thesis entitled: 'Mau-Mau and

the Quest for Freedom in Kenya: Retrieving the History of Revolution-
ary Rebels Versus Ecclesia and the Colonial Government in Kirinyaga
County (1952–60)', awarded in 2015. A remarkable third PhD, this
time in Educational Leadership, was awarded in 2018, and was titled
'Chronic Student Absenteeism: Implications for Classroom Management
and Teacher Leadership'. This wide educational background sheds light
on his extensive research and publications in human and social sciences,
especially with regard to mission historiographies.

In particular, Gathogo's commitment to oral studies seeks to show
Africa's rich oral sources, which can contribute much to both public and
academic discourses of the twenty-first century, particularly when utilized
innovatively and creatively. In his view, creativity, innovation and inven-
tion, spiced with critical thinking, are the panacea for African woes, as no
academic disciplines can afford to ignore this trio.[38] He brings this to his
own work on locales and his wider argument that African histories and
theologies will need to be revisited and rewritten from the perspective of
locals rather than through the perspectives of European anthropologists
and explorers of earlier days. As the African saying goes, unless the lion
learns how to write, every story will glorify the hunter.[39]

While Gathogo's works have been criticized for employing a 'mixed-
bag' approach to scholarship, he shows himself to be a keen student of
Africa's oral and mission historiographies, one who must necessarily
employ a multidisciplinary technique in order to effectively address the
myriad of challenges within his context.[40] He might be compared with
Reinhold Niebuhr (1892–1971), the American scholar based at New
York's Union Theological Seminary who led other scholars to move away
from idealism and drove them to embrace realism in their respective discourses.[41] Niebuhr dallied with ethics, theology, public intellectualism,
political commentary, and analysis of social affairs, all of which contributed to his own multidisciplinary enterprise that was geared towards
problem-solving and a richer understanding of the society of which he was
a part.[42] Niebuhr's trajectory is thus a common occurrence in Gathogo's
works.[43] In addition, Niebuhr's broad-based approach went on to influence the socio-scholarly thinking of key players in American history, and
indeed global history.[44] In other words, he influenced Martin Luther King
Jr, Jimmy Carter, Hillary Rodham Clinton, Madeleine Albright, Barack
Obama, and Steve de Gruchy – among many others.[45] Gathogo's work
has the potential to reach beyond the limited circles of theological discourse. This comes out clearly in his article 'Consolidating Democracy
in Colonial Kenya (1920–63): Challenges and Prospects' in which he
explains the Church's contributions in Kenya's evolution as a nation. He
cites Bildad Kaggia who was initially a pastor but joined the likes of Jomo

Kenyatta, Paul Ngei, Achieng Oneko, Kung'u Karumba and Fred Kubai; they were jointly jailed for their activism in the freedom struggle in the 1950s. In following Niebuhr's trajectory, Gathogo says this:

> While democracy and/or democratic culture is broader than mere elec-tioneering, the article considers electoral processes as critical steps in consolidating democratic gains, as societies now find an opportunity to replace bad leaders and eventually install a crop of leadership that resonates well with their pains, dreams, fears and joys. With its own elected leaders, the article hypothesizes, a society has a critical founda-tion because elected people are ordinarily meant to address cutting-edge issues facing a given society. Such concerns may include: poverty, corruption, racism, marginalization of minority, ethnic bigotry, eco-nomic rejuvenation, gender justice, and health of the people among other disquiets.[46]

He goes on to demonstrate the ecclesiastical role in the freedom struggle, as demonstrated by Bildad Kaggia and some African-instituted churches, thus:

> With the leadership of the African Instituted Churches throwing their full weight behind the main political parties, especially the African National Union (KANU), the overt and covert role in nurturing a democratic process was visible. Bildad Mwaganu Kaggia (1921–2005), for instance, was one of the founders of African Instituted Churches, where he was the leading pastor in what is now called Voice of Salvation popularly called *Dini ya Kaggia* (Kaggia's religion). His new religious outfit embraced Africa's religio-culture, and remained as a protest move-ment against western Christianity, as was propounded by the European missionaries. Since 1946 when he formed his church, Kaggia and his followers in central Kenya were constantly arrested and imprisoned for holding illegal meetings. Nevertheless, 'Kaggia's doctrine' spread to other regions of Kenya, and especially Nyanza where one of the off-spring churches is currently referred to as the *Voice of Salvation and Healing Church* (VOSHC). Kaggia's religio-cultural ideologies spread in western Kenya after Blasio Oking' Mbara from Miwani of Kisumu County and Kefa Usenge from Bondo, Siaya County, both of whom were working in central Kenya, heard from Kaggia and returned to Luo-Nyanza by 1948 to preach his attractive religio-cultural ideologies. Their association was eventually registered on 16 May 1956 as one of the first few indigenous Pentecostal church movements in the colonial

Kenya under the name *Voice of the World Wide Salvation and Healing Revival.*[47]

Further, in demonstrating his broad-based approach (akin to Niebuhr's trajectory), he addresses the plight of Internally Displaced Persons (IDPs), Stateless Persons (SPs), and the refugees in tropical Africa. He cites the United Nations High Commission for Refugees' (UNHCR) 2008 report. The 2008 UNHCR's report shows that Sub-Saharan Africa had a total of 2,257,100 refugees. The Great Lakes region and Central Africa led with 1,086,200 refugees. The East and Horn of Africa had 815,200, West Africa had 174,700, while Southern Africa had 181,000 refugees. He also notes that there were 26 million IDPs globally, 15.2 million refugees, and 827,000 pending cases of asylum seekers by December 2008. In reference to SPs, who, as he says, are part of the peoples whom God so loved (John 3.16), he also says:

> By stateless persons, I mean ethnic minorities who migrated to designated areas in Africa and were unable to return to their ancestral lands but remained largely isolated in their respective host countries. Globally, there are about ten to twelve million stateless people in 2023; while by 2008, there were about seven million cases in at least fifty-eight nations (UNHCR, 2008, Githiga, 2023). The figure keeps growing upfront, as SPs were a paltry 3.3 million in 2007 (UNHCR, 2008). Hence, this is another area where Ubuntu philosophy and/or concept has to stamp out its all-inclusive motif and drive the global community to get concerned and eventually swing into action in arresting the ambiguity. It is equally important that African nations address the challenge by effectively documenting such cases of stateless persons and eventually act within the international conventions and their respective national constitutions, as it will go a long way in appealing to the indigenous forms of hospitality that embraced a stranger in a foreign land. Such a stranger was given the necessary support, which was inherited from the ancestors.[48]

Besides Niebuhr, Gathogo also compares well with the Nigerian poet and prolific writer Christopher Okigbo (1932–67), who rejected the first prize in African poetry that was awarded to him in 1966 on account of his conviction that there is no such thing as a 'Negro' or 'black poet'. Hence, Okigbo was simply saying, 'If my poetry is good, then it's fine across the board; and if it is not up to global standards, then there is no need of awarding me, merely because I am an African.'[49] Likewise, Gathogo rejects adulation.

Conclusion

It was apparently the American civil rights leader Martin Luther King Jr who suggested that if a person hasn't discovered something he or she would die for, they are not fit to live. Gathogo's passion for research in oral history and theo-mission histories has undoubtedly justified his purpose for living.[50] He is certainly one of the leading Anglican scholars in Kenya and indeed Africa. This prolific African-Anglican scholar has addressed numerous historico-missiological themes, alert to Africa's contemporary challenges.

Notes

1 Julius Gathogo, 'Liturgical Initiatives and Moratorium Debates in Africa: An Afro-ecclesiological Perspective', *Stellenbosch Theological Journal*, 8.1 (2022): 1–25.

2 Gathogo, 'Liturgical Initiatives': 18.

3 Gathogo, 'Liturgical Initiatives': 3.

4 Julius Gathogo, 'African Indigenous Knowledge Versus Western Science in the Mbeere Mission of Kenya', *HTS Teologiese Studies/Theological Studies*, 79.1 (2023): 1–8.

5 Jomo Kenyatta, *Facing Mount Kenya* (London: Heinemann, 1938), 42.

6 Julius Gathogo, 'Some Expressions of African Hospitality Today', *Scriptura* 99 (2008): 275–87 (279).

7 Gathogo, 'African Indigenous Knowledge': 2.

8 Julius Gathogo, 'Njega wa Gioko and the European Missionaries in the Colonial Kenya: A Theo-historical Recollection and Reflection', *HTS Teologiese Studies/Theological Studies*, 77.2 (2022): 1–11.

9 Julius Gathogo, 'Were the African Indigenous Resources Rendered Impotent by the Pandemic? A Review of COVID-19 Impact in Kenya, March 2020 to March 2022', *Jumuga Journal of Education, Oral Studies, and Human Sciences*, 5.1 (2022): 1–13 (6).

10 Julius Gathogo, 'The Reason for Studying African Religion in Post-Colonial Africa', *Currents in Theology and Mission*, 36.2 (2009): 108–17.

11 Gathogo, 'Were the African Indigenous Resources Rendered Impotent by the Pandemic?'

12 Julius Gathogo, 'African Philosophy as Expressed in the Concepts of Hospitality and Ubuntu', *Journal of Theology for Southern Africa*, 130.1 (2008): 39–53.

13 Julius Gathogo, 'Mutira Mission (1907–2011): The Birth of a Christian Empire in East Africa', *Studia Historiae Ecclesiasticae*, 37.1 (2012): 171–94.

14 Julius Gathogo, 'Some Challenges in Founding an African Faith: Mutira Mission, Kenya 1907–2012', *Studia Historiae Ecclesiasticae*, 38.2 (2012): 81–99.

15 Julius Gathogo, *Mutira Mission: An African Church Comes of Age in Kirinyaga, Kenya (1912–2012)* (Nairobi: Zapf Chancery, 2011).

16 See also Gathogo, 'The Birth of a Christian Empire in East Africa'.

17 See also Julius Gathogo, 'Karubiu wa Munyi and the Making of Modern Kirinyaga, Kenya', *HTS Teologiese Studies/Theological Studies*, 76.4 (2020): 1–9.

18 See also Julius Gathogo, 'Unsung Heroes and Heroines in Mutira Mission', *Studia Historiae Ecclesiasticae*, 39.1 (2013): 107–27.

19 See also Gathogo, 'Karubiu wa Munyi'.

20 Julius Gathogo, *The Imprints of NITD-Kabete in Mutira Mission, Kenya: Recollections on Josphat Kathogo wa Kamoni (1918–1978)* (Nairobi: Kairos, 2021).

21 See also Gathogo, 'The Birth of a Christian Empire in East Africa'.

22 See also Gathogo, 'Some Challenges'.

23 See also Gathogo, 'Karubiu wa Munyi'.

24 See also Julius Gathogo, 'Environmental Management and African Indigenous Resources', *Studia Historiae Ecclesiasticae*, 39.2 (2013): 33–58.

25 See also Gathogo, 'Unsung Heroes and Heroines'.

26 See also Gathogo, 'Unsung Heroes and Heroines'.

27 See Gathogo, 'Some Challenges'.

28 Gathogo, *Mutira Mission: An African Church Comes of Age*.

29 Julius Gathogo, 'Johana Njumbi (1886–1991): The Pioneer African Leader in Mutira Mission', *Oral History Journal of South Africa*, 1.1 (2013): 74–95.

30 Gathogo, 'Some Challenges'.

31 Gathogo, *Mutira Mission: An African Church Comes of Age*.

32 Gathogo, *Mutira Mission: An African Church Comes of Age*, 155.

33 Gathogo, *Mutira Mission: An African Church Comes of Age*, 156.

34 See also Gathogo, 'Unsung Heroes and Heroines'.

35 Gathogo, *Mutira Mission: An African Church Comes of Age*.

36 Gathogo, 'Some Challenges'.

37 Gathogo, *The Imprints of NITD-Kabete*.

38 Julius Gathogo, 'Memory and History: Oral Techniques in the East African Context', *HTS Teologiese Studies/Theological Studies*, 77.2 (2021): 1–9.

39 Gathogo, 'Memory and History'.

40 Julius Gathogo, 'Theological Education in Tropical Africa', *HTS Teologiese Studies/Theological Studies*, 75.1 (2019): 1–19.

41 Brian Urquhart, 'What You Can Learn from Reinhold Niebuhr', *The New York Review of Books* (26 March 2009).

42 Urquhart, 'Niebuhr'.

43 Julius Gathogo, 'Njega wa Gioko and the European Missionaries in the Colonial Kenya', *HTS Teologiese Studies/Theological Studies*, 78.3 (2022): 1–9.

44 Urquhart, 'Niebuhr'.

45 Urquhart, 'Niebuhr'.

46 Julius Gathogo, 'Consolidating Democracy in Colonial Kenya (1920–63): Challenges and Prospects', *Jumuga Journal*, 3.1 (2020): 1–18 (1). doi.org/10.35544/jjeoshs.v1i1.22.

47 Gathogo, 'Consolidating Democracy': 13.

48 Julius Gathogo, 'Nexus between Refugee Crisis and Ubuntu Concept in the East African Region', unpublished article (forthcoming).

49 Gathogo, 'Njega wa Gioko'.

50 Gathogo, 'Njega wa Gioko'.

7

Winston Halapua

FRANK SMITH

Winston Halapua was born in Tonga. He entered St John the Baptist College in Suva, Fiji, at the age of 20, to begin his theological studies. He has made Fiji his home again on his retirement. But during his career with the Church, his writings communicate his theological ideas. Winston's approach to theology is influenced by the worldview inherited from his forebears and his search for an authentic way to speak of Christ in the Pacific, that part of the world which he calls Oceania.[1] Halapua sees himself as a 'multicultural person', having studied Christian mission and ministry in Tonga, Fiji, England, Israel and Aotearoa New Zealand.[2] This chapter celebrates his work, although I acknowledge that my contribution is a small window into an expansive world of all that Halapua has stood for as a person, a priest and church leader, and educator.

On becoming Bishop of Polynesia in August 2010, Halapua was installed as Archbishop and Primate of the Anglican Church in Aotearoa, New Zealand and Polynesia, a role he held until he retired in December 2018. He was formerly (1998–) the principal of the college of the diocese of Polynesia, a position he assumed having initially joined St John's as lecturer in 1996. The establishment of the college for Polynesia is a direct result of the 1992 constitutional changes of the Anglican Church in the Province of New Zealand, which resulted in the name change – to the Anglican Church in Aotearoa, New Zealand and Polynesia, thus establishing the Three Tikanga (cultural stream) Church. This also enabled the creation of an archdeaconry of the diocese of Polynesia in New Zealand of which Halapua was made archdeacon. In 2005 this archdeaconry unit became a bishopric and Halapua became the Bishop of Polynesia in Aotearoa New Zealand. Thus, he not only led the development of the diocese of Polynesia in New Zealand but also the emerging college of the diocese of Polynesia as a constituent college of the College of St John the Evangelist, which also includes The Southern Cross (Pakeha) and the Te Rau Kahikatea (Māori), thus the Three Tikanga. All of this flowed from the constitutional changes mentioned above. But the Three Tikanga college was not smooth sailing, and in 2010 an enquiry led to structural changes at the college in 2011. Ten years later, there was another college enquiry in 2021. These continuing enquiries into the college suggest a continuing struggle to understand how the Tikanga streams relate to one another in concrete entities like the College of St John the Evangelist, especially when it is seen as a provincial college, as well as sharing resources between Tikanga, an arrangement that needs a deeper level of theologizing about the Three Tikanga Church. Halapua's theological method and the ideas that inform this would be helpful in this endeavour.

In what follows, I explore Halapua's theological thought and its operation in various contexts. I attempt to bring together his treatment of various oceanic concepts as a way of understanding his theological world. I begin with an observation that, for Halapua, the idea of a transcendent and immanent God is imaged in the dynamics of the world's named oceans in relationship to one another. The underlying idea here is of an interconnecting God who is inseparable from creation both human and other-than-human, a God made manifest in the Christ event. So, the interconnectedness of all creation leads to the ideas of human identity as an interconnected being; and that life in the fullest sense must be lived in relational terms for that is how God should be understood, with the relational emphasis already inherent in a Trinitarian understanding of God.

We get a glimpse of interconnected reality from the way oceans relate to one another and to creation, including human creation. The collective term for oceans is *moana*. Halapua uses this term as a metaphor for God; the metaphor also undergirds Halapua's approach to real-life issues. But first let me put this in context.

A Bishop in a Three Tikanga Church

The Three Tikanga Church and the revision of its constitution is a recognition that the 1840 Treaty of Waitangi between the British Crown and the New Zealand indigenous people, the Māori, had not lived up to its covenanting requirements. Thus, at the 1990 Waitangi celebrations, the Bishop of Aotearoa, Te Whakahuihui Vercoe, spoke of these directly to the Queen and her government. To quote:

Some of us have come here to celebrate, some to commemorate, some to commiserate, but some to remember what happened on this sacred ground. But since the signing of that Treaty 150 years ago I want to remind our partners that you have marginalized us. You have not honoured the Treaty. We have not honoured each other in the promises we made on this sacred ground. May God give us the courage to be honest with one another, to be sincere with one another, and above all to love one another in the strength of God.[3]

Historical reviews of this relationship are well documented elsewhere,[4] so I will not discuss them here. But the indigenous Māori reawakening together with the public mood led to a new examination of historical injustices against the Māori. This development influenced the Anglican Church in New Zealand, whose structure up until 1992 had only started to listen to the Māori voice through controlled appointments of assistant bishops in a Māori pastorate.[5] The Māori worldview and ways of doing things had not taken hold in the mainstream – an all too familiar scenario when colonial ideas are embedded in the wider society and indigenous peoples become the disenfranchised. Indeed, it was the monocultural Church (the 'settler church' as the early European immigrant Anglican Church is known) within a multicultural setting that came to face immense pressure to reform. Halapua describes the 1992 revised constitution as a 'redemptive expression of the Anglican Church in Aotearoa, New Zealand and Polynesia. It is a result of addressing unjust structures in which uneven relationships were maintained. It is a move toward justice and respect for Māori and other peoples.'[6] This statement gives us an insight into Halapua's key paradigm of being in the world – namely, the centrality of 'relationships' that undergirds doing theology *moana*-wise.

However, the restructuring resulting from the constitutional changes has been critiqued for supposedly lacking a solid theological framework. For example, Valerie Turner wrote in *The Anglican*, a publication of the diocese of Auckland, that the Three Tikanga model reflects 1980s social and political rhetoric and thinking, and John Wright points out that theology does need to relate to the twenty-first century to be relevant.[7] While there is a point in these comments, I am of the view that Turner's statement exaggerates issues for two reasons. Firstly, such views are premised on a form of a universalist theological approach. Secondly, these theological considerations come after a defining event. For example, it took several hundred years for the Church to come to terms with a shared theological understanding of the Christ event in the Trinitarian understanding of God. So, while it may be true that the Church had not produced a written theological framework on which the constitutional changes are based, the Church had commissioned a report on *Tikanga Rua Bicultural Development* in 1986 and this made way for understanding the rationale for a reformed constitution.[8] The language of this document expressed indigenous concepts and values that are loaded with theological premises as a rationale for structural changes – for example, concepts like *kotahitanga*,[9] *manaakitanga*,[10] *tikanga*.[11] These are terms that have often been translated in single words. But the truth is that these words in languages of Pasifika cultures – including Māori – are multivalent. Thus, single words in English do not capture the essence of these concepts that have far-reaching meanings.

In the next sections, I discuss examples of indigenous ideas and Halapua's theological treatment of these. Here I want to note that the interweaving and intertwining nature of Pasifika languages, the imagery language creates, and the dynamic nature of the *moana* allows Halapua to do theology in Pasifika/Oceania/*moana* mode.

Moana as Paradigm

In the ensuing debate about the Three Tikanga Church and what may be called a 'Three Tikanga theology', Halapua's contribution was to bring an overarching theological framework as a source for further exploration. This is the focus of his article, 'Theomoana: Toward a Tikanga Theology – The Story (talanoa) of the Three Tikanga Church – The Anglican Church in Aotearoa New Zealand and Polynesia'.[12] The St John the Evangelist Theological College took the debate further through two theological Hui (gatherings) about the issue. The first resulted in a publication called *Te Awa Rerenga Maha: Braided River*;[13] a further publication is forthcoming. Halapua's initial essay explored various indigenous concepts inherent in an Oceanic way of life and of doing things – expressions already mentioned here as well as others – in order to provoke theological debate about the new constitution. His understanding of the dynamics of *moana* forms the basis of his theological method.

Moana is explored in his book *Waves of God's Embrace* (2008). Here Halapua lays out his key method of doing theology enshrined in the natural way named oceans (Arctic, Mediterranean, Indian, Atlantic, Pacific) interconnect with one another: 'The largest ocean is the Pacific Ocean, and the Pacific cannot be an ocean without the Atlantic, Indian, Arctic, and Antarctic Oceans ... The oceans are interconnected. No ocean can function without the others. And so, we can only be useful for God's activity if we can do it together.'[14] If *moana* (an ancient term for oceans) is one whole connected body, it is no wonder that despite being named as different oceans occupying specific spaces, they contribute to the life of the other because they flow into one another. There is also an interconnectedness between *moana* as ocean and land and people in Pasifika understanding, as Pacific islands are not isolated islets but part of one big expanse of ocean with lands and people without borders. In this Pasifika way of thinking, the Pacific Ocean and Pacific islands are redefined to reflect interconnectedness. In decolonizing the way Pacific islands are referenced, Epeli Hau'ofa coined the term 'Sea of Islands' to suggest its vastness as a distinguishing form and shape and to convey its influence on Pasifika resistance to thinking about Pacific islands as small and isolated countries.[15] This expansive way of speaking about the Pacific nations arises from an understanding of *moana* as contiguous with land and people. *Moana* is inclusive of oceans, land and people. Thus, when speaking about identity Pasifika people might say that they are of the *moana*. I belong to *moana* because I am given life through my birth to my death in this part of the world where I experience this immense body of water that surrounds – and I am part of it. The reference here is not about smallness but about borderlessness, relatedness, an idea of one-ness. The idea of difference in the cultures that inhabit the islands is also evoked – and thus the idea of diversity within oneness is imaged. Hence, from the experience of Oceanic people who know and live in *moana*, we can say that we experience its depths and mysteries and offerings, its potential destructiveness and its calmness. We interact and depend on it for our very livelihood; and for generations, we have sailed on it to find new homes. We recognize it as contiguous with us, with dry land, and with life itself. For this reason, we can speak of *moana* as a metaphor.[16] *Moana* sustains human life and provides a habitat for thousands of species. *Moana* is home to people as it is to other living entities. *Moana* is identity to oceanic people. This is key to the *moana* model that Halapua emphasizes.

Halapua draws attention to the ways that the 'flow' of oceans creates dynamism. Interconnectedness creates the opportunities for flow of oceans into one another. This provides an image for the relatedness of humanity and the rest of creation, the whole. No one thing can function independently. They all require the other to fulfil their purposes and for fulness of life to be experienced.

From a Pasifika perspective, Christian understanding of God arose out of the experience of the first Christians with Jesus. Jesus made God real in that his teachings and actions spoke to them in a way that made God a reality for them. In Jesus' death and resurrection, they saw powerful images of God's grace and power. This happened in the context of the Jewish story, Jesus' culture, and time. So in our time, the question arises as to how God is made real to us in our experience of the world we now inhabit. For Pasifika people, *moana* is real and the images it evokes in terms of its immediacy, its immensity, interconnectedness, diversity, life, depth, as home but at the same time a mystery, makes the reality of

God accessible to us. Thus, when we speak of the depths of the *moana* we speak of the depth of the love of God in Christ. When we speak of the borderless *moana* as it embraces islands, this images a God who embraces everyone in all our diversity. When we speak of interconnectedness, we image a relational God because that is who we are, rooted in our relations with family, with Vanua (Fijian understanding of land, sea and people) and all of creation. All of these make the mystery of God perceptible to us as Pasifika peoples.

Moana Relationships and Climate Change

Understanding God through the metaphor of *moana* has implications for how human relationships should work out in practice. *Moana* is the identity of human in relational terms. It is belonging to one another and being one at the same time as being different and diverse. These ideas imply having and developing right relationships. All are intricately woven so that the essential hope is for a balance and harmony to exist. These notions of *moana* contradict Newtonian theory that objectifies the world. They have more in common with emerging paradigms through the works of, for example, David Bohm,[17] Fritjof Capra[18] and Margaret Wheatley,[19] recognizing that relationality has a lot to contribute to overcoming a false Cartesian mind–matter dichotomy. *Moana* as metaphor speaks to all situations in which we find ourselves. This is particularly poignant for controversial issues that Pasifika peoples experience. Halapua is particularly interested in climate change, and gender and leadership.

Halapua's interest in climate change is understandable. His country of birth, like the many islands of Oceania, is comprised of islands that are low-lying atolls. Climate changes resulting from global warming causes rising sea levels that are catastrophic for *moana* peoples. Already, this is a reality for Tuvalu and Kiribati. For this reason, when Halapua was Bishop of Polynesia he worked with the government of Fiji to allow for several hundred acres of church property to be set aside for resettlement of the people of Kiribati should the need arise. He has also encouraged debate at the highest level between Church and state in other countries where he had jurisdiction. For example, in 2015 he facilitated the Archbishop of York's visit to the diocese of Polynesia, and brought together government and church leaders to hear John Sentamu speak on 'Leadership and Climate Change'. Halapua then highlighted the climate change issue by celebrating Eucharist on an island devastated by a hurricane just several months previously.

Halapua has also promoted practical ministry projects highlighting climate change, and these have also enabled dialogue around Oceania. One might think that approaches taken by small countries are futile since larger industrialized countries are the ones that make the major contribution as pollutants. Yet the countries that are most affected – which includes numerous Pasifika island states – have needed to find a greater collective voice at world assemblies and have been given profile and encouragements through Halapua's actions and example.

Moana Relationships and Sexuality

Gender is a controversial issue that has put some strain on relationships around the Anglican Communion, especially as the issues of gay marriage and the ordination of gay people came to the fore. Halapua was one of those who were invited to produce theological reflections on homosexuality following the 1998 Lambeth Conference that 'unambiguously declar[ed] any homosexual practice incompatible with Scripture and therefore, a sin'.[20] However, the Lambeth Conference also commended the Anglican Communion to listen to those others who were or are not represented at the meetings. The collection of essays in *Other Voices: Other Worlds: The Global Church Speaks Out on Homosexuality* was published in 2006, and Halapua contributes to this publication. He invokes a *moana* perspective that is inclusive in its approach to homosexuality. Again, his thinking shows that the *moana* concept has far-reaching implications.

Halapua's essay is titled 'Moana Waves, Oceania and Homosexuality'.[21] I quote from his work to illustrate the connectivity between Oceanic values and a *moana* way of thinking and of doing things in relation to sexuality:

> When an understanding of homosexuality is located within Oceanic values and interconnectedness ... homosexuality is accepted and celebrated as one of the many waves of the moana. Waves dance to the currents of the ocean depths and waves faithfully touch the island shores to embrace all small or big, mountainous or flat, volcanic or golden sand, to remind us all that the moana is very much alive ... moana places emphasis on the inclusive embracing of all the richness of human sexuality. A moana perspective is about transformative relationship – about seeing ourselves and others in the context of God's embracing love which is as deep and wide as the ocean.[22]

One can see immediately how *moana* values – for example, interconnectedness, imagery of waves embracing islands and depth of oceans
– translate to ideas about inclusiveness. Halapua laments that the othering[23] of homosexual people is a result of dualistic thinking that came
with the missionaries.[24] This thinking invaded oceanic minds. It is only
recently that new decolonizing paradigms are beginning to take hold.
Moana thinking is one such paradigm.

Moana and Talanoa

On becoming Bishop of Polynesia, Halapua started issuing the diocesan
newsletter under the new title *Talanoa Wave*. The word 'wave' carries
forward Halapua's *moana* imagination. This also coincided with naming the new diocesan headquarters 'Moana Administration and Teaching
and Services' (MAST), and the creation and naming of new ministry
projects beginning with the term *moana*, such as 'Moana Children's ministry'. This shows an embeddedness of the *moana* conceptual framework
in Halapua's worldview. The term *talanoa* is, in simple terms, an open
conversation, a telling of stories. Thus, the *Talanoa Wave* brought stories
of the diocese to the distant places where the diocese is represented in its
parishes and congregations.

The term *talanoa* also has far-reaching meaning and effects with
practical implications, not least in decision-making, education and pedagogy. The academic disciplines that apply *talanoa* frameworks in their
research as well as in their practice, whatever that may be, are discussed
elsewhere.[25] I discuss here *talanoa* in relation to *moana* dynamics and
leadership.

Talanoa is conversation that is open, and not timebound. The term is
composed of the words *tala* and *noa*. *Tala* is about the storying of life
events in the presence of others, so that communication is facilitated.
Noa implies ideas of openness, vast spaces, non-boundedness, wandering.
Halapua links *noa* with space in a manner that enables actions to manifest
– for example, in space-time dimensions that enable respectful communication to occur. Respect is valued in *talanoa* space, in the activity of
dialogue and communication.[26] And underlying this respectful disposition
is an indigenous understanding of another core value in *moana* relations.
This is the idea of *vā* which literally means the space between subjects.
Hospitality is offered through this space out of respect. Respect is offered
because the sacred inhabits the *vā*, the space between subjects. *Vā* recognizes difference. Thus, 'othering' is understood to dishonour the sacred,
the divine, the holy.[27]

Well-facilitated *talanoa*, even though it may be heated, can continue in several directions such that those looking for an answer to a problem may be frustrated. But coming quickly to 'answers' is not what *talanoa* is about and what its dynamics value. Rather, *talanoa* recognizes that participants are all of equal standing with voices to be heard, for unless all voices contribute to the conversation the idea of a common understanding arising out of *talanoa* may not be fulfilled. It follows that one must be present with others at the same time at the same space with all allowed to speak and participate fully. *Talanoa*, then, has space-time dimensions that offer opportunities for hospitality, for conflict resolution, for consensual agreements and for covenant making. Halapua describes these space-time dimensions of *talanoa* as 'divine gifts'.[28]

The Sociologist in Theological Debate

Earlier in his life, Halapua undertook two research projects for his MA and PhD degrees at the University of the South Pacific in Suva, Fiji. His MA focused on issues affecting the Melanesian community in Fiji, people who are descendants of the Melanesia Islanders (from Solomon, Papua New Guinea and Vanuatu) brought to Fiji as indentured labourers by the British colonial power. The Melanesian islanders in Fiji are called 'Solomoni' to distinguish them from Fijians, and most are Anglicans. Halapua's work sought to explain the origins of their present status as marginalized Christians in the Fijian community and the reason why the Anglican Church has responded to their needs as a moral requirement. Halapua's PhD research focused on the coup cultures following the military takeover of Fiji's elected governments. Halapua recognized that the coup culture lay in cultural worldviews, and that the country's military coups are a symptom of a leadership crisis in Fiji.[29] In the context of that research he promoted the idea of *talanoa* as a way of providing a forum for discussion among leaders on whatever issue is at hand.[30]

The focus of Halapua's two research projects shows a deeply held care for the people of a country that is now home to him. These early projects also demonstrate Halapua's long-standing interest in people and the socio-political environments that impact human lives. He has also always been a keen observer of ways in which people do not/are not made to experience wholesome lives. Both of his academic research projects resulted in published works.[31] They also show the undergirding of all his future activities is a *moana* understanding of the world.

Conclusion

This has been a short discussion of Halapua's *moana* approach to issues that include leadership, sexuality, climate change and care for the environment. If theology is 'faith seeking understanding', Halapua's advancement of *moana* as a theological idea has sought to earth Christ in his part of the world, developing what Ilaitia Tuwere and others have also explored from their own indigenous perspectives.[32]

The practical implications of *moana* thinking to ministry create ways of imagining relations with others, of consensual decision-making, of transparency and work towards dissolving hierarchical power structures within organizations, including within the Anglican churches. Yet there is much work to be done to make these changes visible in everyday life. Halapua continues with his research on climate change and attempts to mitigate its effects. He continues to make a key contribution to education in the country he has called home, and throughout the Pasifika region.

Notes

1 This term was coined by the French explorer Dumont d'Urville in 1831 and traditionally includes Micronesia, Melanesia, Polynesia, Australia and New Zealand. It is a catch-all word so does not distinguish between these countries.

2 Lloyd Ashton, 'Humble Beginnings for Polynesia's New Bishop', *Anglican Taonga* (12 May 2010).

3 Lloyd Ashton, 'What Binds This Church?', *Anglican Taonga* (6 May 2016).

4 For example, Allan Davidson, *Christianity in Aotearoa: A History of Church and Society in New Zealand* (Wellington: New Zealand Education for Ministry Board, rev. edn 2004).

5 For example, Bishop Bennet was appointed in 1928 through synodal approval but only as an assistant bishop to a Pakeha diocesan bishop; in 1972 an independent Māori Pastorate was established with its own bishop – of Aotearoa.

6 Winston Halapua, 'Theomoana: Towards a Tinkanga Theology', in *Talanoa Rhythmns: Voices from Oceania*, ed. Nasili Vaka'uta (Wellington: Massey University Press, 2010), 69–101 (83).

7 Both these views are expressed in Valerie Turner's article on John Wright, the former dean of the College of the Southern Cross (a constituent college of the College of St John the Evangelist) in *The Anglican* (diocese of Auckland), 19 June 2005.

8 This is the report that formed the basis for the next stage in the development of the Church Constitution which was finally adopted in 1992.

9 Expresses unity that is rooted in the idea of belonging and survival.

10 Expresses hospitality towards creation (human and other than human) that is rooted in the idea of love; an inherent all-encompassing quality of goodness expressed in action.

11 Expresses a unique way of doing things specific to a people; encompasses the idea of culture, thus speaks about identity.

12 Halapua, 'Theomoana'.

13 *Te Awa Rerenga Maha: Braided River*, ed. Donald P. Moffat (Auckland: Anglican Church of Aotearoa New Zealand and Polynesia, 2018).

14 Winston Halapua, 'Talanoa Wave', *Diocese of Polynesia Newsletter* (28 February 2018).

15 Epeli Hau'ofa, 'Sea of Islands', *The Contemporary Pacific*, 6.1 (1994): 147–61.

16 Winston Halapua, *Waves of God's Embrace: Sacred Perspectives from the Ocean* (Norwich: Canterbury Press, 2008), 9–27.

17 David Bohm, *Wholeness and the Implicate Order* (Abingdon: Routledge, 2005).

18 Fritjof Capra, *The Web of Life* (New York: Doubleday, 1996).

19 Margaret Wheatley, *Leadership and the New Science: Discovering Order in a Chaotic World* (ReadHowYouWant.com, 2010).

20 *Other Voices, Other Worlds: The Global Church Speaks Out on Homosexuality*, ed. Terry Brown (New York: Church Publishing, 2006), ix.

21 Winston Halapua, 'Moana Waves, Oceania and Homosexuality', in Brown, *Other Voices, Other Worlds*, 26–39.

22 Halapua, 'Theomoana', 10.

23 Othering is a sociological phenomenon that defines persons or groups of people against some norms. It is a way of negating others' humanity, thus those who are othered are considered less worthy of dignity and respect. See, for example, John A. Powell and Stephen Menendian, 'The Problem of Othering: Towards Inclusiveness and Belonging', *Othering and Belonging*, 1 (2016): 14–40.

24 Halapua, 'Theomoana', 29.

25 For example, Tomote M. Violeti, 'Talanoa Research Methodology: A Developing Position on Pacific Research', *Waikato Journal of Education*, 12 (2006): 21–34.

26 Halapua, *Waves of God's Embrace*, 54–5.

27 A more extensive treatment of *vā* in relation to the sacred/holy is found in Frank Smith, 'Relational Hermeneutics in the Three Tikanga Context', in *Te Awa Rerenga Maha: Braided River*, 110–13.

28 Halapua, *Waves of God's Embrace*, 64–6.

29 Winston Halapua, *The Role of Militarism in the Politics of Fiji* (Suva: University of the South Pacific, 2002).

30 Another response to the military coups is Ilaitia S. Tuwere, *Vanua: Towards a Fijian Theology of Place* (Suva: University of the South Pacific, 2002).

31 Winston Halapua, *Living on the Fringe: Melanesians of Fiji* (Suva: University of the South Pacific, 2001); Halapua, *Role of Militarism*.

32 See Ama'amalele Tofaeono, *Eco-theology: Aiga – the Household of Life: A Perspective from Living Myths and Traditions of Samoa* (Erlangen: Verlag für Mission und Ökumene, 2000).

8

Kwok Pui-lan

KEUN-JOO CHRISTINE PAE

At the American Academy of Religion's annual conference in November 2021, a group of Christian, Jewish and Muslim theologians and religious studies scholars dedicated a Festschrift, *Theologies of the Multitude for Multitudes*, to Kwok Pui-lan. All the contributors to the book are Kwok's friends, students and mentees who honour her scholarship and appreciate her friendship and mentorship. Rita Nakashima Brock and Tat-siong Benny Liew, editors of the book, note:

> Throughout her remarkable career, Kwok Pui Lan has demonstrated an uncanny ability to work with a multitude of people. Her contributions to feminist theological scholarship and to Asian and Asian American studies of religion and theology are extraordinary both for her publications and for her decades of involvement in grassroot movements that have become enduring organizations ... her ability to move among and across different networks of people in the Global North and Global South is extraordinary as she engages with different habits of thought and praxis between ministry and the academy and across academic fields beyond her own discipline of theology. As a result, she has edited books on the Anglican Church, on postcolonial practices of ministry, on Asian and Asian American women's theologies and religions, and on the 'Third World'.[1]

Writing about an exceptional theologian, critical thinker and prolific writer like Kwok Pui-lan is not an easy task. There is no single word to describe Kwok's life and theology. The 2021 Lambeth Awards, which Kwok received under the category of the Lanfranc Award for Education and Scholarship for outstanding leadership and contribution to Asian Feminist and Postcolonial Theology rooted in an Anglican ecclesiology, might be the Anglican Church's token of appreciation for Kwok's distinctive theological voice. She has written or edited more than 20 books in English and in Chinese. Her teaching and scholarship show a wide range of theological and political topics: Asian/American feminist theology, postcolonial theology, interfaith dialogue, biblical theology, Anglican theology, theological education, pedagogies of global theology, transnational feminist theology, embodied spirituality, and so forth. Kwok interweaves the theological with the political, helping her audiences expand their theological imagination. As a pioneer of Asian and Asian American feminist theology who is in solidarity with Third World theologians, Kwok is a leading voice in postcolonial theology, primarily through the intersections of race, gender, sexuality and class.

This chapter reflects on Kwok Pui-lan's legacy in the Church and theology beyond the Anglican/Episcopal tradition. It includes Kwok's central theological ideas, visions for the Anglican Church, lifelong commitment to mentoring young theologians across the globe, and solidarity with global subalterns. After introducing Kwok's biography, I engage with three interrelated areas of Kwok's theology: feminist theology, postcolonial theology and interfaith dialogue. These three themes are connected to Kwok's life in, and vision for, the Anglican tradition, showing her theological persistence in utilizing gender and sexuality analysis, transnational solidarity, liberation and justice. All point to new understandings and liberative images of God which emerge from the margins. The chapter is based on my critical reading of Kwok's various publications and on interviews with her. To my only chagrin, it cannot fully show the depth and breadth of Kwok's scholarship or her significant influence on theological academia.

Teacher, Mentor, Scholar

I first met Kwok at the annual conference of the Pacific Asian North American Asian Women in Theology and Ministry (PANAAWTM) in 2002 when I was a Master of Divinity student. Kwok is one of the founding members of PANAAWTM, a one-of-a-kind organization that has produced provocative Asian and Asian American feminist theological voices in academia and the Church. Since then, Kwok has been a teacher and mentor to me. I have enjoyed opportunities to listen to her stories, theology and life experiences over the past 20 years. Kwok is undoubtedly a role model for many Asian and Asian American women.

The year 2022 marked Kwok's 70th birthday. After World War Two, her parents moved to Hong Kong from southern China. In the 1950s and 1960s, Hong Kong was a poor Third World country like most countries in Asia. Kwok grew up with seven siblings in a relatively poor household. It was serendipitous for her to be Anglican. Christianity was foreign to her working-class family, and her parents practised popular Chinese religion. She had a neighbour who was a descendant of the first Chinese Anglican priest in Hong Kong and brought Kwok and her sister to a local Anglican church. When she was a teenager, Kwok was baptized at the church. Since then, she has remained in the Anglican faith. At this church, Kwok developed a close relationship with Jane Hwang Hsien Yuen, who would be one of the first ordained female priests in the Anglican Church.[2] It was with the Rev Hwang's influence that Kwok decided to study theology.

In her autobiographical essay, Kwok notes, 'Growing up in a working-class family, I became aware early on that I had to study hard to have better opportunities in life.'[3] Kwok was a serious student full of academic curiosity to explore the intersection of social power and religion. In 1971, she started studying theology at Chung Chi College of the Chinese University of Hong Kong. Her college courses taught European male theologians such as Karl Barth, the Niebuhr brothers, and Paul Tillich, and most theology professors were male missionaries from North America and Europe. Soon, however, as part of the Student Christian Movement's travel seminar, Kwok had the opportunity to visit various Asian countries and to learn about Christian social movements and Asian liberation theologies. For instance, in the Philippines and South Korea, Kwok learned about progressive Christians fighting against the military dictatorship. In Japan, Kwok met courageous Christians who initiated peace movements and remembered wartime crimes committed by their government.[4] This travel seminar, along with student political movements against corruption, police brutality and racial discrimination under the British colonial government in Hong Kong, would challenge Kwok to comprehend that 'theology should not be an armchair exercise but must be related to people's struggles'.[5] At this time, Gustavo Gutiérrez's *Liberation Theology* led Kwok to contemplate the vocation of a theologian.[6]

After completing the Master's programme in Theology, Kwok was invited to the theological faculty at her alma mater, so she taught one of the first courses on feminist theology in Hong Kong. Many people encouraged Kwok to pursue doctoral studies in theology. So in 1984 she started doctoral work at Harvard University because she was attracted to Harvard's vast resources in Chinese studies. It was quite an odyssey for Kwok to embark on a journey to the USA with her spouse and their two-year-old daughter. During her study at Harvard, Kwok expanded her network with feminist and womanist theologians, pondering theological perspectives that were different from those of middle-class white women. Through black women's theological lenses, Kwok critically interrogated issues in church, society and academia and became aware of the racial dynamics of the USA. This awareness led her to co-found an organization that would later become PANAAWTM.

While exploring new intellectual discourses from American women, racial minorities and postcolonial scholars, Kwok focused her doctoral dissertation on Chinese Christian women in the late nineteenth and early twentieth centuries. Her research illuminated Chinese women's agency to reinterpret Christianity on Chinese soil, especially when Euro-American and Japanese empires threatened China. Orientalism portrayed Chinese women as victims of Confucian patriarchy or as exotic temptresses. Since then, Kwok's work has deprovincialized Christianity, critically interrogating Christian theology, rituals and biblical interpretation in the non-Western world. After Harvard in 1989, Kwok returned to Hong Kong and continued to nurture younger theologians. She then took a visiting faculty position at Auburn Theological Seminary at Union Theological Seminary in New York in 1991. Later, she taught theology and spirituality at Episcopal Divinity School in Cambridge, Massachusetts, from 1992 until the school's closure in 2017. Kwok is currently Distinguished Professor of Theology and Spirituality at Candler School of Theology at Emory University, in Atlanta, USA.

Kwok is a beloved teacher, compassionate mentor, and rigorous scholar. As a respected theological educator, she received the American Academy of Religion's Excellence in Teaching Award in 2009. In her statement for the award, Kwok articulated teachers and students as 'co-investigators of the subject under study', adopting Christian educator Parker Palmer's 'subject-centered' model.[7] Kwok has been ever-diligent in adopting new pedagogical tools and creative methods to help students holistically explore theology, God and the sacred. Multimedia, arts, literature, Chinese herbs in Boston's China Town, Chinese drums, and meditation bells are common tools for Kwok to lead students to sense the sacred and, thus, think about God differently. Kwok has not shied away from incorporating body movements such as yoga, chi gong and tai chi, and also mindfulness practices, into her teaching of theology and spirituality. Just as an armchair theologian cannot produce living theology, a teacher who refuses to venture outside textbooks cannot inspire students to explore deeper meanings of life. Most important for a teacher are intellectual curiosity and enthusiasm about learning to be transferable to students. For her, 'teaching is an art and requires much dedication and hard work'.[8] Her aesthetic work has inspired many younger scholars and students to explore feminist and womanist theologies, postcolonial theologies and spirituality. As a result, students have experienced and learned the sacred in non-traditional ways.

Moreover, as the first Asian woman in many academic and church spaces, Kwok has accentuated the necessity to mentor younger generations, particularly Asian and Third World women. Kwok's mentoring reaches beyond national borders. She has formed and participated in the Global Anglican Theological Academy, 'which seeks to provide mentoring and advanced theological educational opportunities for younger women'.[9] In the meantime, mentoring requires mentors to reimagine and rethink religious education and society to open more doors for students beyond the religious field. Kwok's presidential address at the American Academy of Religion in 2011 underscores this: 'To train people that the society has a demand for means that we have to rethink, reimagine, and recreate our discipline and the certification process.'[10] Why the study of religion still matters in our times is a question that should constantly challenge and inspire theologians and religious mentors and educators.

Between *Chinese Women and Christianity 1860–1927*[11] (1992) and *Postcolonial Politics and Theology* (2021), Kwok has published abundant critical discourses on political theology, feminist theology, postcolonial theology, popular activism, interfaith dialogue and intercultural theology. It may not be an exaggeration to say that she has touched every possible theological discourse, expanding the horizon of theology. Many of her publications evince her collaboration with diverse theologians across the globe and her mentoring. What follows are some keys to Kwok's central theological ideas: feminist theology, postcolonial theology, and interfaith dialogue.

Feminist Theology

Feminist theology is central to Kwok's various theological discourses. Her feminist theology begins with a keen awareness of gender oppression in the Church and society. For instance, although gender and sexuality issues are at the centre of recent debates and schisms within the global Anglican Communion, women's voices from the Communion have not been heard or appreciated clearly.[12] Indeed, the marginalization of female-identified people is a shared problem in many Christian churches across the globe.

Kwok's feminist theology can be adequately understood only from a postcolonial and transnational perspective. Her books in the 1990s – when academic studies of religion and theology actively engaged with other disciplines on multiculturalism and postcolonialism – uncovered the hidden stories of Chinese Christian women through archival research and critical gender analysis. For example, *Chinese Women and Christian-*

ity, 1860–1972 accentuates Chinese Christian women's agency to adopt Christianity that is different from Western portrayals of these women (for example, as victims of foot binding practices in patriarchal culture). *Discovering the Bible in the Non-Biblical World*[13] engages with Asian women's critical interpretation of the Bible based on their experiences of patriarchy, colonial violence and political activism. Indeed, the so-called biblical world has resided in European male scholars' imaginations tainted by Orientalism and colonialism. Thus, Asian women have had to invent and reinvent tools to critically interrogate biblical narratives, not merely reacting to white colonialist interpretation but searching for emancipatory wisdom, courage and solidarity. As a trailblazer of trans-nationalism in theological education and scholarship, Kwok has never ceased to interrogate colonial gazes embedded in Christianity and also in feminist theology.

Postcolonialism, according to Kwok, is not just about power reversal (such as transferring power from colonialists to formerly colonized people) but is also about an engaged critique of the structures, ideologies, symbols, mentality and legacy of colonialism.[14] Gender and sexuality, along with race and class, are crucial lenses in analysing the long legacy of colonialism. With critical attention to the academic study of religion's development in the colonial educational system, Kwok first argues that:

> Doing postcolonial feminist theology, it can be argued, is akin to the 'writing back' process in postcolonial literature – only that this time, the writing subjects are the formerly colonized Christian women, and the matter to be discussed is theology.[15]

Kwok acknowledges the epistemological privileges of 'female subalterns who experience the intersection of oppressions in the most immediate and brutal ways' as they articulate more inclusive feminist theology than others.[16] However, this does not mean the exclusion of the (former) female colonizers from postcolonial feminist theology. Instead, Kwok notes 'different entry points, priorities of issues, accents, and inflections' caused by multiple social locations and positions of the producers of postcolonial feminist knowledge.[17] Additionally, male-identified people can be allies of feminist theology owing partly to their lack of experiences of gender-based discrimination and violence.

Kwok suggests three ways of doing postcolonial feminist theology in the twenty-first century: (1) resignifying gender, (2) requeering sexuality, and (3) redoing theology.[18] The resignification of gender highlights the necessity to use gender in analysing cross-cultural and transnational net-works of relations and social movements. Kwok expresses dissatisfaction with white feminist and poststructuralist theological work. American white feminist theology often focuses on language, desire and bodies, destabilizing masculine symbols, metaphors, and languages for God.[19] However, symbols, desires and bodies are not the main concerns of many Third World women who strived to bring material changes in the concrete context. In addition, changes in metaphors and symbols in Christianity do not necessarily induce structural changes or challenge the problems of Christian imperialism. Similarly, feminist poststructuralists' emphasis on desire, bodies and human differences can be easily 'appropriated into a highly individualistic, eroticized consumer culture of American late capitalism'. However, many Third World women understand their liberation and desires in relation to their communities.[20] As a result, many white feminist theologians do not apprehend the complex inter-locking of race, gender, class and sexuality. Namely, gender is not the only structural problem that women of colour and postcolonial women face. By resignifying gender, Christian theologians avoid essentializing gender binarism and search for a new way of conceptualizing feminist theology from a cross-cultural and transnational perspective.

Requeering sexuality essentially destabilizes the binary gender hierarchy. For Kwok, requeering sexuality requires not only criticizing the Church's long history of homophobia and transphobia but also unpacking 'the manifold and entangled relations of homophobia and homoerotic desire to gender, race, religion, and colonialism'.[21] Indeed, white heteropatriar-chal bourgeois sexual morality interwoven with the Christian idealization of abstinence from sex has depicted Native Americans, African Americans and colonized people of colour as sexually promiscuous and hypersexu-alized. Like gender, sexuality should also be placed in more significant categories of politics, such as the global economic structures, political terror, violence, and (neo)colonial power. By doing this, postcolonial feminist theology can trace the sexual history of Christianity (e.g. the convention of Presence-God-Phallus) and Christian imperialism while disabusing Christian sexual moral discourses of controlling the poor and the marginalized.[22]

The processes of resignifying gender and requeering sexuality induce 'redoing theology' – new ways of conceptualizing theology. According to Kwok, postcolonial feminist theology's most important contribution is to 'reconceptualize the relation of theology and empire through the multiple lenses of gender, race, class, sexuality, religion, etc'.[23] More specifically, postcolonial feminist theology should continue to concern (1) the circulation of theological symbols and cultural capital in the colonial period and its permutations in late capitalism (i.e. material analysis of culture for justice), (2) the conceptualization of the religious difference, and

(3) environmental degradation and its impact on the lives of marginalized women.[24] Postcolonial feminist theology still adopts traditional Christian themes as a way to think through theology. Yet, a feminist analysis of the postcolonial condition is a starting point to articulate theological issues and themes.

Postcolonial Theology

Kwok's postcolonial theology is inseparable from feminist theology. Neither is postcolonial feminist theology differentiated from political theology. To expand on the previous introduction to Kwok's postcolonial feminist theology, I now note Kwok's postcolonial methods of interpreting the Bible and producing (feminist) theology. Kwok's investment in Asian/Third World women's critical reading of the Bible produces an essential method for postcolonial feminist theology or what she calls 'postcolonial imagination': historical, dialogical and diasporic imagination. These movements are not linear, but they overlap and interweave in complex ways.[25]

Kwok's historical imagination aims to reconstitute and release the past to make the present liveable. Third World women's collective and embodied memories are powerful in resisting institutionally sanctioned forgetfulness by the colonial and neo-imperial ruling.[26] Historical imagination limns Third World women as agents of writing and remembering painful history and memory. They do not simply find pleasure in asserting their individualist sexuality or sexual freedom, as found in white bourgeois culture. Instead, their pleasure and assertion of humanity come from 'the commitment to communal survival and in creating social networks and organizations' so that they and their communities can be healed and flourish together.[27] Historical imagination allows postcolonial theologians to creatively retrieve their communal and historical sources for global peace and justice and genuinely care about people who retell the stories and memories of decolonizing movements.

As a concept and region, the transpacific captures Kwok's dialogical imagination, which critically interrogates the modes and zones of contact between the dominant and the subordinate, or the relations of ruling. Kwok emphasizes the importance of transnational collaboration between Asian and Asian American feminist theologians. Unlike the common belief shared by the American public, Asia and America are not two separate entities but are 'constantly influencing each other within the broader regional formation of the Asia Pacific'.[28] The Pacific as a concept cannot be separated from European, American and Asian imaginations or fantasies of economic expansion, domination, a clash between civilizations, exoticized indigenous cultures and women, and military operations. For Asians, the Pacific is unthinkable without remembering European and American imperialism. China and Japan's legacies only add Asianized imperialism to the region, while South Korea and Singapore have risen as regional powers, if not sub-empires. In the meantime, the Pacific invokes imperialist nostalgia among Europeans and Americans – wars, conquest and endless wealth. The term 'transpacific' is the most recent effort at naming this forced contact zone.[29] The transpacific offers a transnational feminist lens to reflect on what is happening on American soil that is also happening outside the USA. By re-remembering and rewriting (hi)stories, including those of the Sacred, deeply embedded in the transpacific, Asian and Asian American women open entry points to postcolonial and transnational feminist theo-ethics. Kwok's dialogical imagination illuminates not only 'the fluidity and contingent character of Asian cultures' but also the crucial realities of human life marked with transition and pilgrimage.[30] Thus, dialogical imagination makes transnational solidarity necessary because we, Asian and Asian Americans, can only navigate life's uncertainties and ambiguities in contact zones where our identities and cultures are unsettled but interconnected with dissimilar cultures and identities.

Finally, diasporic imagination destabilizes the centre and periphery and recognizes the periphery as the subject of producing critical knowledge of oppression, war, poverty and forced diaspora. Kwok introduces 'the image of the storyteller who selects pieces, fragments, and legends from her cultural and historical memory to weave together tales that are passed from generation to generation'.[31] Kwok's image of the storyteller shows a female agent accountable to her community while rediscovering the collective wisdom of survival and resistance. A postcolonial woman grounds her transnational solidarity through storytelling and consciously engaging in others' stories of survival wisdom. Furthermore, diasporic imagination critically interrogates diasporic subjects' negotiation of multiple cultures and identities, and the inclusion or exclusion of women and sexual minorities from diasporic recordings. Gender is a signifier of power relations in diasporic memories, whereas negotiation with multiple cultures and religions is required to build transnational solidarity. Kwok's diasporic imagination beautifully elaborates on the interconnectedness of people: 'A diasporic consciousness finds similarities and differences in both familiar territories and unexpected corners; one catches glimpses of oneself in a fleeting moment or in a fragment in someone else's story.'[32] Despite salient differences and power differentials among diasporic and politically vulnerable subjects, they can build alliances for social justice as they see one another's contextual similarities created and sustained by various institutions. Transnational solidarity emerges from diasporic imagination, as diverse diasporic subjects see one another in their particular stories, crossing different times and spaces.

What kind of church would be born out of postcolonial imagination? The following quote may give the readers a glimpse of Kwok's post-colonial vision for a new Anglican Communion:

> If the Church can find a way to live out its commitment to mutual re-sponsibility and interdependence, it can offer hope to a broken world and offer a foretaste for God's Kingdom. Many Anglicans would like to see the birth of such a new church: a church that is more concerned about God's mission than policing sexuality. A church that is not afraid of cultural differences, but welcomes diversity as its strength. A church that is not centralized or hierarchical, but celebrates democracy and participation of all who together constitute the Body of the Christ.[33]

Interfaith Dialogue – Theology of Difference

According to Asian American Catholic theologian Peter C. Phan, Kwok Pui-lan's Asian American postcolonial feminist theology of religious dif-ference is a major contribution to the contemporary theology of religion.[34] Kwok's theology of religious difference surely offers a critical ground for interfaith dialogue for peace-building in the twenty-first century.

Noting that inter-religious dialogue has been dominated by male reli-gious leaders (i.e. clergy), Kwok delineates how to 'demystify myths' concerning religion as an obstacle towards peace-building. Kwok points out three myths regarding religion in international politics. The first myth is political scientist Samuel Huntington's propaganda, 'the clash of civil-izations', which reduces the existence of diverse religions to rivalry and conflict.[35] While popular views on secularism as progress and religion as irrational and incompatible with modernity constitute the second myth, dangerous Islamophobia juxtaposed to Christianity as a peace-loving religion spreads the third myth.[36] All these myths could be demystified first by postcolonial criticism that destabilizes the category of religion, promotes religious literacy, and dissects colonialism's contribution to creating religious rivalry and conflict.[37]

Furthermore, millions of cases show religious people's active partici-pation in global peace-building. With attention to women's inter-religious peace-building on local and global levels, Kwok argues what the commit-ment to peace and inter-religious solidarity requires us: (1) to reclaim traditions of peace, create a new symbolic universe, and tell new stories, (2) to see divine power in relations, in the interstices, or in the spaces between us, and (3) to build relations beyond the binary of us and them.[38] These three requirements are connected to Kwok's concept of polydoxy or divine multiplicity – namely, theology of religious difference.

The term polydoxy captures the idea that 'Christians do not have a monopoly on God's revelation and that divinity should be understood in terms of multiplicity, open endedness, and relationality'.[39] On a basic level, Triune God suggests the multiple forms of God in relation to one another. Unlike so-called orthodoxy, polydoxy draws multiple resources beyond the premature dichotomy of the theological and the secular to engender a multitude of understandings and images of God. Polydoxy liberates God from the tyranny of the 'one' – be it the phallus, the father's law, monotheism, or logocentrism while highlighting multiplicity in Christian tradition and, thus, Divine multiplicity, characterized by fluidity.[40] Kwok emphasizes that the logic of multiplicity resists any permanent and absolute claims of religion, patriotism and identities, which have justified wars, conflicts and violence because the logic 'denies the ontological status of eternity and stasis'.[41]

Polydoxy also highlights the diversity of cultural and religious traditions of the world. The radical recognition of diversity foregrounds the existence of the self only in relation to others. Similarly, a religious tradition can be recognized only in relation to other traditions. Kwok does not uncritically approve that all religions are equally valid. Instead, she asserts that 'we cannot know our own tradition without seeing it in relation to and through the lens offered by other religious and spiritual traditions'.[42] Interrelationality, both as a human reality and as a concept, makes inter-religious solidarity possible and necessary. According to Kwok, Christian churches should critically recognize their 'collusion with the long history of colonialism and cultural imperialism' to strengthen inter-religious solidarity.[43] In other words, inter-religious solidarity, especially practised by the Christian Church, needs a postcolonial perspective. From a postcolonial perspective, Kwok raises a challenging question of 'how to enable the subalterns to mutually recognize one another and create a political narrative to galvanize support'.[44] To answer this question, Kwok pays attention to women's grassroots movements and ordinary people's peace-building activism, such as the Women In Black international solidarity movement, the Occupy Wall Street movement, the Black Lives Matter movement, the Hong Kong protest, the *Minjung* Movement in Korea, and so forth. In these movements, inter-religious solidarity is embodied by activists not through their dialogue on religious doctrines but through the storytelling of and reflections on their struggles and hopes for peace and justice. They are subalterns who give hope to inter-faith dialogue for peace, crossing multiple boundaries.

Conclusion

During my video conference with Kwok, I asked her where we could find hope for the future of the Anglican Communion despite schisms and conflicts over various social issues among Anglicans. Kwok said:

> Being together does not mean that bishops stay together. If we look at only the center, we will lose hope ... If we look at the other sides of the Church, we can see a different picture. Why do we rely on bishops? The Anglican Church does not belong to them only. Sometimes, I feel that we, Anglicans, depend on leadership too much ... I always give the example of hope that Hong Kong ordained the first woman priest when it was a British colony ... That kind of crack from the margin to the center gives me hope for the changes in the Anglican Church ... I once traveled to South Africa and met gay and lesbian laypeople and scholars of gender and sexuality. I learned a lot from them and found hope ... Changes always come from the margin. If we look at the center and the middle, we cannot find hope because changes happen slowly. That's why sometimes we should be patient with God (smile).

Kwok's theology is her consistent and empathetic effort to walk with subalterns and listen to their voices. Despite complex social analysis and challenging postcolonial theories in Kwok's theology, it delivers one consistent message: hope is coming from the margin. Anglican Church history would look a lot different if we empathetically traced ordinary people's lived experiences with God. By consciously rediscovering the stories from the margin of the Church and society, Kwok's theology shares abundant hope with us.

Notes

1 Rita Nakashima Brock and Tat-siong Benny Liew, 'Introduction: Re-Imagining Im-Possibilities All-Together?', in *Theologies of the Multitude for Multitudes*, eds Rita Nakashima Brock and Tat-siong Benny Liew (Claremont: Claremont Press, 2021), 1–20 (1).

2 Jane Hwang Hsien Yuen and Joyce Bennett were the first women ordained to the priesthood in the Anglican Church in 1971. According to the *New York Times*, the ordination of women as priests was certain to arouse controversy among

Anglicans. A world Anglican conference in February 1971 decided, by a one-vote margin, to endorse the Hong Kong Diocese's plan to ordain Hwang and Bennett to the priesthood ('Anglicans Will Ordain First Two Women Priests', *New York Times*, 16 November 1971).

3 Kwok Pui-lan, 'Feminism, Theology, and Academia', *Inheritance Magazine*, 1 August 2017, https://www.inheritancemag.com/stories/feminism-theology-and-academia (accessed 29.1.2024).

4 Kwok Pui-lan, *Postcolonial Politics and Theology: Unraveling Empire for a Global World* (Louisville: Westminster John Knox Press, 2021), 3.

5 Kwok, 'Feminism, Theology, and Academia'.

6 Kwok, *Postcolonial Politics*, 4.

7 Kwok, 'Personal Statement for the American Academy of Religion Teaching Award', https://www.aarweb.org/common/Uploaded%20files/Awards/Award%20for%20Excellence%20in%20Teaching/Pui-lan%20Teaching_Statement.pdf (accessed 29.1.2024).

8 Kwok, 'Personal Statement'.

9 Kwok Pui-lan, Judith A. Berling and Jenny Plane Te Paa, 'Introduction', in *Anglican Women on Church and Mission*, eds Kwok Pui-lan, Judith Berling and Jenny Plane Te Paa (Norwich: Canterbury Press, 2012), xiii–xx (xvii).

10 Kwok Pui-lan, '2011 Presidential Address: Empire and the Study of Religion', *Journal of the American Academy of Religion*, 80.2 (2012): 285–303 (297), https://doi.org/10.1093/jaarel/lfs003 (accessed 29.1.2024).

11 Kwok Pui Lan, *Chinese Women and Christianity, 1869–1927* (Atlanta: Scholars Press, 1992).

12 Kwok et al., 'Introduction', xv.

13 Kwok Pui-lan, *Discovering the Bible in the Non-Biblical World* (Maryknoll: Orbis Books, 1995).

14 Kwok Pui-lan, 'From a Colonial Church to a Global Communion', *Anglican Women on Church and Mission*, 3–20 (13).

15 Kwok Pui-lan, *Postcolonial Imagination and Feminist Theology* (London: SCM Press, 2005), 126.

16 Kwok, *Postcolonial Imagination*, 127.

17 Kwok, *Postcolonial Imagination*, 127.

18 Kwok, *Postcolonial Imagination*, 128–49.

19 Kwok, *Postcolonial Imagination*, 128–37.

20 Kwok, *Postcolonial Imagination*, 135.

21 Kwok, *Postcolonial Imagination*, 141.

22 Kwok, *Postcolonial Politics*, 66.

23 Kwok, *Postcolonial Imagination*, 144.

24 Kwok, *Postcolonial Imagination*, 144–5.

25 Kwok, *Postcolonial Imagination*, 30–1.

26 Kwok, *Postcolonial Imagination*, 37.

27 Kwok, *Postcolonial Imagination*, 37.

28 Kwok Pui-lan, 'Fishing the Asia Pacific: Transnationalism and Feminist Theology', in *Off the Menu: Asian and Asian North American Women's Religion and Theology*, eds Rita Nakashima Brock et al. (Louisville: Westminster John Knox Press, 2007), 3–22 (9).

29 Viet Thanh Nguyen and Janet Hoskins, 'Introduction: Transpacific Studies: Critical Perspectives on an Emerging Field', in *Transpacific Studies: Framing an*

Emerging Field, eds Viet Thanh Nguyen and Janet Hoskin (Honolulu: University of Hawaii Press, 2014), 2–4.

30 Kwok, *Postcolonial Imagination*, 43.

31 Kwok, *Postcolonial Imagination*, 46.

32 Kwok, *Postcolonial Imagination*, 50.

33 Kwok, 'From a Colonial Church to a Global Communion', 18.

34 Peter Phan, 'From Doctrinal Exclusivism to Religious Pluralism: Kwok Pui-lan's Theology of Religious Difference', in *Theologies of the Multitude for Multitudes*, 131–56 (155).

35 Kwok, *Postcolonial Politics*, 170.

36 Kwok, *Postcolonial Politics*, 170–1.

37 Kwok, *Postcolonial Politics*, 172.

38 Kwok, *Postcolonial Politics*, 180.

39 Kwok Pui-lan, *Globalization, Gender, and Peacebuilding: The Future of Interfaith Dialogue* (Mahwah: Paulist Press, 2012), 70.

40 Kwok, *Globalization*, 71, 73.

41 Kwok, *Globalization*, 73.

42 Kwok, *Globalization*, 77.

43 Kwok, *Globalization*, 78.

44 Kwok, *Globalization*, 80.

9

Jaci Maraschin

CARLOS EDUARDO CALVANI

In churches within the Anglican Communion there are several different movements of liturgical renewal. They range from those influenced by more traditionalist strands that refer to certain ancient liturgical forms and patterns, to those that elect postmodern inclinations with free and random forms as their frame. This gradient also includes movements with charismatic and Pentecostal inspiration. We know that Anglican churches follow a liturgical pattern that respects the backbone of ancient liturgies as regulated by each country's Book of Common Prayer (BCP). That is, traditionally, Anglican worship is a standardized experience. Everything is planned – who speaks, when they speak, and how much they speak. At first it looks repetitive. This chapter explores how patterns developed in Brazil, and how the country's social and theological context affected such normativity. It focuses on Jaci Maraschin, as the name that has most influenced Brazilian Anglican liturgy, as well as liturgical movements of other churches in Brazil.

Biography

Jaci Correia Maraschin was born in 1929 in Bagé, Rio Grande do Sul (RS), in the far south of Brazil into an Episcopal family. From childhood, his socialization process developed in different groups of children and young people in his local parish, Paróquia Matriz do Crucificado. There, as a young man, he joined a group of artists who moulded plastics. As a teenager, he took a course in conducting and composed hymns (lyrics and music) for youth choirs. He studied theology full-time between 1951 and 1953 at the Episcopal Theological Seminary of Porto Alegre, RS. And after diaconal ordination in 1953 he was appointed as Coadjunct of the Paróquia da Redenção (São Gabriel, RS). There he began his efforts for liturgical renewal – introducing eucharistic vestments, paraments and candles, as well as the regular observance of feasts and holy days which, although allowed for in the BCP calendar, were not followed by most Episcopal parishes at the time, for reasons that we will clarify later. At the time, bothered by seeing the church as a mere social club that held meetings on Sundays, Maraschin began to lead daily services, even though the presence of the faithful was reduced to two or three people. For the young deacon, the church being closed during the week pointed to a faith that was disconnected from daily life and social problems.

Shortly after his ordination to the presbyterate in 1954, Maraschin went to New York to pursue a Master of Theology at the General Seminary. He enrolled in courses by Paul Tillich, whom he greatly admired. On returning to Brazil, he was appointed professor at the same seminary where he had studied and became the National Secretary for Religious Education of the Episcopal Church. Through this role he organized a curriculum that linked theology, tradition and sociocultural context. During this time, he graduated with another degree, in music, from the Federal University, RS. And between 1964 and 1966 he studied for his doctorate in 'religious sciences' in Strasbourg, writing his thesis on the theology of Frederick D. Maurice.[1]

Starting in the 1970s Maraschin participated in various ecumenical bodies, served as a member of the Inter-Anglican Doctrinal Theological Commission, Theological Adviser to the Lambeth Conference and the Anglican Consultative Council, the Inter-Anglican Theological Commission, the Roman Catholic Anglican International Commission, the World Association of Theological Institutions, and as the Secretary General of the Association of Evangelical Theological Seminaries between 1970 and 1994. His experience as a member of the standing committee on Faith and Order of the World Council of Churches resulted in a precious and highly original book exploring the symbolic language of the Nicene Creed, engaging it with liberation theology, and linking 'symbol' to artistic expression.[2]

Alongside these activities, Maraschin also leveraged his musical talents. In 1959 he was coordinator of the commission that organized the Episcopal Hymnal, selecting and translating ancient hymns for it. In the 1960s he composed the first Brazilian Mass in a samba rhythm and a Mass by St Francis of Assisi, mixing bossa-nova and Gregorian chant. He organized and published different collections of liturgical song. Academically, from 1975 until his retirement, he worked at the Methodist University of São Paulo (UMESP), teaching courses on philosophy, theology and social communication.

Jaci Maraschin, in addition to being a teacher and writer, remained an Anglican cleric throughout his life. He pastored communities in Rio Grande do Sul and served many others in São Paulo and Paraná. He was pastor of some very traditional communities, but also led alternative communities, and until the end of his life he was willing to participate in the internal debates of the Church and to deliver homilies whenever invited. In the 1970s, he ran for the episcopate in the Anglican diocese of São Paulo, having received a significant number of votes from clerics and lay delegations. His was a candidacy that strongly opposed the conservative line. The canonical impasse of not having received the votes by an absolute majority (half plus one) caused the two candidates to resign in favour of a consensus name and, on that occasion, their friend Sumio Takatsu was elected. If he were elected, 'Bishop Maraschin' would have had to balance the role of guardian-of-the-faith with his vocation as an innovative prophet.

Maraschin was at the same time a lover of Gregorian chant in traditional liturgy and an advocate of liturgical renewal. Some people who only knew him from the academic world or from reading his texts were surprised when they saw him dressed in liturgical robes, clapping his hands and on occasions dancing or in absolute silent recollection at other times. He lived his 'piety' in his own unique way – pious, but certainly never pietist or puritan. Married to Ana Dulce Pithan Maraschin, he had two daughters and four grandchildren. He died in 2009, on the eve of his 80th birthday.

Cultural Context

Theological and liturgical movements often respond to specific concerns of their time and context. Some remain incubated only in academic circles, without directly affecting many people's lives. In some cases, it takes years for academic debates to enter the daily lives of the faithful. Relevant as they may be from a theoretical point of view, movements such as the theology of the death of God, atheology, post-metaphysical theology, process theology or even certain issues in biblical exegesis hardly reached local Christian communities in Brazil. Other theological movements, however, because they are more focused on everyday situations, have been more likely to provoke, over time, changes in Christian institutions. This is the case with feminist, queer and ecological theologies; and liberation theology falls into this category. Born in a specific context in Latin America, it caused significant changes in sectors of the Roman Catholic Church and in some Protestant churches. Since the 1960s, Jaci Maraschin was directly involved with liberation theology and his contribution impacted the course of Brazilian Anglicanism.

One of the most common stereotypes in the Brazilian religious field is to imagine that the Episcopal Anglican Church of Brazil (IEAB) is an ethnic church, attended only by the British or Americans who gather in large and luxurious buildings, to the sound of traditional hymns accompanied by organs at services in English, without any close contact with Brazilian culture. This portrait was only true for the nineteenth century. British influence in the IEAB is currently minimal and only in a few cities will you find churches with pipe organs, traditional hymns and English language. The IEAB is a financially fragile church, made up of small communities with great ethnic diversity and no financially dependent relationship with the Church of England. Since becoming an 'autonomous national church', the IEAB has gradually abandoned certain North Atlantic antics, assuming a commitment to incarnate in Brazilian culture without renouncing some historical marks that characterize and identify it as 'Anglican'.

It wasn't always like this. Until the 1960s it was financially and ideologically dependent on North Atlantic references, and not, let's say, so 'Brazilian'. One of the factors that helps understanding of this inculturation was, without a doubt, liberation theology.

The first incursion of Anglicanism in Brazil took the form of religious chaplaincy in the Brazilian colony. From the opening of the ports in 1810, British immigrants (merchants, diplomats, industrialists) organized chapels in coastal cities close to the ports in Niterói, Rio de Janeiro, Santos, Recife, Salvador and São Paulo. They had no proselytizing or growth intentions beyond their ethnic group and were content with celebrations in English and family membership. They understood themselves as temporary visitors to Brazil and respected the Brazilian empire's restrictions on foreign worship services. Many returned to their countries of origin, and those who remained (or their descendants) kept their communities restricted, as ethnic-churches, until the middle of the twentieth century. Anglicanism in Brazil, from 1810 to at least 1890, was simply a 'church of and for Englishmen'.

The first communities in Brazil with the clear intention of missionary expansion began to appear from the 1890s into the early years of the republic, under the initiative of missionaries from the Episcopal Church of the United States, inflamed by an evangelistic ardour that took hold of American Protestant churches in the second half of the nineteenth century. A theology influenced by individualism predominated among them, fruit of spiritual revivals and the strong influence of 'manifest destiny', according to which God chose the Anglo-Saxon peoples to expand his kingdom in the world. Their chosen paths was the preaching of a 'pure gospel' and the education of other people, with an emphasis on universal sin and regeneration through faith in the atoning sacrifice of Christ. This approach included condemning the Roman Catholic Church as an apostate, fighting non-Christian religions, and striving to save pagans from eternal damnation.

This was essentially the nucleus of all preaching from North American Protestant missionaries who arrived in Brazil in the nineteenth century. At that time, the church in Brazil was known not as 'Anglican' but as the 'Episcopal Church', and the members were called 'Episcopals' or 'Episcopalians'. A very common practice for these early missionaries was to conduct 'weeks of evangelism' full of fiery sermons, testimonies and Wesleyan hymns. And this was the model of church that Maraschin knew in his childhood and youth, with Sunday services using the liturgy of morning or evening prayer, an evangelical hymnal, with preaching centred on regeneration in Christ, and at a distance from Roman Catholicism.

The social stratum of the Episcopal communities at the time was weighted to a middle class sufficiently literate to follow the liturgy by leafing through a thick BCP. A reading of the Church's internal newsletter (*Christian Standard*, published since 1893) reveals the way in which the creation of new communities was announced, always exalting the presence of civil authorities, 'upper class people',[3] 'noble gentlemen', 'distinguished and well-educated young people', or extolling the fact that the church had gained adherents from high classes of society. In fact, many communities that emerged in the first half of the twentieth century were formed by families identified with a rising urban social class who had purchasing power that differentiated them from the majority of the population. In this case, the first Episcopal-Anglican communities in Brazil confirmed the thesis of Richard Niebuhr in his classic study of Protestant denominationalism in North America: that 'it's not that they don't have religious purposes. But the fact is that they accommodate religion to the system of classes and castes.'[4]

The Episcopal Church of Brazil only acquired autonomy in 1965. From then on, agreements were made with the Church of England for the incorporation of British chaplaincies and parishes (until then under the jurisdiction of the Church of England), which happened from the 1970s onwards. In general, until the mid-1960s, the Episcopal Anglican Church of Brazil identified itself as a typically Protestant church, with the following marks:

1 Evangelical-minded ecclesiology, with a strong emphasis on individual conversion in a Pietist mould and with a Puritan ethic.
2 Expansionist and conversionist missiology, understanding that the transformation of the sinful character of human beings would bring benefits to society: convert the individual first, so that then, once 'transformed', society could be transformed.

3 Timid investment in social life. Following the traditional Protestant model, the Church invested in the creation of private schools aimed at children of the middle and upper classes, orphanages or homes for the elderly; politically, 'neutrality' was proclaimed but this was not well disguised, especially in the early days of the cold war, when the fear of communism and the fight against Marxist-inspired regimes began to be publicized in the church's official newsletter.

4 The centre of liturgical life was pulpit and preaching, not altar-table.[5] Clerics who demonstrated better speaking skills and greater persuasiveness were most valued.

In short, the first phase of Anglicanism in Brazil was marked by aspirations for growth and expansion guided by an individualistic missiology and soteriology; lack of ecumenical relations with Roman Catholicism; social engagement marked by welfarism; and very little interaction with Brazilian culture with regard to the liturgy. These characteristics only began to change from the 1950s onwards, influenced by three factors: achievement of administrative autonomy by the Brazilian Church in relation to the North American matrix; a growing search for integration with the national culture, mainly through liturgy; and approximation with currents of liberation theology. Jaci Maraschin was key to these emphases, working behind the scenes on administrative issues of autonomy, and in the foreground on liturgical and theological issues.

The achievement of administrative autonomy assured Brazilian Anglicans greater visibility in the national and international ecumenical scene. The Roman Catholic Church experienced its moment of reform with Vatican II and, particularly in Latin America, the first works associated with liberation theology appeared, eagerly read at the Theological Seminary of the IEAB. The new generation that was being formed found in liberation theology a new reference, much closer to the socio-political reality of Brazil. Until then, the theology studied and assimilated by Anglicans in Brazil had privileged doctrinal, liturgical and ethical issues. Such concerns were not dismissed but contemplated in a new light. Theological systems that claimed universal validity were replaced by reflection on the liberating or alienating potential of dogmas. Research on specific themes in the history of Christianity received a new focus, aimed at identifying political forces that determined certain historical options and their consequences. Young clerics of the time, sent to Europe or the USA for postgraduate studies, chose for their dissertation themes related to Christian socialism, human rights and the ecumenical movement. Anglican fondness for liturgical matters moved from debate around preservation of ritual forms traditionally identified with North American evangelical culture to multiple possibilities of inculturation. Liberation theology placed more value on orthopraxy than on orthodoxy and denounced the ideological assumptions of a large part of the North Atlantic theologies, not only those clearly conservative, but also those considered 'liberal'. As a teacher and mentor of this new generation, Maraschin enchanted and nurtured people during the 1970s and in the 1980s began to assume influential positions in ecclesiastical politics – ones previously occupied by leaders formed in older patterns.

This situation, of course, caused tensions. Little by little, liturgical experiences emerged that had never before been imagined among older generations. Maraschin composed the first 'missa-samba', using this rhythm to musicalize the gloria, kyrie, credo, sanctus and benedictus. His innovation required use of percussion instruments, much to the chagrin of organists at the time. Missiology, previously understood as an effort to create chaplaincies and accompany parishioners on migration across Brazil or as growth strategies for local churches, now brought forward new social concerns. It was necessary to place parish structures at the service of all the people (and not just parishioners), even if those same people were indifferent or hostile to the church. Communities located in more rural regions marked by land conflicts or in proximity to indigenous cultures were challenged to approach popular struggles and to value and preserve indigenous cultures and religions as well as popular religiosity. The mission of the church could no longer be understood as conversionist efforts aimed at the emergence of new parishes, but shifted to prophetic witness and the struggle for human dignity against economic, political or social oppression. Brazil was living at the time under a rigid and repressive military regime and the church could not close itself off from the world as if nothing was happening.

Maraschin's Frameworks

Although liberation theology was the main theological reference in context from the 1960s to the 1980s, Maraschin was always attentive to other emphases of a theoretical nature, maturing them progressively and critically. Among them (a) Tillich's 'theology of culture', (b) theological hermeneutics, (c) theology of the body, (d) theology of worship, or the liturgy as an event of joy and openness to life, (e) the limits of theological discourse in the postmodern condition and, finally (f) the exaltation of art as 'salvation'.

When he earned his MA in New York, Maraschin attended classes where Paul Tillich discussed theology and the arts, developing a theological hermeneutics of culture in an attempt to identify and understand the residues of theological vocabulary or religious experiences outside institutional religious spheres. Beginning with Tillich, many theologians were able to free themselves from dogmatic and institutional shackles and expand theology beyond the thematic limitations and restrictions that it had imposed on itself. It was, in the end, a certain 'deconstruction' of traditional concepts of religion, seeking another broader understanding of this enigmatic word. There is a significant shift here. Religion is understood no longer as a particular cultural epiphenomenon, but as content, life, inspiration, the very heart of all cultural expressions. This is its place: not as an external law that imposes itself on culture from a supposed revelation, but as its profound inspiration. Hence Tillich's classic definition: 'religion is the substance of culture; culture is the form of religion'.[6]

Although he translated three of Tillich's books for the Brazilian public,[7] Maraschin developed several criticisms of Tillich's thinking, mainly his obsession with an idealistic language that oscillated between metaphysics and ontology, essentialism and existentialism.[8] In spite of this, Maraschin never abandoned certain Tillichian postulates, such as the notion that the finite is capable of witnessing something of the infinite without the two being confused. Therefore, in mature texts, Maraschin was able to talk about religious languages and expressions in phenomena seemingly so far removed from the religious strata, such as a fan's passion for a football club or the beautiful choreographies staged by samba schools at carnival, many of them with religious themes.

However, Maraschin understood the impossibility of approaching such themes without a certain theoretical basis that would support the theological interpretation of artistic phenomena. Therefore, from the late 1970s to the mid-1980s, he devoted himself to debates on what was then called 'hermeneutic theology'. At this time, he delved into the work of Ricoeur and Heidegger. At first, he basically absorbed the concept of symbol operating in the living movement of culture and human expressions.[9] But after studying Heidegger, he began to understand the limits of ontotheological language and the possibilities of the concept of 'openness' metaphorized by the image of the clearing that drives us not towards 'beyond', but towards excess. This theoretical reflection made way for a new focus towards which Maraschin turned in the 1990s: theology of the body, especially in expression in sexuality and in the arts, especially by poor and oppressed bodies.

An adoption of new emphases did not necessarily mean abandonment of previous ones, but an adaptive incorporation (albeit unsystematic ... after all, Maraschin always rejected any model of 'systematic' theology). So his earlier frameworks from liberation theology and the theology of culture funnelled to the source from which the artistic and liturgical creativity that interested him emerge: the bodies of the poor and oppressed and their artistic expressions. Liberation theology kept sharp his perception that the body is always a social dimension and that its possibilities of expression are capable of overcoming the limitations of culture.

In Brazil, two other theologians of the same generation focused on the body. Rubem Alves, based on Huizinga, proposed a theology of the body from a playful perspective, using games and toys as a strategy to guide society towards a less materialistic and less repressive way of being. Maraschin, more specifically, clarified that a theology of the body is always based on a body, and the body must be thought of as social, polysemic and erotic. Commenting on the Nicene Creed, he asked: 'What can baptism mean for those who are not used to bathing? What can the Eucharist mean for those who have no table, plate, glass, or cutlery?'[10] Barros Neto helps us understand this emphasis:

Maraschin, starting from a critique of theological abstractionism, states that the theological task, insofar as it has to do with a very particular God, revealed in a very particular man, Jesus of Nazareth, is a critical exercise related to the body of people who propose to think. No, not with the generic concept of body, but with 'my body', with 'your body', with 'our body', 'the body of those who are here and now'. And that is why theology is done (and only theology) within the 'body of Christ', not also taken as an 'academic theological' concept, but as that very particular 'body' that makes itself visible here in this place and this time.[11]

This reflection naturally implies due attention to sexuality and eroticism:

I don't know how one could speak of liberation without this fundamental intuition of the body and the corporeal. Thus, the body, which is this polysemic opening, symbolizes the possibility of changing the world. The body is therefore erotic. It wants to express itself beyond itself, but in communion.[12]

The fourth emphasis, constant in Maraschin's academic life, concerns theology of worship, which led him to consider the liturgy as an event of joy and openness to life. In this case, his methodological perspective is clearly guided by an assumption of liberation theology: theology is always a second act. First is revelation in life and in history. Theology comes later, as an elaboration on this experience. This results in the necessary attention to experience and emotions:

In place of the predominance of reason, we have the predominance of experiences and emotions. Hence the importance that churches have always given to worship where art forms have always occupied a preponderant role. The theology belonging to churches is necessarily 'liturgical' in a very broad sense. It deals with expressive forms that go beyond written language. That is why the theology of churches tends to move from being the theology of books to the theology of life.[13]

A longer quote helps us to understand what he initially meant by 'worship theology' or theology of worship:

First, the elaboration of a critique of worship ... Second, a theology of worship presupposes a critique of the worshipping community ... Third, the creation of a theology of worship requires the theologian to examine what we could precariously call the object of worship. We do not, of course, want to suggest that this object can submit to the thinker's critique. If we call it God, it is precisely because it evades any scrutiny of the human mind. God means to us the one who seeks us, judges us, criticizes us, and ultimately forgives us. However, we believe in God at the same time that we know that God's name may not exactly mean the God we worship ... These three criticisms take place, naturally, in the cultural context in which the theologian lives. This context, called 'culture', will serve to filter out the different heritages and stimulate liturgical creativity in churches. The theologian will make use, then, of different data collected by the human sciences and the arts. They will have to compare the semiology of the present with the traditions and possibly develop a theory of symbols ... Finally, a theology of worship will have to discover the meaning of joy.[14]

An emphasis on joy does not mean contempt for human suffering or the pain of the world. Personal, existential, social and ecological vicissitudes are discussed with seriousness, but without losing hope in the possibilities of overcoming that are symbolized in the term 'resurrection'. The incredible human capacity to recognize frailties and overcome them, albeit fragmentarily, manifests itself above all in prophetic expressions of art. When art expresses suffering, it does so precisely because it doesn't want it.

In the 1990s, reading authors identified with what is conventionally called post-modernity, Maraschin signals a new orientation in his thinking, now marked by disillusionment with theological discourses. The first texts that enunciate this transition are *The Critique of Hermeneutics*[15] and *The Aesthetics of the Poor*.[16] But his initial dependence on liberation theology is still not lost. According to Maraschin:

The confusion of aesthetics with wealth transformed the work of art into an object of merchandise and made us think that beauty lay in ostentation and splendor. Modern art and contemporary art have changed the course of these things. They have showed us that art is a part of life as an important element of its manifestation, one that opens worlds for our contemplation, which are not necessarily the worlds prescribed by the powerful and the dominators ... When we say that art does not want to be anything other than what it is – that is, its presence as art – we are, at the same time, drawing the attention of the recipient of the work of art to what remains in an essential way: what makes the work 'art' and not something else.[17]

If, in postmodernity, theology has come to an end, it no longer makes sense to talk about the theology of the liturgy, but only about 'theory of the liturgy' understood from the perspective of art:

today, for me, as theology has ended, one should not speak of theology of the liturgy (because this is always a conceptualization), but of the theory of the liturgy. Postmodernity ends both theology and philosophy. Now, how does the community survive without theology? In fact, you only survive in religion through mysticism and art.[18]

Maraschin further explains this shift:

instead of wasting time on theology and metaphysics, it would be better if we turned to living our religious and aesthetic experiences in order to perceive in its mystery and beauty the presence of the sacred illuminating our lives with its grace. In this sense, religion and art are confused. Although they are not the only expressions of culture, they are nevertheless entrusted 'by the gods', as Heidegger would say, to take us to places and situations where life becomes joyful, beautiful and graced by the power of Eros. These experiences do not need dogmas or catechisms. They belong to the realm of fruition and imagination rather than reason. In this way, I am not discarding the liturgical activities of the churches. But I am proposing that they become moments of beauty that abandon the rationalist trend of pedagogy and apologetics in favor of aesthetics and contemplation. Such experiences have no limits. They include all religions and all cultural spaces. And finally, they belong to the body.[19]

Maraschin already spoke of liturgy as 'non-sense', a community happening without any commitment to clear and rational meanings:

In Oxford at a WCC meeting, I said that the liturgy is not utilitarian. This caused a scandal. It is like art, and only as non-sense is it art. The non-sense of the liturgy means nothing, so it is a work of art. Now, along the lines of the unintelligible, why do neo-Pentecostal movements grow and traditional ones empty? Because, in the traditional, what dominates is the logos/ethics, and in the Pentecostal it is the Dionysian ecstasy.[20]

What would be the impact of postmodernity on liturgical practice? Basically, the enjoyment of the beauty given by God in creation and the awakening of joy. This is the perspective of his 1993 text, *The Aesthetics of the Poor*:

> As theologians we are the hermeneuts of joy. As liturgists we are the creators of joy. And that's exactly what joy is: the enjoyment of the gratuitous beauty given by God. It is also for this reason that the liturgy presupposes communion with God and neighbor, and that it is in the meeting of people in a specific space that singing, color, perfume, gesture, sound and taste are transfigured as if they were coming out of the hand of God for the first time. I spoke at the beginning about the confusion between beauty and luxury. This is a mess that needs to be overcome. Contrast, then, the luxury of Solomon with the luxury of the lilies of the field. Not even that word could be uttered here. For only Solomon could have luxury. The lilies of the field just have beauty. Base communities, in the simple celebration of worship, cannot aspire to luxury. Luxury would prevent them from being what they are. But communities can also be corrupted by the values of our capitalist world, they are tempted to bring into their liturgies the false gloss of surface materials, of copying and mass reproduction such as artificial flowers. There is nothing more beautiful than the elements of nature. The flowers, the green branches, the water from the fountain, the fire of torches and candles, the free singing of Brazilian music, clothing and human warmth are God's gifts for us to organize them in the form of the liturgy and offer them, in the middle of our poverty, the living aesthetic of worship.[21]

Maraschin's Strategy

Among the texts left by Maraschin, one in particular has deeply marked the Episcopal Anglican Church of Brazil. It is the hymnal *O Novo Canto da Terra* (The New Song of the Land). The project was a new musical production for liturgy and had an ecumenical character with clear marks of liberation theology. It includes songs from the Base Ecclesial Communities, draws in each liturgical season and relates to different rituals. Advent exalts the prophets, denounces injustice and announces hope of liberation; Epiphany highlights macro-ecumenism; Lent laments the sin of indifference to social inequalities and human rights; Passover ensures the victory of the oppressed, and so on. Collective confessions for conformity to injustice and oppression find voice. And theological inculturation employs popular rhythms from Brazil and Latin America. Composition workshops were organized to produce this new songbook with Brazilian rhythms – *baião, xotes, guarânias, sambas*. Thus, new songs with new rhythms typical of Brazilian culture gradually began to find space in Anglican worship, sharing space with traditional hymns.

With resources from the Parish of Trindade (New York), this hymnal was released in 1987, containing 201 songs, all with sheet music, at 624 pages.[22] A copy was sent free of charge to all Anglican parishes in Brazil, but only some adopted it. In other parishes, it disappeared for lack of interest from conservative clerics or organists. Yet Simei de Barros Monteiro's comparative study of Brazilian evangelical hymnals highlights *O Novo Canto da Terra* as the only one to be defined by a perspective clearly guided by liberation theology.[23] Today the hymnal is out of print and largely unknown.

During the 1980s and 1990s the musical group 'Gente de Casa' ('People from Our Home') recorded several songs from this hymnal (currently available on YouTube).[24] Years later, the singer, composer and Bishop Flávio Irala recorded another album for dissemination in Brazilian communities.[25]

In 1996, the Association of Evangelical Theological Seminaries paid homage to Maraschin with the publication of a collection of texts by him – *The Beauty of Sanctity* and, later (2010), *On Lightness and Beauty*, works that bring together articles published in the 1980s and 1990s with hitherto unpublished text, written for a conference in London, in which the author elaborates his sense of 'non-sense liturgy', intended to counteract 'heavy expectations that have been imposed on the Christian liturgy for rationalism and activism'.[26] According to Maraschin, a 'non-sense liturgy would be fun and even perverted. Thus, it becomes "subversive" to open "subverted" paths to the experience of the sacred.'[27] In this sense, 'the abolition of the sense (rational sense) represented by the *non* opens the liturgy to the "games and toys" using more of an aesthetic than ethics in the face of mystery, emphasizing the body and its ways and sense, much more on the surface than what was perhaps under it'.[28] This is a clear allusion to the 'indeterminacy', 'randomness' and unpredictability defended by John Cage, who greatly captivated Maraschin when he studied music in the 1950s and 1960s. At the time, Maraschin was responsible for editing the *Episcopal Hymnal* (1962).

The publication of the hymnal included a detail that went unnoticed for a long time – the mention of a hymn (number 222), which has no title, lyrics or score to accompany it. To this day, it is not known whether the aforementioned hymn was censored by the hierarchy of the time or whether it was a mere layout error. Successive editions of the hymnal continue with the same gap between hymn 221 and hymn 223, and the proofs of the original layout was lost after the bankruptcy of the company that originally printed it. In 2008, 46 years after the publication of the hymnal, I asked Maraschin, in an exchange of e-mails, about this 'vacuum'. His answer was subtle and enigmatic: 'You know that, given the impossibility of saying or publishing certain things, we sometimes leave clues for the following generations …' Was it a 'clue' left by Maraschin, indebted to Cage, like Cage's 4:33, without form and void? The theme suggested in the hymnal part between hymns 127 and 226 is 'worship'. The theme is given, but the form is 'open'. In that case, 4:33 could be perfectly adaptable to any fixed part of the liturgy.

The Impact of IEAB

In the 1980s, Maraschin wrote about the importance of the body, emphasizing that

> spirituality is not the absence of body or matter, but the quality that the body has and is capable of expressing as the foundation of existence. The spirituality of the liturgy depends on the spirituality of the body. It is bodies that are spiritual. It is bodies that think, pray, feel joy and sadness, pleasure and pain. And, in this bodily quality, they perform physical acts such as sitting, lying down, kneeling, joining hands, opening their arms, hugging their brothers, kissing them, holding hands, tracing the sign of the cross on their own bodies and singing.[29]

This 'spirituality of the body' and, at the same time, his passion and interest in alternative artistic manifestations has inspired others in several alternative liturgical experiments that include:

São Lucas Parish (Londrina, PR), April 2001 – Foot Washing Office, in Holy Week.

The church building is separated from the fellowship hall by a car-park that has no pavement. We agreed to start the Liturgy of the Word in the hall and, after the prayers, we would leave barefoot, in procession to the church, where the foot washing and eucharist would be celebrated. The idea was for people to get their feet dirty in the red earth of northern Paraná. During the day heavy rain fell on the city, creating large mud puddles in the space to be traversed. Far from being a hindrance, the clay made the moment even more significant, as our feet got very dirty, making it possible to link words from the beginning of Lent – 'you are dust and to dust you will return' – with the foot washing. Those who washed the participants' feet had to put in more effort, even massaging the tired feet of some elderly people. During the ceremony, Maraschin's song 'Foot Washing' encouraged everyone to understand that 'in the dust of the roads of this life, come our feet to wash, so painful, come to give us hands that soothe the wound, of those who, lost, are so far from you'.

Campo Grande (MS), February 2012 – Carnival Liturgy (Transfiguration Sunday).

Maraschin is no longer physically with us. He is transfigured, in the sublime communion of saints. Liturgical space was decorated with streamers, confetti and colourful balloons. Necklaces, sequins, and masks were provided for everyone. The liturgy revolved around the theme 'The Transfiguration Stimulates Us to Shine!' The order was prepared in advance as a samba school parade. (It should be noted that samba schools have a lot to teach us. Each of them works with anticipation on their story and theme that will be developed for that year, carefully rehearsing each section, developing their theme song and lyrics for the year and, mainly, the timing of it all.) While people arrived, there was a time of 'Warming up the tambourines', with old songs from carnival, lending a festive atmosphere to the gathering. Each person received their mask, necklaces and a small bag with confetti and streamers. The leader's greeting indicated the theme of the service and the following moment, called '1st evolution – Liturgy of Praise', in which the opening rites and chants of glorification were sung. This was followed by the Liturgy of the Word, a '2nd Evolution', the reading of scriptures accompanied by soft percussion (played by the *cuíca, agogô* and a tambourine). During a gospel procession, confetti and streamers were thrown on the reader, and the homily highlighted the transfiguration of Christ, reminding that, united with him, we can also shine in the world. Everyone was invited to contribute to that homily, sharing the Word.

After creed and prayers, the eucharistic liturgy (a '3rd Evolution') had an offering to the sound of carnival music and eucharistic prayer to the sound of a soft drumbeat. After the final prayers, the 'Final Evolution – Liturgy of the sending forth in mission' followed, with prayers, warnings, blessing, sending and song (all dancing in a carnival train), followed by a lively carnival ball.

Is liturgical renewal possible by using the resources of art in different communities? Some people might be scandalized by the above descriptions or think the events liturgically irresponsible. There is always this risk – and I have often participated in celebrations that serve only to satisfy the egos of musicians, poets, artists or playwrights. The experience of liturgical renewal in Anglican churches also suffers from these problems and, from a pastoral point of view, it is essential to balance yearning for renewal with pastoral sensitivity. In a talk available on YouTube[30] (in which he also performs on the piano, at minute 6:13, one of his compositions) Maraschin offers practical suggestions on issues related to the difficult trade of liturgists in Christian communities. He suggests that:

1 *Liturgical celebration is a communal act.* It is not a show presented by a single person or a musical group. Nor is it an exhibition of photographs, images or a poetic soiree. As a communal act, liturgy cannot be transformed into a moment of ego satisfaction. In the liturgy no one reads or sings something that pleases them alone. Liturgy is a communal expression of faith professed by a group that is part of a greater communion and, ultimately, of that great communion of saints, which transcends temporal, cultural and denominational boundaries. In liturgical action, we are dramatizing the history of salvation.

2 *Pastoral sensitivity.* Liturgical renewal is necessary, but must always be promoted with pastoral sensitivity. The teaching of liturgy in seminaries has most often been linked to the area of pastoral or 'practical theology', and this is right as a reminder that liturgy is an activity in which expresses the universal priesthood of the faithful who celebrate the sacrifice of Christ for the transfiguration of the disfigured world. In liturgy, the main celebrant is always Christ himself. We are only vehicles, channels of the action of the Holy Spirit, and if this perspective is lost liturgy will distort into some mere literary-musical activity. Liturgy is time in which we are sensorially stimulated to perceive different ways in which eternity touches our history.

3 *Church identity*. In liturgy the identity of the church is revealed. Naturally, each church builds its own identity referents through history. In
churches of the Anglican Communion, these relate to rites of the BCP
and the lectionary that accompanies liturgical seasons, etc. While some
might say a BCP limits creativity, experience can indicate the opposite.
Yet risk of creative processes causing 'scandal' can be minimized if
the seriousness and knowledge of liturgical art is known. This means
paying attention to the tragic moments and seasons of life (funerals,
mourning, penitential services, etc.) and a sensitive liturgist would
never try to force artificial and caricatured joy in such occasions. But
there are infinite resources in the arts to enhance these experiences.

4 *Liturgy group*. Since liturgy is not the action of a single person, but
of a community, the creation of a liturgy group is recommended. This
group must be representative of the whole church (e.g. younger and
older people, from different social situations, musicians, artists and
more). A liturgy group that is cohesive and creative can greatly help a
community as it serves as a 'thermometer' to measure its pulse and the
openness to innovation.

About Artists and Prophets

Artist and prophet Jaci Maraschin seemed to be forgotten by some ecclesiastical leaders in the 1990s who, although they admired his songs,
considered his texts too disturbing, supposedly beyond the limits of 'institutional sobriety'.

This neglect is the burden carried by many artists who are generally
not understood by people with limited horizons. Artists live in a world
of their own, beyond their time. So Nietzsche spoke of 'build[ing] our
nest in the tree of the future; the eagles will bring us sustenance in their
beaks'.[31] Artists live in treetops or on mountaintops, in the solitude of
deserts or in depths of seas: 'Serene is the bottom of my sea. Who would
have thought it hides fun monsters? My depth is unshakeable, but blazing
with enigmas and laughter.'[32] And it is in these hidden corners that the
creative process emerges, 'where loneliness ceases, the public square
begins, where the public square begins, the noise of the great comics and
the buzz of poisonous flies also begin. Flee, my friend, into your solitude;
I see him stunned by the hustle and bustle of the great men and riddled
with the stings of the little ones' – Nietzsche again.[33]

That desert of artists is similar to that of prophets who foresaw
catastrophes but could do nothing to prevent them. They just shouted

and shouted, hoping someone would listen. Prophets and artists have this role, sometimes dazzling and ecstatic, sometimes sad and painful, wanting to smooth out paths without power to change them, but always catching a glimpse of what is hidden in everyday life. Artists do not fix eyes on what they see, aware that it is transitory, but on what is not seen, knowing that it is eternal (cf. 2 Corinthians 4.18). It remains to create, announce, reveal, exercise patience, believe with hope, seeking strength in the desert.

In 2004, on the occasion of a symposium on Anglican theology, the Center for Anglican Studies honoured Maraschin with a special edition of *Revista Inclustividade*, dedicated to his biography, thought and contribution to the IEAB. Later honours continued until his passing in 2009. And Maraschin's last composition, recorded in the year of his death, was the song 'We can choose love'. The impact of Jaci Maraschin on the Episcopal Anglican Church of Brazil was such that the Liturgy Commission in charge of preparing a new BCP inserted into the Brazilian liturgical calendar the commemorative date of 30 June, to remember with thanksgiving 'Jaci Correia Maraschin, Priest of the IEAB. Musician and Teacher in the Faith'.

Notes

1 Jaci Maraschin, *Igreja a gente vive: Uma introdução ao pensamento de Frederick Denison Maurice* (Porto Alegre: Communication Department of the Episcopal Church of Brazil, 1991).

2 Jaci Maraschin, *O espelho e a transparência: O credo niceno-constantinopolitano e a teologialatino-americana* (Rio de Janeiro: CEDI, 1989).

3 Oswaldo Kickhofel, *Notas Para Uma História da Igreja Episcopal Anglicana do Brasil* (Porto Alegre: Metrópole, 1995), 66.

4 Richard H. Niebuhr, *As origens sociais das denominações cristãs* (1929), trans. Antonio Gouvêa Mendonça (São Paulo: Religious Sciences and ASTE, 1992), 23.

5 See Carlos Eduardo Calvani, 'Mesa, púlpito e palco: centros visuais do culto protestante no Brasil – considerações litúrgicas', *Observatório da Religião*, 1.2 (2014): 3–28.

6 Paul Tillich, *Teologia Sistemática* (São Paulo: Religious Sciences, 2005), 610.

7 Paul Tillich, *A era protestante* (São Paulo: Religious Sciences, 1992); *História do pensamento cristão* (São Paulo: ASTE, 1988); *Perspectivas da teologia protestante nos séculos XIX e XX* (São Paulo: ASTE, 1986).

8 Jaci Maraschin, 'A linguagem ontológico-existencialista de Tillich', *Paul Tillich trinta anos depois. Estudos de Religião* 10 (São Bernardo do Campo: IMS, 1995).

9 Jaci Maraschin, 'O simbólico e o cotidiano', in *Religiosidade popular e misticismo no Brasil* (São Paulo: Paulinas, 1984); 'O encontro simbólico do tradicional

com o contextual', in *Simpósio* 34 (São Paulo: ASTE, 1991); 'A crítica da hermenêutica', in *Teologia sob limite* (São Paulo: ASTE, 1992).

10 Jaci Maraschin, *O espelho e a transparência* (Rio de Janeiro: CEDI, 1989), 246.

11 Waldemar Barros Neto, 'Da teologia à pós-modernidade – a trajetória do pensamento de Jaci Maraschin', *Compartilhar*, 37 (Porto Alegre: CEA, 2004): 8.

12 Maraschin, 'O simbólico e o cotidiano', 144.

13 Jaci Maraschin, 'Teologia acadêmica e teologia das igrejas', in *Educação teológica em debate* (São Paulo: ASTE, 1988), 36.

14 Jaci Maraschin, 'Em busca de uma teologia do culto', *Simpósio*, 11 (São Paulo: ASTE, 1973): 4.

15 Jaci Maraschin, 'A crítica da hermenêutica', in *Teologia sob limite* (São Paulo, ASTE, 1992), 124–30.

16 Jaci Maraschin, 'A estética dos pobres', *Revista de Liturgia*, 20 (1993): 32–5.

17 Maraschin, 'A estética dos pobres': 32.

18 Neto, 'Da teologia': 15.

19 Jaci Maraschin, 'A Teologia dos Filósofos Gregos e a Teologia Cristã', *Revista Eletrônica Correlatio*, 5 (2004): 24.

20 Neto, 'Da teologia': 14.

21 Maraschin, 'A estética dos pobres': 35.

22 *O Novo Canto da Terra*, ed. Jaci Maraschin (São Paulo, IAET, 1987).

23 Simei de Barros Monteiro, *O cântico da vida – análise de conceitos fundamentais expressos nos cânticos das igrejas evangélicas do Brasil* (São Bernardo do Campo: ASTE/Religious Sciences, 1991).

24 Album title: *Other Songs*, https://www.youtube.com/results?search_query=Gente+de+casa+outras+can%C3%A7%C3%B5es (accessed 29.1.2024); and album title: *Reliving*, https://www.youtube.com/results?search_query=Gente+de+casa+revivendo (accessed 29.1.2024).

25 *Dança jubilosa*, songs by Jaci Maraschin, https://www.youtube.com/results?-search_query=Fl%C3%A1vio+Irala+dan%C3%A7a+jubilosa+Jaci+Maraschin (accessed 29.1.2024).

26 Jaci Maraschin, *Da leveza e da beleza* (São Paulo: ASTE, 2010), 76.

27 Maraschin, *Da leveza*, 75.

28 Maraschin, *Da leveza*, 76.

29 Jaci Maraschin, 'O espaço da Liturgia', *Estudos de Religião*, 2 (1985): 161.

30 https://www.youtube.com/watch?v=IklB_YK8QPo (accessed 29.1.2024).

31 Fredrich Nietzsche, *Assim falava Zaratustra* (Rio de Janeiro: Hemus, 1979), 74.

32 Nietzsche, *Zaratustra*, 89.

33 Nietzsche, *Zaratustra*, 39.

10

John S. Mbiti

HENRY MBAYA

John Samuel Mbiti, who died in 2019, was characterized, along with others, as exercising a function for Africa as equivalent to that of Barth, Tillich, Niebuhr and Rahner in Europe and North America. This chapter outlines something of the life and career of this remarkable Kenyan Anglican priest. It traces his life from his birth, early educational background in Kenya, and his last years before he died in 2019. It highlights some of Mbiti's fundamental theological themes and scope. Among these is the question of how Africans conceive the Supreme Being. Secondly, it deals with the pertinent issues of the character of religions in Africa and their interrelatedness. Within this framework, it deals with Mbiti's concept of salvation in Africa, of 'an African consciousness', the theological imperative of 'indigenization' of African Christianity, and his approach to ecumenicity and his ecumenical encounters at Bossey Institute in Switzerland.

Mbiti's Life and Background

John Samuel Mbiti was a Kamba. He was born in Mulango in Kitui County in eastern Kenya, 180 kilometres east of Nairobi, on 30 November 1931.[1] Colonized by the British, it was not until 1963 that the country received its independence. Mbiti was one of the six children of Samuel Mutuvi Ngaangi and Valesi Mbandi Kiimba, and he came from a strong Christian background. In Kiikamba, the name 'Mbiti' might literally mean 'hyena',[2] and have symbolic associations of 'a child vowed unto God'.[3] In local law and imagination, hyenas are not associated with gentility or suavity, and the family name Mbiti could signify a sense of misfortune surrounding a person's birth. Parents who have lost children in infancy may give their new-born a 'scary' name, like 'Mbiti', to ward off the stalking death.[4]

According to Myles Osborne, in the 1920s and 1930s many communities among the people of Ukambani were mobile through certain times and seasons of the year.[5] The Akamba valued cattle as wealth. By the time Mbiti was born in 1931, his community had gone through considerable changes shaped by experiences of World War One, not least as fighters alongside the British against the Germans. But Kamba society remained stratified according to age: children, circumcised, youth, warriors, married men and elders, in hierarchy. The top tier of elder was again subdivided into three grades which were achieved through ritual and payments.

In the late nineteenth century, Kenya had been open to the evangelization of the European and North American missions. Among others, including Roman Catholics, it was the African Inland Mission, founded by Peter Cameron Scott in the USA, and a non-denominational mission, that dominated the evangelization of Ukambani in the late nineteenth and very early twentieth century. Christians formed into distinct groups.

It was through the African Inland Mission Alliance high school near Nairobi that John Mbiti acquired his education.[6] His Christian background and his academic training inspired him to write his first novel, *Mutunga Na Ngewa Yake*, while still at high school. Mbiti went on to write a second novel, which the missionaries responsible for assessing and recommending publications lost when it existed only as a single manuscript.

The 1950s, when Mbiti was a young man, were the summit of colonialism in Africa. Mbiti went to the University College of Makerere, then an external college of the University of London, where he graduated with a BA in 1953. He taught for some time at his home school in Kenya. It was during this time that Mbiti began gathering traditional stories and proverbs. He then went to the USA to study at Barrington College (now Gordon-Barrington College), and after a period of two years, 1956–7, he obtained a Bachelor of Theology among other degrees.

He then returned to Kenya to teach at the Teacher Training College at Kangundo, and at the same time engaged in much iterant preaching. But he was offered the William Paton Lectureship, which sponsored his travel to the UK as a visiting lecturer at the Selly Oak Colleges in 1956–60. He stayed in Britain to study for his PhD in New Testament Studies at Cambridge University, and it was during this time that he met his future wife, Verena Siegenthaler. After his studies at Cambridge, he was ordained a priest in the Church of England in 1963, and subsequently he served for 15 months in St Michael's parish at St Albans.

However, Mbiti returned to Kenya at the height of the euphoria of *uhuru* – freedom – in 1964, when his country had just attained independence from the UK. It was a period of optimism, when the door of opportunities seemed to open to young Kenyans. Africans rightly wanted to show that they were as capable as Europeans. From 1964 to 1974, Mbiti was a lecturer, then a professor, at Makerere University, Uganda, teaching New Testament theology, African religion, and other world religions. While professor, he was also involved in the chapel ministry, and it was while Mbiti was at Makerere that he wrote his first book, *African Religions and Philosophy*.

In this book, Mbiti challenged the then widely propagated view that African traditional religions were 'demonic' and 'anti-Christian'. Meanwhile, Oxford University Press published his doctoral research in 1971 under the title *New Testament Eschatology in an African Background: A Study of the Encounter Between New Testament Theology and African Traditional Concepts*. In this period of his life, Mbiti was among 'the first generation of indigenous scholars to take up senior academic posts at Makerere, alma mater to most of them, to which they had returned after earning top qualifications overseas'.[7]

In January 1971, following the overthrow of Milton Obote by Idi Amin, and with the latter coming to power, Mbiti became head of the Department of Religion.[8] According to Derek R. Peterson, barely two weeks after the coup Amin's secretary wrote to Mbiti asking for his views on a proposed new 'Ministry of Religious Affairs', which would have political and administrative powers over religious organizations. Mbiti was required to address a few questions, including: 'Do you seriously think that there is a need for such a Ministry?' and 'What field of responsibility would the Ministry cover in relation to religious affairs?'

Peterson states that 'Mbiti was thrilled at the prospect'. He justified the necessity of such government overseeing on the premise that religious conflicts had been very much part of Ugandan history. 'Some of the conflicts took on political forms, others tribal, some even had backing from outside countries.'[9] So Mbiti suggested that the new ministry could enhance 'reconciliation, mediation, or even [by use] of governmental powers'. Moreover, it would allow for easier coordination between different service agencies; for while universities could enable dialogue in small-scale settings, 'the practical meaning of dialogue would best be achieved under governmental initiative, supervision, and encouragement'.[10]

Peterson then claims that Mbiti set out a theological rationale for Amin's dictatorship. 'African traditional life does not have a division between secular and sacred, between what is religious and what is not,' he argued. 'The division of life into religious and secular compartments was imported into Africa from Europe' under colonial government. So, he went on:

this division has greatly undermined and ignored a basic African philosophy in which the universe and the whole of life are conceived religiously, and in which the spiritual realities and physical realities are only two dimensions of the same basic concept of existence.[11]

According to Peterson, Mbiti sought to apply African principles from his field research on leadership. It is 'unnatural for African people to be made to live a divided life', he told Idi Amin's secretary, 'and we have to safeguard against such a division'. Europe and North America had already paid the price for their secularism, he held, and the evidence could be seen in the 'rebellion of their young people against authority, tradition, and so on'.[12] Then Mbiti, according to Peterson, went on to assert that the new Ministry of Religious Affairs would:

> be a concrete symbol and expression of the basic African philosophy that the whole of life is a deeply religious experience. In setting up this ministry, Uganda would be reasserting a profoundly African heritage which our colonial past has eclipsed and in many ways undermined seriously.[13]

Apparently Mbiti stated: 'We are very fortunate in that our leaders are religious people, and Africans are not embarrassed about expressing their religious life in practical terms.' So, the new ministry was 'consistent with our heritage'.[14]

Again, according to Peterson, in May 1971, subsequent to Mbiti's letter to Amin's secretary, Amin organized a week-long conference which involved Anglican, Catholic and Islamic leaders. It discussed 'the problems facing each religion' and notably 'each committee was chaired by a government minister'.[15] In his opening address, Amin is reported to have said:

> religion must be a source of togetherness ... This government does not believe that any religion or religious organizations should tolerate any tendencies that bring about ... disunity among people who profess the same religion.[16]

Hence Peterson implies that Amin put Mbiti's ideas into practice, and consequently Mbiti played a critical role in propping up the dictator. In this respect, Mbiti might be deemed partly responsible for Amin's excesses. But it must be said that we do not have Mbiti's side of the story on this episode of his life, and so it is impossible to make definitive pronouncements on Peterson's assertions. Nonetheless, Peterson also credits

Mbiti with courage in responding to the threat of Islam in Uganda in 1973. Peterson states that during the visit to Uganda that year of the Libyan dictator, Muammar Gaddafi, Gaddafi offered Amin some funds for the Islamization of the country. Responding to Gaddafi in a sermon addressed to a packed Makerere University chapel, Mbiti asserted: 'Christianity and Africa have fallen in love with each other and intend to live in bonds of a lifelong marriage ... Christianity is here to stay.'[17] This bold stance in fact exposed Mbiti to the danger of losing his life. So, he subsequently fled Uganda and took up the directorship of the Ecumenical Institute in Geneva where he was to spend the remainder of his life.

Theological Themes and Scope

In the 1950s and 1960s, when Mbiti was a young man, he must have read literature that projected and judged African religions as demonic, anti-Christian at best, practised by 'heathens' or 'pagans'[18] – 'labels that had been used to justify imperialism and slavery'.[19] In his own words, Mbiti stated:

> My research into and teaching of African religion has led to another important area of development. In Kenya I grew up in home, school and church milieus that held that the African religious and cultural background was demonic and anti-Christian. In this overpowering environment, one simply accepted this stand and looked at the world from its perspectives. Later, my theological studies in America and England did not challenge this position, since that was not a living issue for my professors and fellow students. But on my return to work in Africa, and on careful study of the religious background of our people, there emerged gradually the demand to examine this issue and to form my own judgment.[20]

Certainly, these notions provoked Mbiti to set out on an academic and 'spiritual' journey – to interrogate African religious and cultural heritage, with a particular question in mind: 'Do Africans not perceive God?' He posed this question in the shadow of the Europeans' assertions that African religion was 'witchcraft' and 'magic'. His answers emerge in *African Religions and Philosophy* of 1969, a book that expanded his lectures to students at Makerere University College, Uganda, and Hamburg University, Germany. He stated that:

Not only did the students in both universities show continued interest in the lectures, but many requested that they be available in book form to meet a need for a text book on the subject of African traditional religions and philosophy. I hope that this book will be a contribution in the study of the subject which is increasingly coming into the curricula of universities, seminaries, colleges and senior secondary schools not only in Africa but overseas as well.[21]

But as he looked around for books on African religions, he found that there were none – hence the beginnings of his own academic journey. He had both a Christian background and 'traditional' religious and cultural background, and his academic questions were also personal. Was being a Christian incompatible with being an African?

African religion(s) and God in Africa

Fundamental to Mbiti's concern with African religion and culture was its core notion of God and understanding Africans' relationship to the Supreme Being. He set out to enquire into the ways that Africans conceived God, but this enquiry led him to related questions about 'salvation': Does African religion and culture hold values that enable Africans to commune with God meaningfully? For Mbiti, an evangelical Anglican, this was critical. Mbiti's reflections on this drew on his observations that Western missionaries seemed to have mixed up culture and the gospel. Thus 'his 1969 book *African Religions and Philosophies* set the parameters for a whole field of scholarly inquiry: it powerfully showed that African philosophical and religious traditions were consistent and sensible, and that they could be understood as a religious system, and not as superstition'.[22] It brought to the fore questions as to if and how African concepts of God were compatible with Western Christian concepts.

The concept of God in Africa and salvation

In *African Religions and Philosophy*, Mbiti argues that a close affinity exists between African traditional religions and Christianity.[23] He claims that values in traditional religions are not at variance at all with the spirit, principles and tenets of Christianity.[24] But in various studies of the concept of God in Africa, Mbiti holds that the notion of the Supreme Being in Africa exists outside the Western theoretical explanation of the God who has revealed himself in the Judeo-Christian Bible.[25] So, for Mbiti the critical issue is: Is African traditional religion *preparatio Evangelica*? And, What values are inherent in African traditional religion that are in harmony with those in Christianity? To bring the questions together: What do the two heritages have in common? Behind Mbiti's questions lie the profound issue of if and how African traditional religion can be considered as a bridge to Christianity,[26] with Mbiti coming to respond to his questions in the affirmative. Writing in the *International Review of Missions*, Mbiti stated:

> African religious background is not a rotten heap of superstitions, taboos and magic; it has a great deal of value in it. On this valuable heritage, Christianity should adapt itself and not be dependent exclusively on imported goods. Here we face the difficult question of sorting out what is valuable preparation for the Gospel and what is not. For that purpose, churches and theological institutions should make it a point to study this African background. Until we understand it well, in the totality of its cultures, languages, and problems, we shall not be able to make a wise judgment on what is for Christianity and what is against it. For too long Western Christianity has condemned the African background, and in so doing has ... thrown out valuable aids to the presence of Christianity in Africa.[27]

It is quite clear that, for Mbiti, Western Christianity had been very unfair in the hostile way it treated African traditional religions, and indeed Western attitudes seemed to border on injustice. For him, African traditional religions had rich resources which Christianity in Africa *needed* to be fully at home with. Kinney asserted that, in his support for this position, Mbiti found evidence in the message of the New Testament where he finds 'the African religiosity in all its richness utterly ignorant and silent'. Hence, in this light, 'African religiosity must assume a listening posture and receive the new Word'.[28]

Totality of life in African heritage

In *An Introduction to African Religion*, Mbiti outlines African beliefs, traditions and cultures. According to him, the ontology of Africans is embodied in the saying 'Africans are notoriously religious'. African life, cultures and beliefs exist as an integrated system. In contrast to Western worldviews in which life is dissected and compartmentalized, Mbiti purports the holistic character of African cultures: a unity between religion and life rather than partitioning of the two. According to Uchenna

Okeja, Mbiti's conception of the totality of life has had a bearing on the understanding of African morality and issues of ethics. He asserts that, according to Mbiti, living a good moral life derives from being 'human', a value that is embedded in the 'religious' dimensions of African culture and traditions.[29] In other words, moral and ethical values emanate from existential and religious imperatives, both sides of the same coin. He states that values and morals 'are part of religion which deals with ideas that safeguard or uphold the life of the people ... there are differences in the values and morals held by different people of Africa, but many of them are similar'.[30]

An African consciousness

Mbiti was an African theologian with a deep sense of African consciousness. In his *Introduction to African Religion*, he begins his book by asserting and extolling the richness of African heritage. He states, 'Africa has a very rich heritage of what past generations of African peoples thought, did, experienced and passed on to their children.'[31] For Mbiti, African cultural and religious heritage has put the continent on a global stage. He states, 'The African heritage spread westwards across the Atlantic Ocean to South America, West Indies and North America ... Much of the African heritage which was exported to the outside world was cultural and religious.'[32]

Thus, it is as if Mbiti considers the 'exportation' of African heritage to the corners of the world as placing Africa in a position of a kind of 'missionary'. He states, 'in spite of the lack of written records in Africa, [Oral] Tradition is better than nothing and some valuable information has reached us through this method though in some cases it is difficult to tell the true from the fictitious'.[33] For such reasons, David Tarus and Stephanie Lowery highlight an African consciousness in Mbiti. They note that the core of Mbiti's theological quest for an authentic African theology is his concern for an African identity and consciousness, and that that this African identity is solely rooted in African heritage.[34]

In Mbiti's view, anything outside an African heritage betrays an African consciousness and identity. He states, 'Even though attempts are made to give Christianity an African character ... its Western forms in many ways are still alien to African peoples.' He concludes, 'This foreignness is an impediment because it means that Christianity is kept on the surface and is not free to deepen its influence in all areas of African life and problems.'[35] This is significant. Mbiti's preoccupation with African heritage seems to derive from his evangelical concerns versus ideologies that appear to undermine it. He states, 'All these political ideologies and economic attempts point to a progress made in Africa.'[36] But in his view, these ideologies are incapable of pervading every aspect of the life of Africans – consequently, not fulfilling their needs and leaving gaps in Africans' lives. That is, these ideologies are incapable of filling gaps they create.

For Mbiti, it is in the indigenous religious heritage that an African acquires their identity and consciousness. Africans can only find meaning in the holism provided in the traditional African heritage where there is no discord between sacred and secular, supernatural and natural.[37]

'Indigenization' of African Christianity – a theological imperative

Although so attentive to African heritage, Mbiti could be highly critical of the African Church. It was, in his view, deficient in relevant theology, it lacked theologians, and was without theological concerns.[38] He urged the Church to engage earnestly with African traditions and religions.[39] In his view, the principal concern of African theology is clearly to communicate the gospel to the African people in 'a manner suitable to African conditions and background'.[40] And in his quest for an authentic indigenous theology, he proposed the following sources of African theology: the Bible, the theology of the older churches, and the major traditions of Christendom, African philosophy and African religious heritages, as well as the living experience of the Church in Africa.[41] So in 1970 he proclaimed:

> The time has come when the Church in Africa must look carefully at the relationship between Christianity and traditional religions. There is a growing interest in traditional religions and culture in many parts of Africa, and those who are showing interest are in fact mainly Christians or people who have been exposed to Christianity. School children, college and university students are all interested in discovering the area of African heritage, which as it turns out, is deeply religious. They are asking many questions which can no longer be ignored by the Church. They are also, at the same time, seeking guidance about how to go about this discovery. There are individuals who even advocate setting up traditional religion in place of Christianity and Islam.[42]

There is no doubt that during the 1970s, in Mbiti's mind at least, the relationship between African traditional religions and Christianity had reached a turning point. Mbiti envisages a balancing task for Christian theology in Africa if it is to retain its integrity – namely, to stamp on

Christianity an African face and character, and to preserve the uniqueness of the universality of Christianity.

His own turning point pivots on some nomenclature for his own project. Early in his academic career, Mbiti had, like various other scholars, used the term 'indigenization' to describe the task for Christianity in his continent.[43] But increasingly he came to refrain from its use. He came to the view that 'I do not think that we need to or can "indigenize Christianity".'[44] Christianity emanates from the encounter of the gospel with any given local or regional community/society:

> To speak of 'indigenizing Christianity' is to give the impression that Christianity is a ready-made commodity which has to be transplanted to a local area. Of course, this has been the assumption followed by many missionaries and local theologians. I do not accept it anymore. The Gospel is God-given. The church in which it is incarnated is made up of people who are, by 'definition', indigenous 'where they happen to be born or live or have their roots'.[45]

He came to see the key question as: Has Africa made a real claim on Christianity? That was the crux of the matter. Put otherwise, Christianity has christianized Africa, but Africa has not yet africanized Christianity. As John Kinney asserts, Mbiti was discontent 'with seeing African Christians as carbon copies of European and American Christians' and believed that Christianity was 'sufficiently unique and flexible to be accommodated in the African environment and that traditional religion is sufficiently compatible with Christianity to give it an African character'.[46]

In his later years, Mbiti focused on the notion of the Spirit in African traditional religion as the core of African religiosity in relation to Christianity. More specifically, he illustrated that dreams constitute an important point of dialogue. In his 'Dreams as a Point of Theological Dialogue between Christianity and African Religion',[47] Mbiti suggests that dreams as a spiritual and sociological phenomenon have implications for understanding ministry and leadership in both traditions. So, in his view, dreams open a new vista in the dialogue between African traditional religions and Christianity: 'There is great potential for inter-religious dialogue between Christianity and African Religion if the dialogue already taking place on the plane of dreams can be developed ...'[48] For Mbiti, there is potential to open a new understanding of two cosmological worldviews, with theological implications for dialogue. He suggests: 'A new cosmology begins to form, when Christianity touches African Religion. This is also evident in the dream-culture which is set in motion by the encounter of the two religious traditions.'[49]

Ecumenism

John Mbiti tends to view theology, religion and life in a broad perspective, and with an evangelical lens. Three interrelated terms seem to characterize this approach to religions, theology and life – namely, 'all-encompassing', 'integration', and 'wholeness'.

The Bible in ecumenical perspective

In his 'An Ecumenical Approach to Teaching the Bible', Mbiti has argued that the Bible is by nature 'ecumenical', and therefore critical in advancing ecumenical initiatives. Because it is ecumenical, so he argues, the Bible must be liberated from North American and European baggage. It cannot be monopolized by one nation. It transcends racial and ethnic boundaries. So he asserts:

> The Bible has now become so thoroughly ecumenical that it cannot be taught meaningfully, nor understood meaningfully, without this ecumenical perspective. We enter into the Bible as individuals, as schools of thought, church traditions or native speakers of particular languages. But when the Bible enters into us, it comes as an ecumenical and multilingual book.[50]

For Mbiti, it is the 'ecumenical' nature of the Bible that makes it possible for Christianity to take shape and form of local cultures and religions. Mbiti calls for a radical adaptation of the Bible to local cultures. He states:

> We cannot afford to read and teach the Bible as though it were exclusively a German or English or Korean or Kiswahili Bible. That would not be ecumenical but provincial; it would be not only a dull exercise, but one that leads ultimately to ecumenical malnutrition and starvation. How can we approach the Bible and teach it in a given context or situation but as a book of the whole world? Teaching the Bible is or should be the opposite of playing in the football world cup competition in which the different teams go on knocking each other out until finally one team wins the golden cup. Teaching and reading the Bible in ecumenical perspectives means that each team starts with the golden cup itself and gives others to drink the water of life out of the golden cup. It is an act of communion (koinonia) and not one of competition, an act of incorporating others and not one of silencing them …[51]

The Bible is open to all cultures. It is available for all and everywhere in the world. It is also this ecumenicity that renders it as supranational, universal. In turn, this renders the Bible as more than at home in Africa. Thus, he asserts, 'Biblical theology will have to reflect the African situation and understanding if it is to be an original contribution to the theology of the Church Universal.'[52]

Ecumenical encounters at Bossey

Mbiti was director of the World Council of Churches Bossey Ecumenical Institute from 1974 to 1980. The Bossey historian Hans-Ruedi Weber wrote that 'the Institute's most creative work during the second half of the 1970s' was a series of conferences on intercultural theology organized by Mbiti. Mbiti outlined their aim as being 'to bring together African, Asian and other theologians for an ecumenical encounter and dialogue'.[53]

The first conference during Mbiti's tenure focused on 'African and Asian Contributions to Contemporary Theology', bringing together over 80 participants in June 1976. According to Weber, while focusing on Africa-Asia dialogue, the meeting was 'an eye opener for theologians from Europe and the Americas'.[54]

The second of the series of these meetings ran under the theme 'Confessing Christ in Different Cultures', held in Bossey in July of the following year. Mbiti is said to have written that the colloquium 'brought together the largest gathering of participants ever to convene at the Ecumenical Institute, Bossey'.[55] Some 110 people from 35 countries attended. A third meeting in this series took place under the theme 'Indigenous Theology and the Universal Church'.[56] Logically, 'Confessing Christ in Different Cultures' had imperatives to transcend the contextual and assert universal implications of confession of Christ expressed in liturgy:[57]

> In an essay he wrote in 1976, according to John Roth, Mbiti framed a pointed question. Theologians from the new (or younger) churches have made their pilgrimages to the theological learning of the older churches. We had no alternative. We have eaten theology with you; we have drunk theology with you; we have dreamed theology with you. But it has all been one-sided; it has all been, in a sense, your theology … We know you theologically! A question is, Do you know us theologically? Would you like to know us theologically?[58]

It is said that these gatherings roused great interest. In explaining why there was such interest, Mbiti is said to have stated: 'Some of us are aware that there is a rapid tilting of Christianity from the northern region to the southern region.' Then in the introduction to the second conference he asserted that this tilting 'is projected to begin after May 1987'.[59]

As an African scholar called to lead the institute of a global ecumenical body, Mbiti pursued and even anticipated intercultural ecumenicity, something equally shared by Philip Potter, former World Council of Churches Secretary General.[60] Mbiti's influence was ongoing, as witnessed in 2001, when Mbiti was involved in the organization of The Pontifical Council for Interreligious Dialogue (PCID) at the Vatican and the Office on Inter-Religious Relations and Dialogue (IRRD) of the World Council of Churches in Geneva, which instituted a joint project to explore Africa's contributions to the religions of the world. Some 25 people were invited by the two offices to form the Standing Committee.[61]

Conclusion

In conclusion, Mbiti's position in African theology is undoubtedly phenomenal. Perhaps the fundamental contribution to the study of African theology was his counter-argument to the negative Western literature and attitudes, his assertion that Africans *do* conceive the Supreme Being. Alongside this, Mbiti insisted that in spite of their diversity African religions operate within a framework of unity. For Mbiti, the diversity of African religions was not so much a problem, but rather an expression of a rich heritage. Mbiti uses this spectrum to invite Christianity to engage in serious dialogue with African religions. In his view, the extent to which Christianity engages with African traditional religions will determine the future of Christianity on the African continent.

Mbiti's own journey moved him forward. He started his research on African religions almost in an 'experimental' way, only to realize that there was a greater need for the critical issues he was concerned with. Over the years, with global forces affecting Africa, Mbiti refined his ideas. While he started out with an evangelical lens, over the years his theological resources became more ecumenical – including embracing other religions. Mbiti's impressive leadership at Bossey Ecumenical Institute demonstrated his commitment to the project of inter-religious dialogue. And, towards the end of his life, Mbiti had just started to occupy himself with the notion of the Spirit in African theology and philosophy. Without time to do the work himself, he exhorted African scholars to engage African religions to dialogue with Christianity on the critical issue of Christology.

Notes

1 World Council of Churches, 'Kenya mourns the late Professor Samuel John Mbiti', https://www.oikoumene.org/news/kenya-mourns-the-late-prof-samuel-john-mbiti (accessed 29.1.2024).

2 Austin Bukenya, 'Prof Mbiti: The Anglican Cleric who dared to Promote African Religions', https://nation.africa/kenya/life-and-style/weekend/prof-mbiti-the-anglican-cleric-who-dared-to-promote-african-religions-212226 (accessed 29.1.2024).

3 FrankTalkBlog 'Bio of the Week', http://sbffranktalk.blogspot.com/2016/01/bio-of-week.html (accessed 29.1.2024).

4 Bukenya, 'Prof Mbiti'.

5 See Myles Osborne, *Ethnicity and Empire in Kenya, Loyalty and Martial Race among the Kamba, c.1800 to the Present* (Cambridge: Cambridge University Press, 2014).

6 FrankTalkBlog, 'Bio of the Week: John Mbiti'.

7 Bukenya, 'Prof Mbiti'.

8 Derek Peterson, 'Reading John Mbiti from Uganda', https://africasacountry.com/2019/10/reading-john-mbiti-from-uganda (accessed 29.1.2024).

9 Peterson, 'Reading John Mbiti from Uganda'.

10 Peterson, 'Reading John Mbiti from Uganda'.

11 Peterson, 'Reading John Mbiti from Uganda'.

12 Peterson, 'Reading John Mbiti from Uganda'.

13 Peterson, 'Reading John Mbiti from Uganda'.

14 Peterson, 'Reading John Mbiti from Uganda'.

15 Peterson, 'Reading John Mbiti from Uganda'.

16 Peterson, 'Reading John Mbiti from Uganda'.

17 Peterson, 'Reading John Mbiti from Uganda'.

18 See, for instance, studies by Edward Tylor, such as *Primitive Culture* (1871), which relegated African religions to the category of 'animism', 'paganism', 'savage', 'tribal' and 'pagan'. James Frazer (1854–1941) asserted that religion, including African varieties, developed from magic, from which modern people had graduated to science (Edward B. Tylor, *Primitive Culture: Research into the Development of Mythology, Philosophy, Religion, Language, Art and Custom*, 1920).

19 Richard Sandomir, 'John Mbiti, 87, Dies; Punctured Myths About African Religions', https://www.nytimes.com/2019/10/24/world/africa/john-mbiti-dead.html (accessed 29.1.2024).

20 John Mbiti, 'The Encounter of Christian Faith and African Religion', https://www.religion-online.org/article/the-encounter-of-christian-faith-and-african-religion/ (accessed 29.1.2024).

21 John Mbiti, *African Religions and Philosophy* (Oxford: Heinemann, 1969), xi.

22 Peterson, 'Reading John Mbiti from Uganda'.

23 John W. Kinney, 'The Theology of John Mbiti: His Sources, Norms and Methods', *International Bulletin of Mission Research*, 3.2 (1979): 65–7.

24 Kinney, 'Theology'.

25 Kinney, 'Theology'.

26 Kinney, 'Theology'.

27 John Mbiti, 'Christianity and Traditional Religions in Africa Mission', *International Review of Mission*, 59/236 (1970): 430–40.

28 Kinney, 'Theology'.

29 Uchenna Okeja, 'Mbiti and Current Issues in African Philosophy', *Journal of Traditions and Beliefs*, 2 (2016), https://engagedscholarship.csuohio.edu/cgi/view content.cgi?article=1051&context=jtb (accessed 29.1.2024).

30 John Mbiti, *Introduction to African Religion* (Oxford: Heinemann, 1975), 11.

31 Mbiti, *Introduction to African Religion*, 2.

32 Mbiti, *Introduction to African Religion*, 3.

33 Mbiti, *Introduction to African Religion*, 4.

34 David Kirwa Tarus and Stephanie Lowery, 'African Theologies of Identity and Community: The Contributions of John Mbiti, Jesse Mugambi, Vincent Mulago, and Kwame Bediako', 311, https://www.degruyter.com/document/doi/10.1515/opth-2017-0024/html (accessed 29.1.2024).

35 Mbiti, *Introduction to African Religion*, 184–5.

36 Tarus and Lowery, 'African Theologies of Identity and Community', 311.

37 Tarus and Lowery, 'African Theologies of Identity and Community', 311.

38 John Mbiti, 'Some African Concepts of Christology', in *Christ and the Younger Churches: Theological Contributions from Asia, Africa, and Latin America*, ed. G. F. Vicedom (London: SPCK, 1970), 51–62.

39 Mbiti, 'Christianity and Traditional Religions in Africa': 430–40.

40 Mbiti, 'Some African Concepts of Christology'.

41 John Mbiti, *New Testament Eschatology in an African Background* (Oxford: Oxford University Press, 1971).

42 Mbiti, 'Traditional Religions in Africa'.

43 Kinney, 'Theology'.

44 Kinney, 'Theology'.

45 Kinney, 'Theology'.

46 Kinney, 'Theology'.

47 John Mbiti, 'Dreams as a Point of Theological Dialogue between Christianity and African Religion', *Missionalia* 25.4 (1997): 511–22.

48 Mbiti, 'Dreams'.

49 Mbiti, 'Dreams'.

50 John Mbiti, 'An Ecumenical Approach to Teaching the Bible', https://onlinelibrary.wiley.com/doi/abs/10.1111/j.1758-6623.1987.tb01434.x (accessed 29.1.2024).

51 Mbiti, 'An Ecumenical Approach to Teaching the Bible'.

52 Mbiti, *New Testament Eschatology*, 189.

53 'WCC commemorates life of former Bossey director John Samuel Mbiti', https://www.oikoumene.org/en/press-centre/news/wcc-commemorates-life-of-former-bossey-director-john-samuel-mbiti (accessed 29.1.2024).

54 'WCC commemorates ...'

55 'WCC commemorates ...'

56 'WCC commemorates ...'

57 'WCC commemorates ...'

58 John Roth, 'Learning from African Theology', https://www.goshen.edu/wp-content/uploads/sites/59/2020/03/March-2020-Rhizome-Digital.pdf (accessed 29.1.2024).

59 'WCC commemorates ...'

60 'WCC commemorates ...'

61 'WCC commemorates ...'

11

Jesse Mugambi

JULIUS GATHOGO

This chapter considers the Kenyan Anglican Jesse Ndwiga Kanyua Mugambi, a remarkable pan-Africanist scholar of theology, philosophy and African studies. His work has both debts to and disagreements with that of John Mbiti, and he has produced a number of significant texts such as *African Christian Theology: An Introduction*[1] and *African Heritage and Contemporary Christianity*.[2] He has had a significant role in the reconstruction of postcolonial Kenya, a concern that is clearly signposted in his book *From Liberation to Reconstruction: African Christian Theology after the Cold War*.[3] This chapter sets his work in context, by attending closely to the social and political contexts in which Mugambi's theology was formed and which it addresses powerfully, as it would need to.

Mau-Mau War of Independence

The Mau-Mau war of independence (1952–60) is of immeasurable significance in Jesse Mugambi's scholarly formation, for several reasons. Firstly, the Kenyan-African returnees of both World War One (1914–18) and World War Two (1939–45) eloquently spoke their mind about the future of a postcolonial Kenya in a manner that would inspire the young Jesse Mugambi, who listened to them from a very tender age. Growing up in an agitated society had its mixed fortunes, as it enlightened as well as led Mugambi to wrestle with several unanswered questions. Some of these questions would include: How did Kenya and Africa end up a colony of other people? Who failed in history? Where was God, and was God neutral in Africa's history, in slavery, colonialism, land expropriation, religio-cultural humiliations, and 'colour-bar' as Kenyan apartheid was called? Secondly, the Mau-Mau war led to Kenya's first republic, declared the 34th African state on 12 December 1963. The second republic was pronounced on 27 August 2010, when a people-driven constitution was promulgated. Hence, Mau-Mau provided a historical landmark to Mugambi, just as it does to the general populace. As the war of independence divided the people of Kenya in terms of collaborators versus freedom fighters, especially in Mugambi's central Kenya region, its huge impact also led some to become poets, inquirers, seekers of a laissez-faire society, while reducing others to depression, among other impacts. Jesse Mugambi belongs among those who remained inquisitive, energetic, inspired, and were positively driven beyond expectations by this war. Thirdly, seeing Mau-Mau martyrs, which are comparable to the Uganda martyrs – a people who died for their faith in God – also contributed to Mugambi's scholarly and social formation. In retrospect, Mau-Mau guerrilla rebels, who were operating from the forests near Mount Kirinyaga (renamed Kenya in 1948, when Mugambi was barely a year old), would require evangelical Christians to recant their Christian faith and undertake a Mau-Mau oath of loyalty to the war of independence. Anyone who refused to take the oath was beheaded or otherwise killed. Interestingly, lots of proselytized and converted Christians were more than willing to die for their Christian faith. Equally, colonial authorities killed Mau-Mau rebels with abandon, hence it almost turned out to be a civil war within central Kenya, as brothers in different camps in the politics of the day turned against and killed one another. Spy systems operated, churches and schools were burned, social facilities collapsed. This was the context in which Mugambi was raised.

Mugambi the Man

Jesse Mugambi was born on 6 February 1947 at Kiangoci, in the Embu district of eastern Kenya. Kiangoci is near Kigari, a vibrant centre of the Anglicanism given that the Kigari Mission Station was established in 1909–10 by missionaries from the Church Missionary Society (CMS). While two Canadian missionaries from Ontario established the station, another, T. W. W. Crawford, resided at Kigari from 1910 to 1915, training the first generation of six evangelists. From 1915 to 1939, John Comely, an English CMS missionary, lived at Kigari, training local evangelists and introducing new ways of living. During Comely's long period of service, the Emmanuel Anglican Church was built at Kigari, which Mugambi's parents (Jemimah and Timothy) attended. Several out-stations were also established, and over 20 evangelists were trained and assigned to train others. In 1937, at the same Kigari campus, the CMS established St Mark's Normal School for the training of primary school teachers. This was the forerunner of the present St Mark's Teachers' College, a public institution sponsored by the Embu diocese.

Culture

As with St Paul in the New Testament who had an able Jewish teacher in Gamaliel, Mugambi had his maternal grandfather, Mzee Njeru wa Kanyenje, who taught him to respect his African identity. His grandfather had little appreciation for the British as a result of their seconding him to the war-effort, which to his mind had no relevance to Africa, and he was well informed about the events of his day. In particular, the British had told him that the Germans were cannibals who, if not defeated, would invade Kenya and capture Africans for meat. This was meant to encourage Africans to see World War One as being to their own benefit.

When Kanyenje arrived at the war-front, he discovered that the description of Germans as cannibals was a British propaganda tool meant to garner the support of Africans for what was essentially a European war. In addition, he and his peers found the Germans were fellow tribesmen with the British, only that they perhaps belonged to a different clan. Kanyenje therefore concluded that the British administrators must have been liars. In view of this, he felt that the British and the Germans ought to have resolved their tribal dispute at home in Europe, and should not have involved Africans.[4] He felt that the European powers could have avoided war if they had paid attention to African heritage. That is, they would have sat together and sought consensus on their problems and thereby reconcile,[5] a phenomenon that is well emphasized in the *Ubuntu* philosophy.

Kanyenje's discovery that Germans were like other nations finds echoes in John Mbiti's understanding of authentic human nature:

> By nature, Africans are neither Angels nor demons; they possess and exercise the potentialities of both angels and demons. They can be kind as the Germans, but they can be murderous as the Germans; Africans can be as generous as Americans, but they can be as greedy as the Americans; they can be as friendly as the Russians, but they can be as cruel as the Russians; they can be as honest as English, but they can be equally hypocritical. In their human nature Africans are Germans, Swiss, Chinese, Indians or English – they are men.[6]

For Mbiti and Kanyenje, Europeans and Africans (or any other peoples) are human beings and as such possess negative human traits such as hatred. Furthermore, the human race is divided into various 'clans' whose worldviews sometimes differ.

Following his return from World War One, Kanyenje reportedly came back with great pride for Africa, its religious heritage and identity. Consequently, he was willing to preach about the goodness of African religion vis-à-vis other religions that had subjected him to 'fight their fellow clans'. But Kanyenje rejected Christian baptism. He only came to finally accept it shortly before his death in 1976, as a result of persuasion from his grandchildren whom he did not want to disappoint. His acceptance was on rational grounds, arguing that the persuasion by his grandchildren indicated the cultural and religious success of the Europeans over Africans!

With opinionated grandparents who were very proud of their African cultural heritage, Jesse Mugambi's interest in African religion versus the Christian faith of his immediate parents was stirred. This interest made him, as a scholar in later life, seek a correlation between Christianity and African culture, resulting in his book *African Heritage and Contemporary Christianity*.[7] This early exposure to African heritage likely led him to his assertion that it is not possible for a foreigner to understand Africans in their entirety, just as an African can never be fully assimilated into Euro-American culture. He therefore stresses that only 'Africans can make the best authorities for their own heritage'.[8]

Liberation Movement

The Mau-Mau liberation movement struggled for emancipation from the early 1940s to the early 1960s, in protest against the injustices of colonial rule. These injustices can be explained in various ways. First, the five million Africans who lived in the British colony of Kenya had failed to gain any meaningful form of political representation; and there was the suppression and banning in 1940 of emerging political movements such as the Kikuyu Central Association (KCA). As David Anderson has noted, political dissent found expression for over three decades prior to the Mau-Mau uprising, as Africans voiced their 'plangent political concerns despite the obstruction of an unsympathetic colonial state'.[9]

Some of the issues that dominated African politics included the low wages, which were kept to a minimum by the European settlers eager to remain competitive agricultural producers. Africans were also agitating against the forced carrying of the *Kipande* – that is, an identity card and passbook that were introduced after World War One, without which no African could leave home to seek employment. Frequently, European settlers would punish 'errant' African workers by tearing up the *Kipande*, thereby making it impossible for them to get further employment.[10] In addition, the European settlers punished labourers with the *kiboko* – that is, a whip made of rhinoceros hide. As Anderson notes, 'By the early 1920s, the deaths of several African servants from beatings at the hands of their European masters earned Kenya's white settlers an unenviable reputation for brutality.'[11]

These injustices led Africans to retreat to the forests and form bands of guerrilla fighters. As the war went on, brutality and torture were prevalent. As Caroline Elkins has noted:

> Torture, or fear of it, compelled oath takers to give details about their ceremonies, including names or revealing the locations of the caches of arms or food supplies for Mau-Mau fighting the forest war. Some of this intelligence was accurate and some [was] pure fiction, fabricated on the spot by Mau-Mau suspects trying to save themselves. The colonial government nevertheless used the information to convict some thirty thousand Kikuyu men and women of Mau-Mau crimes and sentence them to prison, many for life.[12]

Mzee Mbūūrī wa Kīnyua, of Ndia Division, Kīrīnyaga District of Central Kenya, concurs with Elkins's assessment:

> Among the things that I am unable to forget, however much they invoke painful memories, is the screening exercise that was administered to us – during the Kenyan quests for self-rule. Those British, who worked with the sellers of the land (*African traitors*), were never satisfied with us (*we*) who were being screened; they just wanted more information from us but we didn't have more to give. But they just beat us and beat us in the police station, in their detention camps, and (*embarrassingly*) in the villages (*before our wives and children*). Screening was hell.

Jesse Mugambi was shaped by these critical moments in Kenya's political history, at the peak of colonial brutality. Nelson Mandela, speaking at an African National Congress (ANC) Conference on 21 September 1953, clearly describes the Kenya of Mugambi's childhood days:

> The massacre of the Kenyan people by Britain has aroused worldwide indignation and protest. Children are being burnt alive; women are raped, tortured, whipped and boiling water poured on their breasts to force confessions from them that Jomo Kenyatta had administered the Mau-Mau oath to them. Men are being castrated and shot dead. In the Kikuyu country there are some villages in which the population has been completely wiped out.

Mandela went on to say:

We are prisoners in our own country because we dared to raise our voices against those horrible atrocities and because we expressed our solidarity with the cause of the Kenyan people. You can see that there is no easy walk to freedom anywhere, and many of us will have to pass through the valley of the shadow of death again and again before we reach the mountain tops of our desires.[13]

This environment of Mau-Mau liberation had obvious effects on Mugambi's whole life, having been surrounded by Mau-Mau freedom fighters who knew the cunning of colonial powers. His environment introduced him to 'liberation' and 'democracy' and other concepts that are key to him. As he has said for himself:

These events greatly shaped my childhood. I started school in the middle of the Emergency (1954), and spent eight years of my childhood in two concentration camps (Kigari and Kirigi in Embu). I have known oppression since my childhood! They confirm that what I went through was also experienced by a whole generation of Kenyans. Unfortunately, there has not been anything similar to the South African Truth and Reconciliation Commission; so much of the experience of this generation remains unexpressed within the public domain.

Conversely, Mugambi's experiences with the missionary enterprise in which suppression of African culture in the Church were also not positive. He observes:

During that period, 1952 until 1962, the missionary agencies fully supported the colonial regime. In school and at the church they (as citizens of the empire) taught us to be docile subjects of Her Majesty the Queen. Yet they expected us to respect them. Rather than winning respect, they instilled fear in us. While accepting the Gospel, we rejected its ideological misappropriation by the missionary establishments. Thus long before I began to study theology I knew and understood the difference between oppression and liberation.

Although the young Mugambi's zealous Christian father was part of the political agitation prevalent at the time – he was busy preaching – young Mugambi was taking in the agitation, listening to the injustices, the decrials of racism, stories of torture, witnessing land-grabs. A contemporary, Zablon Nthamnuri, describes the scene:

I remember growing up as a small child in one of the small towns in Kenya. There was a 'white only' restaurant in town with the inscription 'Africans and dogs are not welcome'. From the very beginning you were made to understand that you are not fully human. You were classified with the dogs, and that is the treatment you got.[14]

State of Emergency

An event that had a profound effect on Mugambi's life was the State of Emergency, declared following the arrival of Evelyn Baring as the crown's newly appointed colonial governor of Kenya in October 1952. Jesse Mugambi entered the formal education system at Kigari in January 1954. His movement was restricted from dusk-to-dawn, and even during the daytime. Mugambi's school was very overcrowded as Kenyans were forced to move from their ancestral homes.

The immediate cause of the declaration of the State of Emergency was the brutal killing, on 9 October 1952, of Chief Warūhiū, a known sympathizer and collaborator of the colonial government. Coupled with this, there was general tension in the country following skirmishes between Mau-Mau fighters and colonial forces resulting in much bloodshed.

The situation for Kenyan nationals got worse by the day. Between January and April 1953, Baring instituted dozens of extreme and wide-ranging laws, referred to as the Emergency Regulations. These included communal punishment, curfews, influx control and, as Elkins relates:

> The confiscation of property and land, the imposition of special taxes, the issuance of special documentation and passes, the censorship and banning of publications, the disbanding of all African political organizations, the control and disposition of labour, the suspension of due process, and detention without trial.[15]

It was a state-organized reign of terror in a state-sanctioned police state. In addition, emergency legislation controlled African markets, shops, hotels, and all public transport, including buses, taxis and bicycles. In addition, Baring created concentrated villages in the African reserves, and barbed-wire cordons in African towns, including the city of Nairobi. He also established mini-detention camps on settler farms in the so-called 'White Highlands'. Above all, Baring sanctioned inhumane treatment of Mau-Mau suspects that was devoid of any humanity.

Anderson contends that 'the most punitive measure of all was surely villagization' – a term that refers to 'the compulsory resettlement of people from their scattered, ridge-top farms, into centralized, regulated villages, situated at key points along the busier roads'.[16] While some villages were principally meant to protect the loyalists, most of the 854 established villages or camps were in reality mass detention camps intended to punish Mau-Mau sympathizers.

The speed with which the villages or camps were established was astonishing and suspicious. Between June 1954 and October 1955, a period of just 15 months, 1,077,500 Africans were resettled in 854 villages. Kenyans were forced to abandon their farming projects to settle in overcrowded environments where life was extremely difficult to manage. On villagization, punishments and rewards would be applied depending on the willingness of villages to cooperate. Villages that did not cooperate would have curfews imposed, while those that did collaborate received certain benefits, including:

> Agricultural services, the reopening of shops, and the lifting of curfews to allow (*some*) night-time activities. More than anything else, villagization allowed the government to stamp its authority on the countryside, destroying the last elements of passive wing support for the forest fighters.[17]

Women suffered greatly. In a bid to impress their white superiors, the Home Guard (black patrollers in the village) abused African women, especially during the daily forced labour sessions. Home Guards would also brutally hit those who lifted their heads or who sought a break from hard labour, treating them as ancient slaves. This was meant to remind a person that 'you should always be working without rest'.[18] The forced labourers were prohibited from singing, drinking, talking, eating or any other activities while working in trenches.

African women would compose stanzas mocking the brutality of the Home Guards and white 'Johnnies' (as the British soldiers were generally called). In their songs, they would point out the colonial injustices and beg for humane treatment. When the white colonial District Officer (DO) visited Gatung'ang'a village, in the Nyeri District of Central Kenya, the women who dared would condemn him in a song about his detention of their husbands at Manyani detention camp, leaving them to die while digging the trenches. One such song was:

> Women tell Kariuki (the headman)
> So that Kariuki may tell Gatoto (the sub chief)
> And Gatoto may tell Karangi (the chief)
> And Karangi may inform the DO
> That this trench digging is going to kill the women.[19]

Such songs form an essential part of African traditional practice and culture, expressing inner fears or joys, admonition, ridicule, values. Mugambi himself explores the importance of songs in African religiosity in his major works, including *African Christian Theology: An Introduction*, *African Heritage and Contemporary Christianity*, and *From Liberation to Reconstruction*.

Another dimension of the war of liberation is that women who were suspected of continuing to feed the Mau-Mau guerrillas were sometimes brought into the village square and shot or hung as a warning to the rest. Such practices compare with the Nigerian terrorist group Boko Haram's killing of their targets, enemy spies and rival armies.

In considering the two sides that were battling it out from 1952 to 1960, it was not always easy to tell who the real terrorists were, as unorthodox methods were employed on both sides of the divide, including the burning to ashes of General Kubukubu of Kianjokoma-Embu near Jesse Mugambi's home, in September 1956. Similarly, the colonial government burned to ashes the body of General Chui wa Mararo of Kamuiru-Kirinyaga, close to Mugambi's Embu County, in May 1956. In both cases, women were invited to bring heaps of firewood to roast their own ram, only to discover that they were being tricked to burn the bodies of their freedom fighters rather than give them decent burials. Such bizarre methods of scaring the rival combatants has had far-reaching effects to date, via the trauma and poverty that it triggered. Jesse Mugambi stands out as one of the lucky few who overcame huge trauma and moved on to become global scholars of no mean repute. Ironically, such events inspired him to think critically, creatively and innovatively.

Besides the above, the colonial authorities in Mugambi's Embu district would sometimes have local people beaten by the Kenya Police Reserve, King's African Rifles, and Kenyan Regiment, sometimes collectively called 'British savages'.[20] Sometimes, Mau-Mau fighters would be roped to the back of the Land Rovers and be driven around the concentrated villages to scare women whose husbands had been detained in other parts of the country. Local women were also raped by the military, together with their daughters in the same hut. They would be asked at gunpoint to choose between death and rape. Women also had to watch their own children 'slaughtered and their remains skewered on spears and paraded around the village squares by the Home Guards'.[21] Use of excrement-based torture was also widespread, as one woman who experienced this ordeal relates, 'The Johnnies would make us run around with toilet buckets on our heads', contents 'running down our faces, and we would have to wipe it off and eat it, or else we were shot. Even then, some people were killed anyway.'[22]

Fortunately, the East African Revival Movement (EARM) was active in the concentration villages during the struggle for freedom and human dignity. This Christian movement operated within the Anglican, Methodist, Presbyterian and other colonial-friendly established missionary-initiated churches. Begun in Rwanda 1927, it spread throughout Uganda into Kenya, reaching Western Kenya in 1937.[23] As during Mugambi's childhood, it was characterized with calls to be 'born again', its focus being on the heavenly kingdom; repentance and the confession of sin; 'heavenly pursuits' as opposed to 'earthly' ones.

In evaluating this war, which had such great impact on Jesse Mugambi's life, we realize that this was not a race war between Europeans in Kenya and the Africans. Rather, it was a socio-political war, where the oppressed sought liberation from the dominance of foreigners who had dehumanized them by occupying their land and property, among other things. Although the Mau-Mau uprising was principally directed against Europeans, according to some reports of the rebellion only 32 European civilians were killed as a result of Mau-Mau attacks. Another 26 were wounded. When this is contrasted with the murder of 1,819 African civilians (mainly collaborators) by the Mau-Mau, and the wounding of a further 916 civilians over the same period, even though the latter figures do not include the many hundreds of Africans who disappeared without trace, many more Africans than Europeans were killed.

Although the Mau-Mau lost the war militarily, they won the war politically and ideologically. As a result, Kenya has lived peacefully for many decades now as a sovereign state without *coups d'état* such as those that have beset surrounding African nation states. Kenya is not only a stable country politically, but is also stable economically, as was evidenced by the fact that, after 42 years of constitutional independence, the finance minister David Mwiraria, in June 2005, could deliver the national budget without factoring in any 'donor' support.

Land Tenure

Another major event that had great impact on Mugambi's life was that of Kenya's land tenure system. The outcome of the Kenyan state of emergency saw a change in the colonial administration's attitude towards the system of African land tenure and the production of commercial crops. The 1953 reform referred to as 'the Swynnerton Plan' proved unjust towards Africans. Named after R. J. M. Swynnerton, Kenya's assistant director of agriculture, its original aim was to address the 'unsolvable' land problem, and find a way that would 'make the reserves more agriculturally productive'.[24] With Baring's support, Swynnerton secured £5 million from the Colonial Development Fund, in order that 'intensified agricultural development in all African Areas of Kenya with due emphasis to the loyal tribes' could be made.[25]

Unfortunately, the plan envisaged European experts to direct Africans in cultivation and animal husbandry techniques, failing to be aware that Africans had managed their land and livestock successfully prior to the arrival of the British in the late 1800s. Anderson contends that the Swynnerton Plan was crafted with the sole aim of rewarding those Africans who were loyal to the colonial government, and who contributed to the downfall of the Mau-Mau forces.[26]

The government exploited its villagization process by securing clan lands (land belongs culturally to various clans) deserted by the people who were incarcerated in the colonial camps. It subdivided and allocated the land to loyalists under the guise of an improved agricultural development programme. Consequently, as the loyalists benefited, the convicted Mau-Mau rebels were excluded from these illegal land reallocations. Unfortunately, the repercussions of the Swynnerton Plan are still felt today, after decades of constitutional independence.

In Mugambi's view, the Swynnerton Plan was aimed at legitimizing the alienation of primal land in Kenya by British settlers and forcing Africans to share the 'native reserves' among themselves. Consequently, Kenyans found themselves in overcrowded areas that were infertile and thereby unsuitable for arable farming. Land marginalization was one of the major factors that drove the freedom fighters to the forests to reclaim their inheritance.

Declaration of Independence

Another major event that had a great impact on Mugambi's life was the Kenyan National Declaration of Independence on 12 December 1963. For the adolescent Mugambi, this was the beginning of a future filled with hope. Jomo Kenyatta, who had been released from colonial detention in 1961, became Kenya's first elected president.

As Mugambi watched Kenyatta being reintroduced to the world in April 1961, Kenyatta told a packed press conference, 'I have been greatly misrepresented by some of you, but today I hope you will stick to the truth and refrain from writing sensationalist stories about me.'[27] He then rejected the Corfield Report (on Kenyatta and the Mau-Mau), which had been released to the public domain a year before his release in early 1960.

The author of the report, F. D. Corfield, relying on British and loyalist sources, employed the usual colonial terminology in describing British enlightenment and African darkness. He declared Mau-Mau to have been 'wholly evil' and Kenyatta its chief protagonist. But Kenyatta dismissed the Corfield Report as 'a pack of lies'. He assured the various ex-patriots (including Indians, Europeans and Africans) living in Kenya of security 'under Kenyatta'. This indicated a very different persona from the 'terrorist Kenyatta' that the European-dominated media had consistently portrayed. Kenyatta also focused his attention on the issue of vengeance.

Signifying the same magnanimous spirit of reconciliation as Nelson Mandela would later show in 1990 following his release from prison after almost three decades of detention under its apartheid regime, Kenyatta emerged from detention preaching forgiveness and reconciliation. Inter-estingly, the presumed leader of the 'darkness and death' borrowed freely from the words of Jesus, 'Father, forgive them, for they know not what they do' (Luke 23.34).[28] Kenyatta went on to say, 'I have never been a violent man. My whole life has been anti-violence. If I am free I will con-tinue to do so.' He then shouted a word that became the slogan of Kenya liberation, '*Uhuru!*' (Swahili for 'freedom!').

Kenyans wept a mixture of joy and disbelief as they witnessed Kenyat-ta's release from detention. As one former detainee, Hunja Njuki, could explain many years later:

> I wept, I wept with joy when word got around very quickly when he was released, and we danced and celebrated into the morning. Our leader was free, and he was going to save us from the colonial oppressors. *Ngai* (God) had answered our prayers.[29]

As he toured triumphantly throughout Kenya following his release, Ken-yatta delivered a series of reconciliatory and unitary speeches, such that even the remaining white settlers began to hail him as a great African leader and person of state. This went on until 1963 when the declaration of independence was made with Kenyatta as the first leader of a self-governing Kenya.

Two years after his release, Kenyatta was reintroduced to the world. As he stood on the podium of Nairobi's Uhuru gardens, Lang'ata, on 12 December 1963 he delivered an electrifying speech to a crowd of around 50,000 ecstatic people, mainly Africans, stating unequivocally: 'This is the greatest day in Kenya's history and the happiest day in my life.' With oratorical prowess, Kenyatta refused to read his prepared address in English and chose to speak extemporaneously to his eagerly await-ing people in Kiswahili (the popular language of the east and central African countries). Masses of people in the stadium became virtually uncontrollable in their anticipation, to the amazement of dignitaries from around the world who had all come to Kenya to witness Africa's 34th country achieve its constitutional independence from European rule.[30]

Kenyatta led the post-independence reconstruction by adopting the philosophy of 'Harambee' (meaning 'let us pull together') as the national watch-word.[31] Ogot describes the essential elements of Harambee as being participation in self-help efforts towards the generation of a spirit of self-reliance, free from the mentality of the begging bowl. He states:

> This is done both at the national and at the local levels. At the national level, '*harambee*' means a policy, which does not rely for development finance entirely on foreign sources. Domestic resources must be mobilized. For instance, in 1963/64, 82 percent of the total development budget originated in external sources; in 1972/73, this proportion had fallen to 46%. At the local level, *harambee* consists of self-help activities such as educational institutions, water projects, public health schemes, community institutions, etc.

Apart from the philosophy of Harambee, Kenyatta would portray his role in postcolonial reconstruction by telling his audience, 'Na tusahau yaliyopita tujenge taifa' ('let us forget the past and build (read – reconstruct) the nation!'). His was a reconciliatory approach specifically designed to create a harmonious and enabling atmosphere for development as opposed to merely seeking revenge for the past. As a young man, Mugambi watched Kenyatta as he encouraged Kenyans to take destiny into their own hands and make a clear break from the colonial past (read – 'start reconstructing yourselves – you now have what it takes to do so!').

As Kenya's founding father, Kenyatta led the postcolonial reconstruction of Kenya on a stable course. In particular, Mugambi recalls that the economy and other sectors of the national fabric did well. He observed this unfolding scenario with keenness and appreciation, probably wondering whether the whole of Africa could be similarly engaged in the process of social reconstruction.

Some of His Books

Mugambi is among the most quoted Kenyan scholars in the clustered fields of philosophy, history and theology, and *From Liberation to Reconstruction* is his best-known book. He urges African scholars in theology to shift their methodology and focus more on reconstructive motif as the effects of the end of Cold War (in 1989) gave Africa a chance to reconstruct herself without necessarily blaming her woes on the meta-phorical pharaoh (oppressive foreigners and colonialists). As the key symbol of liberation, Nelson Mandela was released from South Africa's apartheid jails in February 1990; Mugambi saw it as evidence of the end of Cold War polarization in Africa that was foreign induced. The con-testing groups of West (North Atlantic Treaty Organization (NATO) group) versus the Eastern group (Warsaw pact), in Mugambi's view had a huge socio-religious implication on Africa. To remake Africa, he argues, African countries embrace the culture seen in the biblical figure of Nehemiah who led in the reconstruction of the walls of Jerusalem on his return from Babylonian captivity. In building on theo-cultural recon-struction, Mugambi insisted on revisiting our previous agenda, including theological training to align it to the new realities, across the diverse sectors of society (socio-economic domain).

Another important book by Jesse Mugambi is *The African Heritage and Contemporary Society*. He understands the African heritage by drawing comparatively on other religio-cultural dialogues such as the trans-formation of Judaism by Jesus versus the Judaization of Christianity. He also considers the Hellenization of Christianity versus Christianization of Hellenistic traditions, Romantization of Christianity versus Christian-ization of Roman culture, etc., so as to prepare scholars to understand his inculturation paradigm in African Christianity. Like John Mbiti, Mugambi endeavours to demonstrate the value of African indigenous cultures as raw materials for the gospel of Christ in the African context.

In *African Christian Theology: An Introduction*, Mugambi employs theo-historical design to understand the liberation theological paradigm in African Christianity. He uses strong language akin to the famous Marcus Garvey's dictum, Asia for Asiatics and Africa for Africans. He dismisses European expatriates working as missionaries, church admin-istrators and as African scholars as incapable of doing African theology effectively, as only the wearer of the shoe knows where it pinches. It is in later publications, as in the case of *From Liberation and Reconstruction* and *Christian Theology and Social Reconstruction*,[32] that he now appears to appreciate the role of non-indigenous Africans in the reconstruction of Africa. It is in these latter publications that he redefines an African, where even those voluntary and involuntary guests to Africa become critical members of the society in its reconstructive task.

In his post-liberation works, Mugambi views the terms 'Africa' and 'African' as in need of new hermeneutics, hence they should be inter-preted ideologically rather than racially.[33] This is, however, a revision of his earlier works (those before 1990) such that in *African Christian*

Theology he almost excludes non-black Africans from articulating African theology. In so doing, Mugambi appears to be saying, 'In adopting the new paradigm of reconstruction, we in Africa and beyond must redefine ourselves in the new dispensation, as we must now see our diversity as strength rather than as a weakness.' He thus states:

> At the beginning of the third millennium, it is important to strongly affirm that [the] African identity transcends race and religion. While it is true that the continent is the native home of one large community with numerous representatives in the Diaspora scattered throughout Europe, Asia and the Americas, it is also true that there are cultural minorities who have made their home in the continent and interacted with their voluntary and involuntary hosts. The rich diversity of African culture and identity may become the salvation of the human race in the third millennium.[34]

In building his faith on African resources, Mugambi published most of these publications in Kenya and East Africa, thereby making it affordable and cheaper for his local readership. As a result, he became a great inspiring individualist who was revered greatly, as he was the socio-scholarly think-tank of the local context whose presence provided theological direction just as St Paul did in the New Testament. He became the beacon that mapped out direction for most of the active scholars and a huge constituency in African contexts and beyond. On one occasion he wrote of St Paul thus:

> Christian theological reflection is essential for the healthy development of any church. A church that is incapable of producing its own theologians cannot be said to be mature. In the New Testament we find St Paul addressing himself to the doctrinal, pastoral and organizational problems that faced the churches he had helped to start. It is clear in the epistles that the congregations to which St Paul writes looked up to him for theological guidance, because they did not have their own theologians to discern conclusive solutions to the problems pertinent to each local church.

It might also be noted that Mugambi addressed himself to the doctrinal, pastoral and organizational problems of churches in which he had much influence. Moreover, Mugambi goes on to say:

> African churches have for a long time depended on theological mentors from the parent denominations in Europe and North America, just

like those churches of the Mediterranean region during the apostolic period depended on St Paul for theological leadership and guidance. One important question that African Christian theologians must ask themselves at the end of the twentieth century and at the beginning of the twenty-first, is whether African churches should continue to rely on theological packages designed for other cultures and historical contexts.

As he went into retirement in 2020, though remaining strong and active for consultations, did Mugambi prepare his successor in African Christianity, or was that beyond his province? Did he overtake Professor John Mbiti, his mentor, at one stage? Who inspired him? This drives us to the next sub-section.

Scholarly Inspiration and Contest

An important figure that inspired Mugambi's academic life was Stephen Neill, the founder chairperson of the Department of Philosophy and Religious Studies (1970–3) at Nairobi University. Mugambi later succeeded him as the fourth chairperson of the Department (1986–90). Neill taught him as an undergraduate (1971–3). Mugambi describes his teacher as being an articulate and prolific author who lived to the age of 86 years and published 80 books, thereby writing on average one book per year! Neill challenged him, and others in his class, to do serious academic work, always responding positively and constructively to their queries. In Mugambi's view, Neill was a public speaker of a high calibre. He was once quoted as saying that when he was young he 'liked writing and disliked preaching, then had much preaching and little time for writing; now when old, like preaching and dislike writing, but have little preaching to do and endless writing'. He had, however, a very low opinion of African writers for, as Mugambi recalls, Neill used to say frequently and openly that an African did not make a good scholar. This discouraging remark from his teacher became, however, a blessing in disguise, in that Mugambi sought to one day prove Neill wrong by endeavouring to publish renowned, scholarly works. Fortunately, his resolve was encouraged by the impressive eloquence and wide knowledge of Ali Mazrui who later visited the University of Nairobi. In Mazrui, he saw a true African match for Neill, even though the bishop, in Mugambi's estimate, would not have willingly accepted this.

Even though Mugambi's works, in general, do not appear to build on John Mbiti's work, he nonetheless considers him one of his mentors. Mbiti was to publish Mugambi's first research paper. Mbiti also encouraged many other African students to conduct research on their cultures and histories, and took the trouble to publish research papers – often under severe financial constraints. He issued more than 20 volumes of Occasional Research Papers at Makerere University, and was the prime mover for *Dini na Mila*, the journal of the Department of Religious Studies at Makerere in which Jesse Mugambi's paper was published in 1971.

Mugambi recalls one morning when Stephen Neill came to deliver a lecture on comparative religion. As the lecture went on, Neill promptly drew a religious map of the world, showing the continents and assigning major religions, one for each region. In his allocations, Protestantism was assigned to Europe and North America; Roman Catholicism was assigned to South America; Islam was assigned to the Middle East; Hinduism was assigned to India; Buddhism was assigned to South East Asia; Confucianism was assigned to China, and Marxism assigned to Eurasia. Neill then went on to explain to his eager students that the religious map of the world was now complete without Africa! As classmates, they looked at one another and wondered quietly, has the professor forgotten something? Interestingly, most of the students had individual copies of Mbiti's book *African Religions and Philosophy*, and took Mbiti's works seriously. In low voices, they nominated the oldest member of the class to ask Neill to explain the omission. As Mugambi recalled, the conversation went as follows:

> 'Excuse us, Professor Sir; it seems that your map is incomplete!' 'No! No! This religious map of the world is complete!' 'Excuse us, Professor Sir; we do not see Africa on your map!' 'That is correct, dear students! There is no African religion!' 'But excuse us, Professor (Bishop), Sir, Professor Mbiti has written much about it.' 'Listen to me! There is no African religion!' they were told.

The students finally listened as they were ordered, but they did not respect his view. For Mugambi, this experience became one of the turning points of his academic career, for he was convinced that Neill had not bothered to read any of Mbiti's books. Mugambi therefore vowed 'to read more, research more and publish more, so that there could be more scholarly evidence to document the African cultural and religious heritage'.

Another person who inspired Mugambi's socio-scholarly formation is Ghanaian philosopher Kwasi Wiredu, whom Mugambi met in 1974. Their relationship had been established when Wiredu expressed, indirectly, his appreciation for the insights that Mugambi articulated in a paper entitled 'The African Experience of God'. When they finally met, they talked about some philosophical ideas for about three hours, their dialogue focusing on an African understanding of reality and the role of religion in morality. In his paper, Mugambi had suggested that 'relation' be considered the most fundamental concept in African thought, thereby deviating from Mbiti's argument. Wiredu's suggestion was for Mugambi to develop this argument further.

With regard to Mugambi's ecumenical tutelage, John Gatu, former Moderator of the Presbyterian Church of East Africa, and the first person to call for a moratorium on Western missionaries, became his mentor when they served as the only Kenyan members of the WCC Commission on Faith and Order, 1974–84. At the Mission Festival in Milwaukee in the USA in 1971, Gatu argued, 'The continuation of the present Missionary Movement is a hindrance to the selfhood of the Church.'[35] During his time at the WCC Commission on Faith and Order, he reminded Mugambi of the necessity to root academic theology in the lives of Christians and churches at home and abroad.

Evaluation

Clearly, Jesse Mugambi's socio-scholarly background led him to have an early encounter with most of the themes that his works address. An illustration of this: on the gospel and culture, his father and his maternal grandfather clearly provided this. From his father, who was a committed Christian, Mugambi who is not only a scholar but also a preacher had something to inherit; and from his grandfather, who strictly adhered to African religion, he learnt much about African culture – which he propounds, in his work, with clarity of thought. On liberation and reconstruction, he scores highly, as he has lived with these concepts through his experience of the Mau-Mau liberation movements and post-independence period of Kenya's reconstruction. Sadly, he appears to have learnt very little from women, in particular his mother and grandmother(s). Neither in his e-mail correspondence, nor oral interviews, does he reflect on the role of women in his journey to his present position as a scholar. Even though Elizabeth his wife 'has been the silent half of my personality! She has supported me all along', little of this appears in his published works. Could it be that Mugambi overvalues privacy to the extent that exposing his grandmother, mother and wife would go against the very culture that his grandfather taught him? However, the theologians and teachers that inspired his theo-philosophical outlook were all men. Were there no women who could inspire him? What about St Teresa of Calcutta, or Coretta Scott King? What about the Kenyan women who struggled for Constitutional Independence, as in the case of field marshal Muthoni

Kirima? What about his favourite teachers' wives, such as Daina Muthanji Kivuti?

Secondly, although Mugambi claims to have been inspired by John Mbiti, he appears to be critical (sometimes over critical?) of Mbiti's work. For example, he is critical of Mbiti's contention that Africans are notoriously religious, yet most would agree with Mbiti. For Mugambi, Africans 'are not notoriously religious', but rather they are reputably religious.[36] Or is this disagreement akin to the case of Aristotle who differed with his teacher, Plato, on the 'theory of forms', but they still remained friends?

Conclusion

In this chapter we have explored the roots and formative factors that shaped Mugambi. We have noted that his background provided him with early engagements with the concepts of liberation, culture, justice, freedom, and reconstruction among others. We have focused on the background from which Mugambi was later to participate in the rebuilding of post-colonial Kenya. His strength when calling for a shift of theological gears following the end of the Cold War was strongly felt in Kenya. Viewing the liberation of Southern Africa, the unfolding scenario was like history repeating itself in a disguised form. This gives us a reason to take his work more seriously.

Notes

1 Jesse Mugambi, *African Christian Theology: An Introduction* (Nairobi: Heinemann, 1989).

2 Jesse Mugambi, *African Heritage and Contemporary Christianity* (Nairobi: Longman, 1989).

3 Jesse Mugambi, *From Liberation to Reconstruction: African Christian Theology after the Cold War* (Nairobi: EAEP, 1995).

4 From my written interview with Jesse Mugambi, November 2004.

5 Mugambi, *From Liberation to Reconstruction*.

6 John Mbiti, *African Religions and Philosophy* (Oxford: Heinemann, 2nd edn, 2005).

7 Mugambi, *African Heritage and Contemporary Christianity*.

8 Mugambi, *African Heritage*, 188.

9 David Anderson, *Histories of the Hanged: Testimonies from the Mau Mau Rebellion in Kenya* (London: Weidenfeld and Nicolson, 2005), 9.

10 Anderson, *Histories*, 9.

11 Anderson, *Histories*, 78.

12 Carolin Elkins, *Britain's Gulag: The Brutal End of Empire in Kenya* (London: Jonathan Cape, 2005), 78–9.

13 Nelson Mandela, *Long Walk to Freedom* (Boston: Little Brown, 1994), 42.

14 Zablon Nthamburi, *The African Church at the Crossroads* (Nairobi: Uzima, 1991), 5.

15 Elkins, *Britain's Gulag*, 55.

16 Anderson, *Histories*, 294.

17 Anderson, *Histories*, 294.

18 Elkins, *Britain's Gulag*, 243.

19 Elkins, *Britain's Gulag*, 243.

20 Elkins, *Britain's Gulag*, 247.

21 Elkins, *Britain's Gulag*, 247.

22 Elkins, *Britain's Gulag*, 247.

23 Mugambi, *From Liberation to Reconstruction*, 126.

24 Elkins, *Britain's Gulag*, 125.

25 Elkins, *Britain's Gulag*, 126.

26 Anderson, *Histories*, 294.

27 Elkins, *Britain's Gulags*, 357.

28 Elkins, *Britain's Gulags*, 359.

29 Elkins, *Britain's Gulags*, 359.

30 Elkins, *Britain's Gulags*, 359.

31 B. A. Ogot, *Historical Dictionary of Kenya* (London: Scarecrow Press, 1981), 69.

32 Jesse Mugambi, *Christian Theology and Social Reconstruction* (Nairobi: Acton, 2003).

33 Mugambi, *Social Reconstruction*, 113.

34 Mugambi, *Social Reconstruction*, 112–13. Jesse Mugambi's other work includes: *Text and Context in New Testament Hermeneutics* (Nairobi: Acton, 2004); *Responsible Leadership: Global Perspectives* (Nairobi/Geneva: Acton/WCC, 2005); *Church-State Relations: A Challenge for African Christianity* (Nairobi: Acton, 2004); *Christianity and African Culture* (Nairobi: Acton, 2002); *Interpreting the New Testament in Africa* (Nairobi: Acton, 2001); *Jesus in African Christianity: Experimentation and Diversity in African Christology* (Nairobi: Acton, 1998), among others.

35 Julius Gathago, *The Truth about African Hospitality* (Mombasa: Salt, 2001), 74.

36 See Mugambi, *From Liberation to Reconstruction*.

12

Nyameko Barney Pityana

JAMES TENGATENGA

Nyameko Barney Pityana was born on 7 August 1945, in the Eastern
Cape, South Africa. He was educated at the University of Fort Hare,
where he was expelled during the student revolt of the early 1970s when
Desmond Tutu was chaplain at the same university. Pityana studied
Law at the University of South Africa (UNISA) and graduated with a BA
(Law) in 1975 and BProc degree in 1976. After his release from prison
and his friend Steve Biko's murder by the police, he went into exile in the
UK. In 1982 he graduated from King's College, London, with a Bachelor of Divinity and proceeded to Ripon College Cuddesdon, Oxford, to
train for the priesthood in 1983. In 2001 he earned his Masters in Law
from UNISA in South Africa. Even though he was qualified, the South
African apartheid government would not allow him to be admitted to the
bar and practise law in South Africa. So it was not until February 1996
that he was finally admitted as an attorney of the High Court of South
Africa and allowed to practise. On his return to South Africa, he studied
for his doctorate in religious studies at the University of Cape Town and
was awarded it in 1995. He remained at this university as senior research
officer in the Department of Theology and Religious Studies until the
Truth and Reconciliation Commission was set up, when he left to work
alongside Desmond Tutu, who chaired the commission.

Pityana has received many honours for his life and work. In 1996,
Trinity College, Hartford in Connecticut, USA, awarded him an honorary
Doctor of Divinity degree. The University of Buenos Aires also honoured
him with a doctorate. Rhodes University awarded him a Doctor of Law
honoris causa. The Psychology Society of South Africa awarded him a
life membership in 2000. In 2001 he was honoured with the Tribute
Achievers Award for Leadership. Kings College London appointed him
a Fellow in 2002. That same year, he received an honourable mention in
the United Nations Educational, Scientific and Cultural Organization's
Prize for Human Rights Education. In 2006, he was awarded the order

of the Grand Counsellor of the Baobab in silver for his 'excellent contribution to a just and democratic South Africa'.

Barney Pityana has skilfully straddled the worlds of religion, academia, law and human rights. He was involved in the South African Student movement of the 1970s and together with Steve Biko and others, he led the secession of the South African Student Organization from the national multiracial student organization. While Biko was chair, Pityana was the Secretary General from 1970 to 1973. Among other things, they founded and led the Black Consciousness Movement in South Africa. This activism led to the arrest and murder of Steve Biko and Pityana's exile. After his priestly formation at Cuddesdon, he worked in parish ministry in England from 1982 to 1988. He then left for Geneva, Switzerland, to take up the job of Director of the Programme to Combat Racism at the World Council of Churches (WCC), 1988–92. After this, he returned to South Africa and studied again at the University of Cape Town. From 1995 to 2001, he chaired the South African Human Rights Commission. He was a member of the African Commission on Human and Peoples' Rights, 1997–2003.

He also once served as Deputy President of the Academy of Science of South Africa (ASSAf) and the General Secretary of the Network of African Academies of Science (NASAC). As an academic, he worked at Cape Town and as a professor at the University of South Africa (UNISA) before he became its principal and vice-chancellor from 2001 to 2010.

> During Pityana's decade as Vice-Chancellor, he exercised a resolute resistance to government and ruling-party influences that sometimes resulted in conflict with the Ministry of Education and the ANC. Yet, Pityana was a determined driver of the government's mandate to transform higher education, instituting changes at Unisa that ranged from a firm anti-racism policy to active Africanisation – including the successful creation of Unisa's satellite campus in Ethiopia.[1]

On his retirement from UNISA, he became rector of the Church of Southern Africa's College of the Transfiguration in Makanda, South Africa (2011–15). He currently runs his consultancy on theology, human rights and law. His specialty about which he has spoken, lectured and taught is black consciousness, black theology (South African), human rights, and human rights education. He continues his engagement with the black consciousness movement, and is a regular speaker in the media on matters of youth engagement in society and culture, especially with respect to African identity, education and employment.

Barney Pityana has yet to produce any monographs of note, but he has edited numerous volumes and many speeches and addresses from which his thoughts and theology can be gleaned.[2]

Black Consciousness

Barney Pityana's thinking is born from his experience in apartheid South Africa. Black consciousness is resistance to legalized black inferiority, an act of affirmation of blackness, and an appreciation and deployment of one's cultural heritage towards self-determination and liberation.[3] He says:

> Black Consciousness has identified the great myth designed to rob the black man of his soul and his human dignity, brought about by the white settlers with the able assistance of their handmaiden, the Church, through blood and tears, in suppression and humiliation, through dishonest means, by force and subjugation of the sons of the soil. It is the liberating effect of this self-knowledge and awareness that we refer to as Black Consciousness.[4]

The African nationalist movements on the continent had long espoused the concept of Pan-Africanism, and in the theological arena there was a development of African theologies that claimed African thought and African culture as a vehicle of Christian theology. In many ways, this was nothing new in the South African context. I am referring to the resistance movements from early colonization and white proponents of African culture as a vehicle for Christian theology. The most famous example is that of John Colenso, the Anglican Bishop of Zululand in the middle 1800s, who dared say that Zulu culture can be such a vehicle – for which he elicited many remonstrations from his contemporaries. Barney Pityana and his colleagues (including Biko), while appreciating the role and place of such proponents and allies, believed that 'salvation' comes primarily from the African, not from allies. For that to happen there needed to be a re-membering of Africanness,[5] which would form the basis for discourse and activism. In this vein, he writes:

> Black Consciousness calls for a decultured being in the black society. It means 'a whole new vision. A totally different perspective, a penetration to the depths beneath the depth of blackness' (Lerone Bennett). Black Consciousness implies a vision of the heritage of our forefathers. It is the beginning of a new search for roots to anchor us firmly in the midst of a military struggle. It is not only a search for humanity but it is an assertion and affirmation of the worth and dignity of the black man. Black Consciousness is indeed a hunger for solidarity with the oppressed

people of this world. The real black people are those who embrace the positive description 'black' rather than the negatives of others who set themselves up as the standard, the criterion and hallmark of value. It is a positive confrontation with the self. Black Consciousness seeks for a social content of the lives of others, for this has been the cornerstone of the traditional black community.[6]

It is this that leads to the formation of the black consciousness movement. The movement opposed the condescension that was the creation of Bantustans and the patronizing and acquiescent white liberals in South Africa. His reaction to all this leads to the phrase associated with the student movement: 'Black man, you are on your own'. He opines:

In their place we were being asked to recognize as leaders, quislings and collaborators with the repressive legislation. The system who saw no need for resistance and acted as agents of disempowerment. The Bantustans were the Big Lie of the apartheid system that claimed that there was anything like separate but equal, or that there was designated land that belonged to the black people, who had to be divided up into enclaves of despair and abandonment. Gradually, there emerged into this mix of ideologies a strange mix of bedfellows in the name of the English press and the white opposition parties that claimed the mantle of the Cape liberal tradition who were now arguing for an alleviation of the bad aspects of the system of repressive legislation, in other words who emerged as spokespersons of the oppressed majority.[7]

He describes the times as 'the best of times because such periods saw the flourishing of ideas and of idealism. It was a time of searching for the authentic and of discovery of the ideal of unity and solidarity. It was also a time of affirming values. It was a counter-assertion of the right to human dignity.'[8] In all this, he nevertheless acknowledges the influence of Western thinkers. As well as ascribing black consciousness to sources in African cultures and religion he also acknowledged debts of thinking to the likes of Hegel and Gramsci, Martin Luther King Jr, US-based black theology and post-Vatican II liberation theology. Yet he emphasizes the critical influence of the movement's location in South Africa itself:

Based as we were in Durban with many Gandhian activists in our midst, one must not forget that training in Mahatma Gandhi's Satyagraha principles were very important. At Phoenix Settlement originally founded by Gandhi as an ashram for satyagraha activists. One must never underestimate the ethical force of Gandhi's seven deadly sins: Politics without principle; Wealth without work; Commerce without morality; Pleasure without conscience; Education without character; Science without humanity; and Worship without sacrifice ... [The] approach was not a wholesale condemnation of religion and the church. Instead, he drew from a long history of Christian resistance by Black post-missionary Christians to the hegemony and control of the church by European missionaries. For that he had some powerful examples in Nehemiah Tile and the Ethiopian Movement, in the apocalyptic millenarian movements of the Mgijimas and the Nazarites in Bullhoek, in John Colenso and the challenge of cultural interpretation of the Bible among the Zulus, and of the more contemporary mass indigenous churches of Shembe and Lekganyane, even to the manifestations of independent theological thought of the African indigenous churches of the Zionists, charismatic and healing churches.[9]

In doing so, Pityana also introduces readers/listeners to different Christian movements within South Africa. He locates black consciousness within black theology: 'Black Theology then is an extension of Black Consciousness. Theology is the study of God, but it also studies the relationship between man and man, and thus it must have an existential and social content.'[10] In this, he demonstrates not only a knowledge of the movements but also respect for a novel form of ecumenism (and interfaith cooperation) that is possible in his South African context, which has yet to flourish. He concludes, 'If the Church is the greatest cause of the misshapen state in our country, the blackness of souls and culture of alienation, it must in future work for the culture of liberation. It must go back to the roots of broken African civilization, and examine the traditional African forms of worship, marriage, sacrifice, etc., and discover why these things are meaningful and wholesome to the traditional African community.'[11] I will return to the implications of this ecclesiology and the ecumenical praxis in the liberation of South Africa in the last section of this chapter.

Youth

Inasmuch as the black consciousness movement has universal implications, it began as a student movement and, thus, a youth movement. Its concern was to ensure that indigenous South African youth knew who they were and that their future (and indeed the country's future) needs to be, and will be, shaped by them. Pityana continued to hold the same view, lamenting: 'In South Africa at the present, it is fair to suggest that we are in danger of growing a generation of young people without hope of a better future.'[12] In this respect, he is very much in the realm of the ideas of the 'decolonization of the mind' and 'conscientization', as this idea was propagated at the height of the Freirean era. Pityana's call is for youth to be actively engaged

> in the manner in which society is governed, and the manner in which public resources are being used. That is of value not so much because invariably students and youth are affected by corruption and the paucity of ideas to drive the economy in a progressive manner, but also that the moral character of society lays the foundation for a society that values education, offers prospects for advancement, assures professional opportunities, and creates an environment where they may grow their own values and futures.[13]

He is harking back to the 1970s era and the culmination of the 1976 student uprising in Soweto, which gave expression to such an attitude. He fears that the current situation in South Africa is in danger of growing youth with no hope. Pityana worries that this has led to the youth being used by unscrupulous leaders for their ends and, in turn, has made the youth into suckers for patronage from these same politicians. The plunder of resources in both public and private spheres creates a sense of despair and the prospect of a dismal future. He observes:

> Third, control of public resources means that so many young people and students aspire not so much for education at the highest level they can achieve, but to become millionaires through tender-preneurship and not by innovation, entrepreneur, and opportunity. This then means that young people shadow their elders and work towards patronage that would be the only lifeline to change their condition.[14]

In this, he is contrasting the current generation of youth with his generation. This is the generation the world over, which was engaged in many demonstrations as a voice to the conscience of their nations. He says:

> The idea of Black Consciousness reflected a generation of students in our country wrestling with the fundamental questions of human existence. It was a search for answers, answers that each generation must needs ask of its leaders. In some sense, these were the questions that were never answered definitively because the questions kept arising each time the question was asked.[15]

He believes this search for answers is lacking in this generation of youth in South Africa.

Pityana is much concerned with the development of the youth in their own self-understanding, which would lead to engagement in society. He desires that they act not from other people's notions of personhood and humanity but from a basis of self-knowledge and ubuntu. Ubuntu is based on knowledge of one's culture and values while at the same time not negating the influence of others. This is where he leans on understanding allies as allies who know their place in the relationship. Self-determination can be thwarted when allies confuse their position with those they are aligned with and begin to see themselves as champions of the cause over and against those concerned. Sometimes this leads to the concerned people being emasculated and continuing a subservience mentality perpetuating their subjugation. As mentioned earlier, the famous mantra for the organization was 'Black man, you are on your own'.[16] This led to black students breaking away from the multi-racial student movement of his day. So, he is for activism and theologizing based on one's self-understanding – and pride of being – informed by one's culture. Thus, for Pityana, black consciousness, black power and black theology come together to inform the praxis of youth participation; for he speaks from a position of faith and philosophy.

Ecclesiology

In 'Culture and the Church: The Quest for a New Ecclesiology',[17] Pityana sets out the task of reimagining the Church in the wake of the end of the struggle against apartheid, during which the Church had a significant role. He says, 'All this activity points to two factors in our national and church life: an acknowledgement that there have been significant changes in the sociopolitical environment and a resultant need for the church to review its ecclesiology.'[18] In his estimation, the Church 'emerged bruised and battered' and the miracle is that it 'has emerged to tell the tale and learn some lessons'. His saw the churches ecumenically responding to the challenges of the day, and affirms continuing ecumenism. So he observes:

> Particularities of denominations were there and generated some loyalty, but I want to suggest it was no greater loyalty than of being together in struggle. We can continue to appreciate the level of common spirituality and devotion detected in the songs and dances and style of prayer and preaching which continues to sustain many communities even in changed circumstances. There is an ecumenical spirituality which is spontaneous and which is not the property of any one denomination. It has left the people a wonderful legacy of togetherness.[19]

He went on to speak of a further lesson, also a cause of rejoicing,

> that there are lay people who have learned leadership in the streets.
> They are assertive, articulate, and industrious. The language of political
> struggle has become the language of theology, workshops, networking,
> accountability, transparency and are some of the trademarks of this
> new Christian layperson. Ordained ministers have to deal with a differ-
> ent calibre of layperson from whom they have to learn.[20]

A third point he makes is that

> the church has had to cope with a more assertive cultural expression,
> especially in African congregational life. Church life has been predomi-
> nantly European in theological substance, liturgical practice, and church
> order. Popular culture has found expression in church life, even though
> insufficient recognition of this has been provided for. As a result the live-
> lier worship – songs sung spontaneously with dancing and *ex tempore*
> prayer – have been added to the formal and stuffy European worship
> of our traditions. Further, it is noticeable that many African people
> including devout Christians, practice African traditional customs and
> rituals without any sense of dichotomy or disregard for devotion. More
> and more African Christians have become both African and Christians
> without shame or a feeling of being torn apart.[21]

However, he then decries that the Church and its theology 'has taken no
account of this and our theology has not begun to deal with it'. In addition, he observes that even though women make up the majority, they
had not been allowed to take leadership positions and are discriminated
against. This, he noted, contrasts with the secular sphere where female
leadership is acknowledged and accepted.[22]

Then he suggests an ecclesiology faithful to these lessons, employing
the concept of 'consciousness' that has defined his epistemology from the
beginning of the black consciousness movement. He ends this discourse
with suggestions about how to use the concepts so derived as 'a tool for
unlocking' theological consciousness.

Throughout, Pityana's primary concern is that the Church, having
learned and engaged in a liberative and liberating praxis during the struggle, does not revert to the old ways of cosying up with denominationalism,
pietism and knee-jerk reactions to social woes from an uninformed position. The Church's engagement must now be determined by a desire for
neutrality rather than prophetic engagement, and must not reintroduce
restrictions on the clergy's engagement in politics. This itself could only
lead to the Church's loss of credibility with the populace.[23] He suggests,

'The ideal speech situation implies an ideal form of life which sits uneasily with the hermeneutic of suspicion.'[24] Invoking the Boff brothers' concepts of a liberating theology – in which they speak of theology needing 'to articulate the discourse of society, of the oppressed, of the world of popular, symbolic and sacramental signs with the discourse of faith and the normative action of the church' – Pityana holds that

> liberation theology shifted the paradigm of theological inquiry. It begins by taking a serious account of the context since this raises fundamental questions about faith not much different from Anselm's faith seeking understanding. The inspiration for doing theology, therefore, is not the book, a classic text or way of believing but 'from present realities and future possibilities' (Bevans, 1992, 64) On this understanding, theology is an *activity*. It is about *doing* and not the Cartesian cogito 'I think; therefore I am.' Praxis is reflected-upon action and acted-upon reflection. Praxis, then, is a model of contextualization in theology (Boff and Boff, 1987, 11ff).[25]

He claims that he is not suggesting anything new. The South African Church has 'never been short of theological ideas for transformation: black theology, contextual theology have been movements for change within the church throughout the years of intense struggle against apartheid'. And he compares this to the movement within the Roman Catholic Church when the election of new bishops was done in such a way that new appointees would move the Church away from liberation theology to ways of non-engagement. If the Church is to be a Church that is in touch with and serves the people, it simply must desist from such a trajectory.[26] And to prove his point, he refers to critiques by South African theologians Itumeleng Mosala and Simon Maimela.[27]

Pityana also suggests that humility is called for if the Church is to be this kind of church: 'The church would need to be a little humble: to recognize both the strengths and the weaknesses of the institution; to acknowledge its own failures in the past and to recognize its need to be part of wider society.'[28] In this, he holds that the Church cannot stand aloof and imagine itself as standing apart from society. It has to recognize that it is an integral part of society and that its membership stretches across all structures of society. As such, the Church is well-placed to serve the people and speak truth to power. He believes that should the Church renege on this stance and responsibility, it will have chosen to be irrelevant and become just a proverbial purveyor and dispenser of platitudinous prayers. He is critical of any such reneging, which he thinks would come hand in hand with people having 'no expectations of the church' because the Church could 'become invisible in their lives'. That is, they would think that their moral conduct was no business of the Church, and that the Church would be confined to what happens on Sundays, at those platitudinous prayers.[29] He also adds that a denominationalism has crept back into the Church after an era of active ecumenism during the struggle, and that the denominationalism was a danger to national unity and reconciliation. To make his point, he quotes another South African theologian, Malusi Mpumulwana, who sees the Church's potential in the humanization of society:

> the possibility exists of reconciling the evangelical priorities of the various sectors of the South African church around the common goal of ensuring that a society emerges based on social values and social practices that are in keeping with its implications. With the 'new South Africa' in mind, I want to call for the mutual discovery of our churches in the embrace of prophetic theology in a church praxis that both gives life and advocates for institutional structures that are lifegiving.[30]

Moving his focus from an activist Church to a Church in Africa, he points out that even though the Church came to Africa with missionaries and colonialists, it must become a genuinely African Church to become a Church of the people. In his own context, the Church in South Africa must

> learn from the history and theology of the African indigenous churches – something that could be the basis for an extended and truly African dimension of ecumenism ... A relevant contextual ecclesiology for South Africa can never be meaningful without seeing culture as the very source of the theological enterprise. Such a cultural expression of theology requires active participation by the proponents and practitioners of culture.[31]

In so suggesting he is alert to the dynamism of culture and so warns against a static view of culture. And even with that alertness, he is not oblivious to the globalized society of which the Church is part. Aiming at church culture influenced by Christian movements from the USA, he says:

> In fact, non-African forms of culture which we have imbibed have bequeathed to us other dimensions of conservatism. The Americanization of youth culture, for example, makes up what I would call the 'Dallas' and 'The Bold and the Beautiful' culture. This model of acculturation also finds expression in evangelism. Both result in superficiality, disengagement and conservatism. They constitute a serious threat to evangelism in our country.[32]

As is evident in this extract, his concern for young people is active in his ecclesiological views. These points recur in much of his commentary on South African society in his many speeches and lectures.

In his build-up towards his proposed ecclesiology, Pityana asks, 'Can a leopard change its spots? Yes, argue the liberation theologians and the critical social theorists.' On that basis, he presents his *tour de force*. As he imagines the Church, he is conscious that he is writing in the wake of the *Kairos Document*[33] with its critique of the Church in South Africa and he acknowledges that it has significance for a prophetic ecclesiology for South Africa and a helpful impetus for 'the leopard' to change its spots. He concludes by saying:

> In a new South Africa conscious of its place and role as part of the continent of Africa, the possibility of the church as a mutually support-ive and moral community is compelling. This community is one that is continually under construction, correcting and reforming itself. It is a moral community because it seeks to build on the moral resources that all humanity possesses for the good of all. It is mutually beneficial because it recognizes that 'an injury to one is an injury to all' – a slogan adopted by the labor movement in South Africa which resonates with Pauline theology. This is quintessentially *ubuntu* in African idiom, *koinonia* in New Testament language. The church is the community whose existence we already anticipate and which could be an example of human living. A relevant community for South Africa today should be one without walls, which looks out to the world. It has to be an inclusive community. The challenge for the church should be continu-ously experimenting and living these different expressions of commu-nity.[34]

Conclusion

Another South African theologian, introducing his book on missiology and proposing a new paradigm, said: 'Our missionary practice is not per-formed in unbroken continuity with the Biblical witness, it is an altogether ambivalent enterprise executed in the context of tension between divine providence and human confusion. The church's involvement in mission remains an act of faith without earthly guarantees.'[35] However, that faith has to be imagined and worked out in every generation. Each genera-tion must ensure that the next carries the mantle as it breathes new life into old forms. Johan Baptist Metz talked about the dangerous memory that remembers a future that is still outstanding – a *memoria passionis*

Christi. There is a Nguni saying, '*Inkunzi ise matholweni*' (literally, '*a bull is in the calves*') – as in the future leadership for, indeed, the future is in the potential of the youth. These, put together, give us a vignette into Nyameko Barney Pityana's teaching, social, political and human rights activism, and his theology. Self-knowledge leading to self-determination and action expressed in the black consciousness movement is based on taking our *ubuntu* seriously, and expressed in the beloved community established by Jesus Christ. A church *ngabantu* (is people), and as such it takes its humanity and its responsibility to society seriously while reflecting and engaging with the culture and religion of its context. It must confront its denominationalism (thus taking its ecumenicity seriously), its tendency towards Western hegemony, its apathy towards youth, its clerical bias, and its dismissal of women, and must recognize that it is a crucible for the formation of a moral society. Pityana's activism, always informed by his faith, expresses his theology. For him, God is the creator of 'the rainbow people of God', and so the Church is a beloved kaleidoscopic community.

Educator and educationist, lawyer, activist, priest, theologian: Nyameko Barney Pityana staddles all these characteristics as a servant of Christ and the Church.

Notes

1 https://www.unisa.ac.za/sites/corporate/default/Unisa-History-and-Memory-Project/Personalities/All-personalities/Barney-Pityana (accessed 29.1.2024).

2 For the sections that follow on black consciousness and youth, I glean from Pityana's 'Black Consciousness, Black Theology, Student Activism and the Shaping of the New South Africa', a lecture he gave as the Steve Biko Inaugural Lecture at the London School of Economics in 2012; the speech he delivered at the 3rd Annual Thabo Mbeki Africa Day Lecture at UNISA (also in 2012); 'Human Development and an Ethical Life: The Challenge of the Modern University' at the University of Mpumalanga, Mbombela, (2017); 'Redefining Understandings of Racism', a keynote address to the NIPILAR Annual Duma Nokwe Human Rights Awards Ceremony on the International Human Rights Day 1999, and his chapter, 'What is Black Consciousness?' in *Black Theology: The South African Voice*, ed. Basil Moore (London: Hurst and Co., 1973). For his ecclesiology, see 'Culture and the Church: The Quest for a New Ecclesiology', in *Being Church in South Africa Today*, eds Barney Pityana and Charles Villa-Vincencio (Johannesburg: South African Council of Churches, 1995).

3 Barney Pityana, 'Black Consciousness, Black Theology, Student Activism and the Shaping of the New South Africa', The Inaugural Steve Biko Lecture, London School of Economics and Political Science, London, 9 October 2012. For more on the movement and the times, see Steve Biko, *I Write What I Like* (Portsmouth, New Hampshire: Heinemann, 1987); Saleem Badat, *Black Man, You Are On Your Own* (Johannesburg: Real African Publishers, 2010) and *Black Student Politics:*

Higher Education and Apartheid from SASO to SANCO, 1968–1990 (Abingdon: Routledge, 2016).

4 Nyameko Pityana, 'What is Black Consciousness?', in *Black Theology: The South African Voice*, ed. Basil Moore (London: Hurst and Co., 1973), 60. (Notice that here he goes by his African name, Nyameko, which was a trend among the woke Africans of the so-called nationalist era; it was a claim of their personhood, humanity and ubuntu. One of the famous people who has done that is Ngũgĩ wa Thiong'o, who was originally called James Ngugi.

5 See Ngũgĩ wa Thiong'o, *Decolonising the Mind* (Portsmouth, New Hampshire: Heinemann, 1986) and *Something Torn and New* (New York: Basic Cavitas, 2009).

6 Pityana, 'What is Black Consciousness?', 61.

7 Pityana, 'Black Consciousness', 2–3.

8 Pityana, 'Black Consciousness', 3.

9 Pityana, 'Black Consciousness', 10–11.

10 Pityana, 'What is Black Consciousness?', 62. See also his Inaugural Steve Biko Memorial Lecture, 10–11.

11 Pityana, 'What is Black Consciousness?', 62.

12 Barney Pityana, Steve Biko Memorial Lecture at the London School of Economics, 2012, 24.

13 Pityana, 'Black Consciousness', 17.

14 Pityana, 'Black Consciousness', 18.

15 Pityana, 'Black Consciousness', 1.

16 See Badat, *Black Man, You Are On Your Own*.

17 Barney Pityana, 'Culture and the Church: The Quest for a new Ecclesiology', in *Being Church in South Africa Today*, South African Council of Churches, eds Barney Pityana and Charles Villa-Vincenio (Johannesburg: Council of Churches, 1995).

18 Pityana, 'Culture', 85.

19 Pityana, 'Culture', 90.

20 Pityana, 'Culture', 90.

21 Pityana, 'Culture', 90–1.

22 Pityana, 'Culture', 91.

23 Pityana, 'Culture', 91.

24 Pityana, 'Culture', 93.

25 Pityana, 'Culture', 92, citing Stephen Bevans, *Models of Contextual Theology* (Maryknoll, NY: Orbis Books, 1992) and Leonardo and Clodovis Boff, *Introducing Liberation Theology* (Maryknoll, NY: Orbis Books, 1992).

26 Pityana, 'Culture', 94.

27 Pityana, 'Culture', 94.

28 Pityana, 'Culture', 94.

29 Pityana, 'Culture', 95.

30 Pityana, 'Culture', 95.

31 Pityana, 'Culture', 97.

32 Pityana, 'Culture', 97–8.

33 *The Kairos Document* (Braamfontein: The Kairos Theologians, 1985).

34 Pityana, 'Culture', 98–9.

35 David J. Bosch, *Transforming Mission: Paradigm Shifts in Theology of Mission* (Maryknoll: Orbis Books, 1991), 9.

13

John Acland Ramadhani

PATRICK BENDERA, MAIMBO W. F. MNDOLWA AND FERGUS J. KING

John Acland Ramadhani was born on 1 August 1932, in the village of Gongoni on the island of Zanzibar; he was the last born of five children who survived to adulthood. He died on 12 September 2022, and was laid to rest in the small cemetery at Christ Church cathedral, Mkunazini, Zanzibar.

John's father Augustino Ramadhani was a teacher, and little is known of his background. His paternal grandmother was Naomi Mayakayeni from Mbweni, but there is little information about his grandfather. His mother was Margaret, the fourth child of Cecil Majaliwa and Lucy Mgombeani.[1] They were married by Frank Weston, later Bishop of Zanzibar, in 1904. Cecil was originally from the Yao people, a freed slave subsequently brought up in mission circles. As Jerome Moriyama has noted, missionaries of the Universities' Mission to Central Africa (UMCA) entertained hopes that Cecil might be the first indigenous bishop for the Church,[2] but this never transpired, for various reasons: personal, political and ecclesial. No matter what missionaries based in the country might have hoped, the apparatus of the Church would not countenance such 'preferments' until the second half of the twentieth century.[3]

This family background meant that John Ramadhani's upbringing and education were shaped in the strongly Anglo-Catholic environment of UMCA. Much of his early education took place in Anglican mission schools. From 1938 to 1942, he attended St Monica's School, Zanzibar, then, in 1943–9, St Paul's Kiungani, Zanzibar. For his secondary education, he went to the mainland, entering form 1 at St Andrew's College, Minaki, in 1950, where he would remain, completing form 4 in 1953. He then entered Grade I Teacher Training, Minaki, from 1954 to 1955, going on to Grade II at the college at Kiwanda. He taught Religious Education at Minaki (1958–9), before appointments at St Paul's, Zanzibar, and St Paul's, Kidaleko (1960–1). In 1962–3, he studied overseas at Moray House College of Education in Edinburgh, Scotland, earning a diploma in teaching English as a second language. On his return to Tanganyika, he was a student at the University of East Africa (1964–7), from which he graduated with a degree in Arts and a licence in teaching. Two teaching positions followed: Principal of St Andrew's Teacher Training College, Korogwe (1967–9), and then at the Institute of Education in Dar es Salaam (1969–73).

In 1973, Ramadhani's call to ministry resulted in a change of direction. He went to England for his theological education, undertaking degree studies at the Queen's College and the University of Birmingham, where he was awarded a Diploma in Theology. He was also able to pursue further studies before his return, and attended a consultation on African and Asian theology at Bossey, Switzerland, 8–14 June 1976, commenting: 'It has been a new way of theologizing of which I have not been aware during three years of theological studies in Britain.'[4] He was greatly encouraged in his vocation by John Sepeku, who had hopes that he might succeed him as Bishop of Dar es Salaam.

On 29 June 1975 Ramadhani was ordained to the diaconate in Birmingham by Bishop Lawrence Brown. Several former and current missionaries from the United Society for the Propagation of the Gospel (USPG – into which the UMCA had by then been incorporated) were able to attend. Returning to Tanzania in 1976, he joined the staff at St Mark's Theological College under Martin Mbwana, who had been his own former student. Again, this was the work of John Sepeku who hoped that the new deacon would quickly assimilate church government and be crucial in Dar es Salaam diocese becoming a senior see. Ramadhani was ordained priest at Christ Church Cathedral, Zanzibar, on 17 October 1976. When Martin Mbwana was appointed provincial secretary, Ramadhani took up an appointment as principal of St Mark's, working alongside Mathiya Mbulinyingi and Charles Mwaigoga. During this period, he also served as a Prison Chaplain at Ukonga.

On the retirement of Yohana Jumaa as Bishop of Zanzibar and Tanga, Ramadhani was elected as successor, and was consecrated on 27 January 1980, the feast of St John Chrysostom. This frustrated John Sepeku's plans. Charles Mwaigoga's election to South-West Tanganyika prompted Sepeku to recall Ramadhani to St Mark's for a second stint as principal, much to the consternation of the Zanzibar and Tanga's diocesan standing committee, who dreaded his loss. However, after the arrival of Michael Westall as principal at St Mark's in 1984, Ramadhani returned to Zanzibar and Tanga and served there until 2000. When the diocese was split in November that year into the two dioceses of Tanga and Zanzibar, Ramadhani served briefly as Bishop of Zanzibar until the consecration of Douglas Toto in 2002. In addition to diocesan duties, he served as Archbishop of Tanzania from 1984 until 1998. This marked a precedent that has yet to be equalled: tenure as archbishop is normally restricted to a maximum of two five-year terms. But his fellow bishops simply felt unable to identify a successor who could match his abilities.[5] Ramadhani was also an active office bearer within the Christian Council of Tanzania, including a term as chairperson.[6] In his sermon at John Ramadhani's requiem at Christ Church Cathedral, on 17 September 2022, the emeritus Archbishop Donald Mtetemela commented that this work revealed a man devoted to the Church of Christ, not denominations.[7]

After retirement, Ramadhani lived on Zanzibar at the cathedral close, and was often consulted by, and gave advice to, the House of Bishops. His mentoring has been particularly appreciated by his successors both in Zanzibar and Tanga.

A Tanzanian Anglican

The account of John Ramadhani's life indicates that his formative years were spent on Zanzibar, and his secondary and tertiary education in Tanganyika. Both territories were under British jurisdiction at this time. Zanzibar had been a British protectorate since 1890, and briefly became an independent constitutional monarchy in 1963. This was short-lived: the revolution of January 1964 saw the sultan deposed and the institution of a republic. In April 1964, this would merge with the newly independent mainland Tanganyika to form the United Republic of Tanzania. Tanganyika had been a part of German East Africa since the partitions enforced on Africa at the Berlin Conference (1885),[8] ceded to the British under mandate by the League of Nations after World War One in 1922, and latterly a United Nations Trust Territory under British control after World War Two, gaining independence in December 1961.

An early piece of evidence from his time predominantly as a student and educator shows Ramadhani's commitment to the fledgling Tanzania. In 1966, a play written by one John Ramadhani entitled *Mgomo wa Mazinde* (Strike at Mazinde) was 'commissioned by the federation of trade unions from mainland Tanzania to be performed in 1966 at the celebrations to commemorate the foundation of the ruling party Tanganyika African National Union (TANU)'.[9] German scholars had sketchy information about the writer: a name, born in 1932,[10] a student at the University of Dar es Salaam, and later employed by the ministry of education,[11] but no further details. While it would seem likely that Ramadhani was the author, he would later confirm this in an email.[12]

Unfortunately, no printed Kiswahili form seems to have been preserved, but a German translation exists.[13] The historical basis of the play was a strike on the sisal estate at Mazinde which started on 25 November 1958, and lasted for 68 days.[14] It tells how a group of workers on a British-owned farm strike for – and win – their rights after joining a trades union. While theatre critics describe the play as 'characterized by "a striking representation of social-political fronts and developments, and flat character-types" reminiscent of agitprop theatre in Europe and Northern America ...',[15] it is possible that a particularly Anglican heritage may also have influenced this writing. Frank Weston, Bishop of Zanzibar (1907–24), much underrated as a theologian in his own right,[16] gained a certain notoriety for both his opposition to higher criticism and his role in the Kikuyu controversy.[17] Yet there was a radical edge to Weston's version of the gospel and its application to critiques of society: he lambasted racist tendencies stemming from the simplistic adoption of post-Enlightenment values within liberal theology.[18] He also provided a robust critique of German colonial practice.[19] No more enamoured of the British rule that followed, he penned a follow-up[20] which made a significant contribution to the successful campaign for reforms of colonial economics.[21] While it may not be possible to prove a direct connection between the tradition of Weston and the writing of Ramadhani, it certainly remains plausible that ideas promulgated by as deeply a formative influence as Weston may well have continued to circulate.

However, from a relatively early age, John Ramadhani was aware of the diversity of the Anglican tradition across Zanzibar and Tanganyika. Early exposure to this occurred in a visit to one of his elder brothers:

My first encounter with the Church in CMS area was in June 1951, as a secondary school student at St Andrews's College, Minaki. My brother who happened to teach at Mpwapwa Secondary School, asked me during my holidays to carry a typewriter to him from Dar es Salaam. I worshipped at Mpwapwa Parish Church for two Sundays. We had Matins conducted by Pastor Yohana Omari, a very lively preacher and committed man. He shocked me in his address when he said it was not enough to be baptized and confirmed. One had to be sure whether Christ has saved him/her. That idea gave me a big jolt for many years, till I came across a book *This is Conversion* by Joost de Blank, later. The book said simply that conversion in the New Testament is a lifelong process – past, present and future. It is an ongoing process.

I am aware of similar shocks which students from CMS areas had when they came to Minaki Secondary School for their School Certificate education. They encountered practices and beliefs in our worship and tradition which made them restless. These were pains of growing together as a Church.[22]

His subsequent experiences as a student at Queen's in Birmingham, then one of the few ecumenical institutions for Anglican formation in the UK, further exposed him to the diversity of Anglicanism.[23] He remained committed to that UMCA tradition, even if sometimes uncomfortable with decisions made elsewhere over the ordination of women and human sexuality, and has never entertained notions of schism. However, as his remarks make clear, he has long been well aware of the deep investment that people may have in their faith tradition, and of the difficulties in moving and negotiating between them.

Church and State

Points of resonance between the emergence of Tanzania as a nation and the path taken by the Anglican Church during the same period suggest strong parallels in the ideologies that would come to be known as *Ujamaa* (African Socialism)[24] and ecclesiology. Maimbo Mndolwa has noted that in several respects the Anglican Church of Tanzania (ACT) mirrored the political and ideological tenor of TANU.[25]

The production of *Mgomo wa Mazinde* suggests that John Ramadhani was a supporter of TANU and, presumably, the enlightened views that Julius Nyerere incorporated into that movement: that it would be open to Tanganyikans from every ethnicity and background. If Nyerere aimed to build a nation out of the 130 ethnicities found within Tanzania, the Anglican Church similarly sought to be a Church for the nation, and this programme was pursued by all the archbishops from John Sepeku onwards. For his part, Ramadhani was a key player in a number of these endeavours, notably liturgy and theological education.

The development of a national liturgy was one means by which a Tanzanian identity was pursued. The mission pre-history of Anglicanism in Zanzibar and Tanganyika had seen two different ecclesial traditions merge: the high-church or Anglo-Catholic UMCA (Coast – *Pwani*), and the more evangelical CMS (Inland – *Bara*).[26] The latter would be shaped by the work of three mission agencies with a shared trajectory: the CMS-UK, its Australian counterpart (CMS-Australia), and the Bible Churchmen's Missionary Society (BCMS – later Crosslinks). The two traditions shared neither a common liturgy nor style of worship. This appeared highly unsatisfactory:

The use of three distinct liturgies within a single province was somewhat of a scandal, and worked against the witness of the Anglican church in a country that espoused the philosophy of Julius Nyerere – *ujamaa ni watu*, 'Community is humanity'. Dioceses from both missionary traditions saw the need for one liturgy, and efforts to unite them resulted in the *Common Liturgy of Tanzania*.[27]

Its development in Kiswahili, which served as both the national and official language, also mirrored Nyerere's use of Kiswahili to foster a national identity.[28] The final version of the new national Kiswahili Prayer Book would be published in 1995, in Ramadhani's time in office as archbishop.[29] Donald Mtetemela described this prayer book as one of the most significant elements of his legacy.[30]

Theological education also revealed inherited divisions as the UMCA/ *Pwani* tradition sent candidates for ministry to train at St Mark's in Dar es Salaam, while their counterparts from CMS/*Bara* mainly went to St Philip's, Kongwa. In the 1990s, integration was attempted in two ways. Firstly, a common curriculum was approved: the first of these was introduced in 1986, and a second, which was less Eurocentric, in 1997.[31] Again, Mtetemela identified this as significant, commenting that Ramadhani's focus on rigorous formation for ministry was intended to spare the Church suffering at the hands of clergy and leaders who might behave like wolves.[32]

More contentious was the attempt to merge the two colleges which was proposed in 1994. Both struggled financially and found difficulties in recruiting staff. The problem was exacerbated by the proliferation of diocesan Bible colleges which meant that qualified clergy were increasingly retained by these institutions. The initial recommendation from the House of Bishops was to close St Mark's. But, not surprisingly, given his long association with St Mark's, Ramadhani recognized that this was an intensely painful decision. The decision was quickly reversed, and no closure was made. This turn of events caused Ramadhani to note that 'there were players who were in the open but there are others who were not in the open ... There are big brothers who are not in the House of Bishops but make decisions on our behalf.'[33] This might imply that there were powerbrokers within the Church who influenced the decisions made, but also possibly from outside. While USPG, Crosslinks and CMS-UK left the decision in the hands of the Tanzanian leadership, it seems that 'CMS-Australia was ready to interfere much more in decisions made in Tanzania. Perhaps they felt they could tell the Tanzanians what was right and wrong. They were not ready for any sort of amalgamation ...'[34] Such actions by expatriates and outsiders did not, however, lead Ramadhani ever to consider anything approaching a moratorium on mission. Equally, he did not think that mission partnerships should be mercenary affairs. In an interview recorded in the *Bulletin of Tanzanian Affairs*, Andrew Ashton noted:

> When I asked Archbishop John Ramadhani if missionaries were still needed in Tanzania he replied that they will always be needed because Christians need to be constantly reminded that they are worldwide church and, as partners, have much to learn from one another.[35]

He also encouraged mission agencies to work with the ACT, though not all agreed. A bilateral consultation held with USPG in 1995, in which he played a key role, consolidated the principle that the agency should entertain support across the whole ACT, not just the dioceses that had formerly belonged to the UMCA tradition. Such a strategy did not receive endorsement from all the other agencies.

Ramadhani's views also resonated with those of Nyerere, who rejected isolationism,[36] but equally recognized the dangers of becoming subject to foreign interest.[37] His sympathy with Nyerere's cosmopolitan outlook may be seen particularly in the ecumenical and international appointments to St Mark's which he supported during and after Michael Westall's time as principal when he was a governor of the college. The presence of staff and students from traditionally CMS/*Bara* dioceses also bridged the UMCA/CMS divide.[38] A further resonance is seen in the stress placed on development for women when Ramadhani was the bishop. Joyce Luhui Ngoda gave the following account of development within the diocese of Zanzibar and Tanga:

> The Diocese under the leadership of the Most Revd John Ramadhani has recently committed itself to the development of 'the whole person', consequently a development unit has been set up and 40% of the development committee members are women. The church is also aware of the unjust practices in the community and within the church structures that in the last synod which was held last year two laws were passed to improve women's status. Widows have the right to own the property which belonged to the couple during their married life and that women representation in the church committees/councils should be consciously increased.[39]

This allies, too, with Nyerere whose 'cosmopolitan thinking also appears in his writings criticizing women's inequality in "traditional" African society and his effort to involve women in Tanzanian political life',[40] basing *Ujamaa* on an understanding of equality that eschewed uniform-ity.[41]

A further hallmark of Nyerere's nation-building was the condem-nation of *ukabila* (ethnic rivalry or conflict)[42] which he denounced as 'very stupid and very evil'.[43] The election of John Changae as Bishop of Victoria-Nyanza (DVN) in 1991 was controversial and mired in this issue. *Ukabila* was evident in the claims brought by the majority Sukuma people that they were being discriminated against, and seen as a prime motivating factor in the complaints against the bishop,[44] although his style (and, in particular, his Anglo-Catholicism which meant he didn't abstain from alcohol) was also cited.[45] Ramadhani would also be accused of *ukabila* for not cancelling the election, on the grounds that both he and Changae came from the same region: Tanga.[46]

Attempts to re-elect failed, and legal complications added to the problem.[47] Nor did Changae's behaviour after both his election and consecration help matters.[48] Eventually, sections of the diocese would secede from jurisdiction under Changae, and the Mwanza deanery ended up under alternative episcopal oversight. In 1993, Ramadhani accepted Changae's resignation, but this was immediately retracted.[49] An episcopal tribunal was held in 1994, but no verdict was brought by the House of Bishops, who left Ramadhani isolated with the advice to do as he thought fit.[50] Without their support, his hands were tied. Changae would survive a vote of confidence held by DVN in 1996.[51] Ramadhani would write to him that year: 'The discussion which took place in Dodoma during the tribunal had to do with the whole question of your episcopacy. I was not on your side. To date my views have not changed. Our differences notwithstanding, you are not my enemy.'[52] Later, in 1997, he would sug-gest that Changae might consider an appointment as assistant bishop within the diocese of Tanga, but this was refused.[53] Amid the rancour, Ramadhani modelled pastoral behaviour, attempting to find a resolution to an intractable situation when the avenues of law and church govern-ment had closed.

Uamsho

The East African Revival (EAR) had its origins in the 1930s, spreading from Rwanda and South-West Uganda around Lake Victoria into Kenya, the Congo and Tanganyika.[54] Many of those influenced by it remained members of oldline churches, and adopted the discipline that the move-ment enjoined. It must be admitted that it had a limited, if any, influence on the UMCA style of Christianity. A residue of that has been described already, in the denunciations of John Changae by members of the DVN because he was believed to drink alcohol. However, the influence of revival (*uamsho*) within the UMCA diocese was greatly increased by the ministry of Edmund John. The brother of John Sepeku, Edmund, who worked for Radio Tanzania in Dar es Salaam, had a vision in July 1967, left his job, and returned to his home area of Tanga where he commenced a healing ministry. He returned to Dar es Salaam in 1969, starting an itinerant ministry from which the parish of St John the Baptist, Minyonyoni, was established. Edmund himself preached, visited and prayed for the sick. This work evolved into the movement known as *Huduma ya Nyumba kwa Nyumba* (*HNN* – House to House Ministry) which continues until the present, now under the leadership of Cyprian Salu. *HNN* members are encouraged to remain within their own denominations, repent of all sin, trust Jesus, pray, abstain from alcohol, tobacco and witchcraft, and fast on Fridays.[55]

While *HNN* has sometimes been treated with suspicion by those associated with the UMCA tradition, Ramadhani welcomed both Edmund John and Cyprian Salu to missions and to speak within the diocese of Zanzibar and Tanga. In part this is because *HNN* offers a return to the discipline of the old UMCA tradition which has sometimes been neglected and replaced with liturgical formalism.

Conclusion

John Ramadhani's upbringing on Zanzibar occurred in an environment strongly shaped by the UMCA mission. The details of his ancestry show that there was no specific alignment with an ethnic identity beyond the description of Cecil Majaliwa as a member of the Yao people, separated from his roots by slavery. This lack of an ethnic component of identity is likely to have placed more emphasis on his identity as a descendant of slaves, and as an Anglican. James Tengatenga thus noted after meeting him in 2016: 'In a very interesting and paradoxical way Bishop Ramadhani reminds one of the celibate and saintly UMCA clergy of the missionary era.'[56] Michael Westall, who knew John from his time at St Mark's College and later as Bishop of South-West Tanganyika, similarly noted a profound spiritual depth:

> One of my memories is when he was in the College for a meeting in 1991. The new chapel had recently been consecrated. I happened to enter the chapel when I thought it was empty. However, the archbishop was there, sitting in what I can best describe as a restful attentiveness.

In 2018 my wife and I spent just one night in Zanzibar. By now Bishop Ramadhani was 86 years old. And yet he was in the Cathedral at 6.00am for Morning Prayer and the Eucharist. It is the primacy of prayer and worship in his life which leads to the courtesy, the simplicity of life and the other qualities which I have mentioned.[57]

This is reiterated by Donald Mtetemela who noted that it was the priority which Ramadhani gave to liturgy and his spiritual devotions, so often neglected by others in the face of busyness, which shaped his character.[58]

A memoir from Jean Howe, a USPG missionary who worked alongside Ramadhani for many years, further indicates his qualities:

> One Sunday, I had the great privilege of travelling with him to a certain village for a confirmation. He was given presents: a goat, chickens, bananas and more. On the journey back he frequently stopped the car to give those presents to people he saw were in need. When he returned home, he had a single hand of bananas left. He gave half of them to his driver.[59]

At his funeral, numerous speakers, including Mtetemela,[60] commented on the way in which John Ramadhani would himself provide them with courtesies usually provided by domestic staff: he embodied a servant leadership in even the smallest matters. His incarnational theology and spirituality, shaped and crafted by values from the UMCA tradition in which he was raised, the disciplined self-reliance and care for the other which was recognized in *Ujamaa*, and a lifelong concern for education, so manifestly clear to those who have had the privilege of working and praying with him, are his enduring legacy for the Anglican Church of Tanzania.

Notes

1 This account differs from the oft-repeated claim that Supreme Justice Augustino Ramadhani (1945–2020) was his brother (e.g. 'Augustino Ramadhani'), https://en.wikipedia.org/wiki/Augustino_Ramadhani (accessed 20.9.2024). This first-person account should be preferred.

2 Jerome T. Moriyama, 'Building a Home-Grown Church', in *Three Centuries of Mission: The United Society for the Propagation of the Gospel 1701–2000*, ed. Dan O'Connor (London: Continuum, 2000), 330–42 (338).

3 Maimbo W. Mndolwa and Fergus J. King, 'In Two Minds? African Experience and Preferment in UMCA and the Journey to Independence in Tanganyika', *Mission Studies*, 33 (2016): 327–51 (331–6).

4 John A. Ramadhani, 'Comments', in *African and Asian Contributions to Contemporary Theology: Report of Consultation held at the World Council of Churches Ecumenical Institute Bossey, 8–14 June 1976*, ed. John S. Mbiti (Céligny: Ecumenical Institute, 1977), 140.

5 'LIVE : IBADA PAMOJA NA MAZISHI YA ALIYEKUWA ASKOFU MKUU ANGLIKANA JOHN AUCKLAND RAMADHANI 17/09/2022', Joy Gospel TV. Online at https://www.youtube.com/watch?v=g-2zqodXkZw (accessed 29.1.2024). Donald Mtetemela's sermon includes an anecdote about the election held in 1998 to find Archbishop John's successor. Mtetemela went to John to withdraw his name from the list of candidates. The response was simple, yet profound: 'Donald – why don't you leave the Holy Spirit to take your name out?' Mtetemela was elected.

6 *The Europa World Year Book Volume II: Kazakhstan-Zimbabwe*, ed. Joanne Mahar (London: Europa, 45th edn 2004), 4108.

7 'LIVE: IBADA'.

8 Colin Reed, *Walking in the Light: Reflections on the East African Revival and its Links to Australia* (Melbourne: Acorn Press, 2009), 9.

9 Uta Reuster-Jahn, 'New Responses to Old Problems: How the German Translator-Publisher is Making Swahili Literature Available in a Notoriously Difficult Market', *Swahili Forum*, 25 (2018): 138–57 (142), citing the work of Joachim Fiebach (ed.), *Stücke Afrikas* (Berlin: Henschelverlag Kunst und Gesellschaft, 1974), 326.

10 Archives et Musée de la Littérature, 'John Ramadhani', http://aml-cfwb.be/catalogues/general/auteurs/134750 (accessed 29.1.2024).

11 Reuster-Jahn, 'New Responses', 142, fn. 9.

12 Personal email to Fergus King, 13.10.2021: 'I remember my attempt to write a play in Swahili in the past, with a title of Mgomo wa Mazinde'.

13 John A. Ramadhani, 'Streik in Masinde', in *Stücke Afrikas*, ed. and trans. Joachim Fiebach (Berlin: Henschelverlag Kunst und Gesellschaft, 1974), 325–46. The author himself had kept no copy.

14 Opoku Agyeman, *The Failure of Grassroots Pan-Africanism: The Case of the All-African Trade Union Federation* (Lanham: Lexington Books, 2003), 93.

15 Reuster-Jahn, 'New Responses', 142.

16 Donald M. MacKinnon, *Borderlands of Theology and Other Essays* (London: Lutterworth, 1968), 112.

17 Mndolwa and King, 'In Two Minds?', 336–8.

18 Mndolwa and King, 'In Two Minds?', 338–9.

19 Frank Weston, *The Black Slaves of Prussia: An Open Letter Addressed to General Smuts* (Boston: Houghton Mifflin, 1918).

20 Frank Weston, *The Serfs of Great Britain: Being a Sequel to 'The Black Slaves of Prussia'* (London: Universities' Mission to Central Africa, 1920).

21 James Tengatenga, *The UMCA in Malawi: A History of the Anglican Church 1861–2010* (Zomba: Kachere, 2010), 227.

22 John A. Ramadhani, 'Foreword', in *Nuru na Uzima: Essays Celebrating the Golden Jubilee of the Anglican Church of Tanzania, 1970–2020*, eds Fergus J. King, Emmanuel Mbennah, Mecka Ogunde and Dorothy Prentice (North Augusta: Missional University Press, 2021), vii–viii.

23 'John Ramadhani: Hadithi ya Maisha Yangu', ed. Patrick Bendera (unpublished manuscript), 40.

24 Particularly associated with the Arusha Declaration; see *The Arusha Declar-*

ation and TANU's Policy on Socialism and Self-Reliance (Dar es Salaam: TANU, 1967).

25 For a detailed study, see William Fabian Mndolwa, 'From Anglicanism to African Socialism: The Anglican Church and Ujamaa in Tanzania 1955–2005' (unpublished thesis, University of KwaZulu-Natal, 2012).

26 For an overview, see Colin Reed, '"God Made It Grow": The Origins of the Anglican Church of Tanzania in the Modern Missionary Period', in *Nuru na Uzima*, 13–29.

27 Esther Mombo, 'Anglican Liturgies in Eastern Africa', in *The Oxford Guide to the Book of Common Prayer: A Worldwide Survey*, eds Charles Hefling and Cynthia Shattuck (Oxford: Oxford University Press, 2006), 277–86 (280).

28 Karsten Legere, 'Marehemu Julius Kambarage Nyerere and Kiswahili', *Kioo cha Lugha*, 5.1 (2007), https://www.ajol.info/index.php/kcl/article/view/61489 (accessed 21.9.2021).

29 Mombo, 'Anglican Liturgies in Eastern Africa', 280. Only Eucharist was prepared in an English version.

30 'LIVE : IBADA'.

31 Mndolwa and King, 'In Two Minds?', 345.

32 'LIVE: IBADA'.

33 Mkunga H. P. Mtingele, *Leadership and Conflict in African Churches: The Anglican Experience* (Frankfurt: Lang, 2017), 71.

34 Mtingele, *Leadership and Conflict*, 71.

35 Britain-Tanzania Society, *Bulletin of Tanzanian Affairs*, 44 (1993): 21.

36 Bonny Ibhawoh and J. I. Dibua, 'Deconstructing Ujamaa: The Legacy of Julius Nyerere in the Quest for Social and Economic Development in Africa', *African Journal of Political Science*, 8.1 (2003): 59–83 (64).

37 Ajay Kumar Dubey, 'India-Africa Relations: Historical Goodwill and a Vision for the Future', in *India and Africa's Partnership: A Vision for the Future*, eds Ajay Kumar Debey and Aparajita Biswas (New Delhi: Springer, 2016), 11–40 (26).

38 Michael R. Westall, 'St Mark's College, Dar es Salaam, and the Anglican Church of Tanzania', *Nuru na Uzima*, 109–16 (114–15).

39 Joyce Luhui Ngoda, 'Go to Your People ...', in *All Africa Council of Churches: Church Women's Consultation on Economic Justice 1990, Kitwe*, ed. Michele Rokotoarimanana (Nairobi: All Africa Council of Churches, 1990), 34. Note that in several societies widows could be dispossessed by their late husband's family.

40 David T. Suell, 'Review – Development as Rebellion: A Biography of Julius Nyerere', *Contemporary Political Theory* (2021). https://doi.org/10.1057/s41296-021-00468-y (accessed 29.1.2024).

41 Innocent Simon Sanga and Ron Pagnucco, 'Julius Nyerere's Understanding of African Socialism, Human Rights and Equality', *The Journal of Social Encounters*, 4.2 (2020): 15–33 (24).

42 The Kiswahili *ukabila* is used in preference over the more common English 'tribalism', in light of Ngũgĩ wa Thiong'o's comment: 'It is fair to say "tribe", "tribalism", and "tribal wars", the terms often used to describe conflict in Africa, were colonial inventions. Most African languages do not have the equivalent of the English word tribe, with its pejorative connotations that sprung up in the evolution of the anthropological language of the eighteenth- and nineteenth-century European adventurism in Africa. The words have companionship with other colonial

conceptions, such as "primitive", the "Dark Continent", "backward races" and "warrior communities"', in Ngũgĩ wa Thiong'o, *Secure the Base: Making Africa Visible in the Globe* (New York: Seagull Press, 2016), 9.

43 Godfrey Mwakikagele, *Nyerere and Africa: End of an Era* (Dar es Salaam: New Africa Press, 2010), 22.

44 Mtingele, *Leadership and Conflict*, 84.

45 Mtingele, *Leadership and Conflict*, 80; Mndolwa, *From Anglicanism to African Socialism*, 244.

46 Mtingele, *Leadership and Conflict*, 79–80.

47 Mtingele, *Leadership and* Conflict, 80–4.

48 Mtingele, *Leadership and Conflict*, 81, 84–5.

49 Mtingele, *Leadership and Conflict*, 86.

50 Mtingele, *Leadership and Conflict*, 87.

51 Mtingele, *Leadership and Conflict*, 88.

52 Mtingele, *Leadership and Conflict*, 199.

53 Mndolwa, *From Anglicanism to African Socialism*, 244.

54 Colin Reed, *Walking the Light: Reflections on the East African Revival and its Links to Australia* (Brunswick East: Acorn Press, 2007), 7, 11.

55 Fergus J. King, 'Edmund John', in *Dictionary of African Christian Biography*, https://dacb.org/stories/tanzania/edmund-john/ (accessed 29.1.2024). For a full account, see Joseph Namata, *Edmund John, Man of God: A Healing Ministry* (Canberra: Acorn, 1996); *Edmund John, Mtu wa Mungu* (Dodoma: Central Tanganyika Press, 1980).

56 James Tengatenga, 'Slavery, Monuments, Memory and Reconciliation: My Pilgrimage to Mkunazini', in *Nuru na Uzima*, 143–60 (152).

57 Michael R. Westall, 'Bishop John Ramadhani', 2. Unpublished reflection sent to Fergus J. King, September 2020.

58 'LIVE: IBADA'.

59 Bendera, *John Ramadhani*, 3. Translated from the Kiswahili.

60 'LIVE: IBADA'.

14

Harry Sawyerr

HERMAN BROWNE

Harry Alphonso Ebun Sawyerr (9 October 1909–August 1986) was a Sierra Leonean pioneer African theologian.[1] He studied initially at Fourah Bay College, later moving to England to study at Durham University. He successively earned BA (1933), MA (1936) and Master of Education (1940) degrees, and became principal of Fourah Bay College (1962–74) and Vice-Chancellor of the University of Sierra Leone (1970–2).

Sawyerr was mentored by Thomas Sylvester Johnson, the first assistant Anglican Bishop of Sierra Leone, and was considerably influenced by the works of J. B. Danquah, especially his *Akan Doctrine of God* (1944).[2] As the son of missionaries sent to the Mende heartland, Harry grew up in traditional Africa and never lost his love or fascination for the Mende language and traditions. His father, the Revd Obrien A. D. Sawyerr, served as missionary and pastor at Boma Sakrim. But, as a Krio of Sierra Leone, Sawyerr's perspective included a long history of Christian identity and missionary activity. His Mende culture, into which he was socialized from infancy, became the *praeparatio evangelica* for incarnational African theology, emphasizing the uniqueness of Christ. He combined a strong Christological emphasis with his experience of a traditional African point of view – as he was one of few Krios fluent in Mende, and was uniquely positioned to see the strengths of a truly indigenized African Christian theology as well as possible solutions to problems that may arise.[3]

As a youth, Harry attended the Prince of Wales Secondary School in Freetown. There Bishop T. S. Johnson discovered him as a bright young man suited for training to teach. When Johnson began to teach at Fourah Bay College, he took Harry with him. Johnson instilled in Harry Sawyerr his vision for a comprehensive education, which included science, theology, economics and Greek. As John Pobee has noted,

> He considered science or economics alone insufficient for Sierra Leone to take its rightful place in the world. Ignorance of European intellectual streams would be more detrimental to African intellectual development

than would be the idea that some such forms of study were irrelevant to Africa.[4]

Sawyerr would later insist on Greek, classical theology and biblical studies for his students. Having immersed himself in biblical languages, the church fathers and an Anglo-Catholic tradition in Durham, his return to Fourah Bay saw a few things change for the better. He continued with Johnson's vision of the necessity of incorporating theology within the university, and not relegating it only to the study of religious practices. Andrew Walls makes clear that Sawyerr held this view with passion:

> That part of Africa's liberation lay in taking hold of the whole *corpus* of learning and in developing the faculties of scholarship and research. For him, there were no areas of study or learning that could be treated as inappropriate to Africa. He was not particularly afraid of the implicit colonialism that might arise from the form and content of Western learning. His [actual] fear was the colonialism that arose from ignorance, under resourcing, and the patronizing judgment that certain expressions of intellectual activity desirable for the West were unnecessary for Africa.[5]

So, no longer under the jurisdiction of the Church as a result of financial crises and subsequent reconstitution, Fourah Bay took its place in the University of Sierra Leone. The theology department developed an ecumenical ministerial programme, a licentiate in theology, continuing education for clergy during periods of vacation, and there were various publications. Sawyerr principally studied and taught New Testament, becoming a conspicuous figure at gatherings of the international (but at that time almost entirely Western) society of New Testament scholars, the Studiorum Novi Testamenti Societas. He was awarded an honorary Doctorate of Divinity by Durham University in 1970, marking a lifetime of service to theology and higher education.[6]

Context

There were several momentous trends and movements on the rise in the 1950s through to the 1970s that form the milieu in which Harry Sawyerr worked. The world saw the struggles for independent Africa as individual countries fought for political independence. The general opinion of this period was that much had not yet happened to decolonize the mind, 'emancipate from mental slavery', or articulate a rage or distaste for the (racist) Western cultural ideology that had entrenched colonialization.

Those educated abroad were clearly determined that African religious systems – and their reflections on them – were not to crumble under the burden of Western neglect or be repressed by racist disdain.

It should be remembered that great efforts in Sawyerr's era had been made to accentuate discontinuity and incongruity between African beliefs and practices and Christian beliefs and practices.[7] More charitable arguments ran along the lines of T. Cullen Young's:

> Rites and ceremonies are just fruits of belief ... and what African thought illustrates in its rites and ceremonial is a theory or a principle, or a policy of clanmanship and association: a gradation of initiation into a social system based on comradeship, and in adult life, a series of group functions illustrative of that system ... Radically and inescapably, as we now see, Christian belief differs from [African] at the very heart. [Christian religion] founds upon God in a personal relationship, and all else is incidental or consequent. Bantu belief on the other hand, founds upon indestructible human relationships, and at no central or vital point is any idea to which we could truthfully apply the title 'God' anything more than incidental.[8]

During this period, what we now know as 'African theology', 'African Christian theology' or 'African liberation theology' or 'black theology in Africa' had not yet been articulated in any significant way. Basic questions of whether God was at work in African religious systems and practices, or among African peoples, and indeed whether Africans were themselves able to identify any continuity between their God and 'Yahweh', were still unsettled questions when Sawyerr began. With the data gathering and analyses of ethnographers and anthropologists,[9] the stage (at least in academic circles) was set for interpreting the empirically descriptive phenomena in a theologically useful and insightful way. The work of theologians in both demonstrating the value of African religious practice to the advance of the Christian faith, as well as establishing their biblical warrant and authenticity from the Christian scriptures, began in earnest. Bursting on to the scene with wit, rigour and a passion to resist the *denigrating of authentic African spirituality*, major works emerged from the likes of John Mbiti (1969), Bolaji Idowu (1965), Kwesi Dickson (1965) and Harry Sawyerr (1968).[10] It was not until later that anything like the liberation strand[11] of African theology would emerge, and Sawyerr, along with these others, operated in a period dominated by this need to self-assert, affirm and position the theology that underlies African religious practice as a *legitimate* source of Christian theological reflection and interpretation.

Sawyer asserted the *legitimacy* of employing concepts native to the continent, and raised the *credibility* of African religious practice. He argued that Africa is no less authentic a source of theological reflection than the concepts employed in the Judaeo-Roman religion called Christianity by the spiritual descendants of the Hebrews. Following this logic, African religious practice, as a 'religious' phenomenon, is rightly studied at the level of the university. But for Sawyerr, this was not enough. For central concepts intrinsic to these religions should also rightly become a prism through which theological study in Africa is pursued. While it was easier for Sawyerr's insistence to relapse neatly into a religious studies department of a university, he saw the proper value of African traditional religions to lie in the scope, depth and evangelistic potential of their theological insights. As he wrote, 'The answer lies in the rigorous pursuit of systematic theology based on a philosophical appraisal of the thought-forms of the African peoples.'[12] So Sawyerr pioneered exploration of a number of central concepts that emerged from the cultural-religious world of his Mende people – and he consistently correlated these with other ethnographic studies from Western, Central, East and Southern Africa. Chief among these were the concepts of sacrifice, ancestor, elder brother, real presence and omnipotence.

Themes

In what follows, rather than reproducing Harry Sawyerr's argument, I identify insights from indigenous religion that he believed would appeal to Africans and also be entirely consistent with the Christian gospel. For him, the task of the theologian was to draw out the full implication of these insights for Christian living on the continent. So, two cultural-religious practices are used to illustrate Sawyerr's sense of that task: sacrifices, and the world of the ancestors.

Sacrifice

The ritualized offering of sacrifice is a frequent and familiar practice in the Old Testament, modelled, perfected and eventually abrogated by the one perfect act of Christ's self-rendering to God, as the New Testament would have it. In West Africa, sacrifice continues to be offered for the preservation of health, for the appeasement of vengeful spirits, to celebrate deities or for veneration of ancestral spirits; in times of peril, joy or uncertainty.

Ultimately, the intended result of a sacrifice is either to win favour or forestall disapproval. Analytically, sacrifices then limit and control antipathetic forces and, in intent, can be classified as acts of incorporation (conjunctive) or repulsion (disjunctive). *Conjunctive* sacrifices strengthen and intensify relations with community dwellers or ancestors or protective forces.[13] *Disjunctive* sacrifices keep at bay anger or spiteful caprices of spirits, community dwellers or ancestors. These expiatory and purificatory sacrifices 'sweep dirt', keep evil away. The overall benefit of sacrifice is to call on the protective forces of one's ancestors to secure one's flourishing in such a way that forestalls and prevents what frustrates or undermines one's success.[14]

The dynamic operating here is the giving up of something of oneself to God and expecting something from God as a consequence. The giving and receiving dynamic is lodged in the religious practice and is helpful as a pattern of relationship, and thereby helpful in speaking of communion with God. Additionally, most conjunctive sacrifices involving blood establish a covenant between a suppliant and the gods. In Sawyerr's words:

> Since blood is a gift ... is a vehicle of life offered to another, it not only revives the life of the recipients, but it also gives a new life to the donors. The reciprocal gift to the offeror is accordingly of the highest order. He receives greater power than in the case of vegetable and other inanimate objects.[15]

The mutual consumption of blood establishes the strongest covenant and is the highest form of power transfer. One is incorporated into a covenant by participating in the consumption. Sawyerr's point is that in taking more seriously the African religious practice of sacrifice, the gospel message of deep communion and blood covenant with God would be better communicated and more readily believed and adopted by Africans because of the religio-cultural resonance of its validity.[16]

The world of the ancestors

The world of the ancestors is our world, and the world in which we live is inhabited by seen and unseen forces and powers all around.[17] In Sawyerr's parlance, we apprehend these powers as an inexplicable 'presence', or a 'medley of presences'. Whether in nature or in the immensity of the firmament, the healing powers of herbs or the awesome dead, we are surrounded by a kind of presence or presences that have boundless power beyond ourselves. Those who are able to harness such presence for good (herbalists) or bad (wizards) are also all around us, as are talismans they possess, totems they identify, and charms they wear.

So, apprehension of presence is 'something', but it refers to the 'hereness' of the thing more than a specific awareness of what that thing is. The world of the spirits is created to explain or interpret these external influences affecting human persons for good or ill:

> The reality of life is thus conceived as an encounter between man and other spirit-influences which are generally different from and in some cases resistant to man. So there develops a concept of power as an aspect of presence ... residing in some object or [another] man other than [oneself].[18]

For Sawyerr, God in West Africa is seen as the supreme Presence, the omnipotence from which all else derives its power and potential to make itself felt. The gospel is not preached nor the Christian life lived in neutral space, but space that may be spiritually debilitating and exacting. Sawyerr depicted how densely populated our environment is with unseen presences – a reality that may at various times infuse one with a sense of dread and anxiety, or confidence and hope. It is in this African context that the power of Christ's sacrifice must be preached to Africans, in order to demonstrate Christ's enabling grace.

Hence, Africans were never without an awareness of God. The God whom the Hebrews would recognize as their God had been working with and through Africans before Christianity arrived by sea.

Incarnation

Three comments are worth making here. The first is that the value of the belief that God became human, for Harry Sawyerr, lies in the fact that that Christ did not just come *to* us. Rather, Christ is *with* us, and because he *becomes* us, he is therefore one *of* us. And in some ways, it is to be expected that Jesus' humanity would be the most valuable asset of the incarnate God:

> In the African situation the Incarnation should be so presented as to emphasize that Jesus Christ was the manifestation of God's love for man, God's share in human sufferings, God's victory over death and all disastrous influences which throng man's everyday experiences ... born as I was, grew up as I did ... suffered death because of his unflinching loyalty to God. But God raised him from the dead, because he was that man in

whom God lived and acted (and still does act) human-wise. In this way, we could affirm our Lord's affinity to man as a basis of presenting the church as 'the Great Family' of which Jesus Christ is the head.[19]

The second comment is that Sawyerr views the incarnation as God's self-offering akin to a priestly act of self-consecration. In fact, it is this view that dominates his Christology.[20] It is not the sorrowful death of Christ to which African Christians should look. Instead, the focus should be the painful birth of Christ who chose to lay down his life and dedicate it to us *for* God. 'For their sake, I now consecrate myself that they too may be consecrated by the truth' (John 17.19). Christ is elder Brother and head of the family and does what he does for the good of the family, selflessly and in a way that no one else can, because no one else is, nor can ever become, the 'first fruit'.

The third comment relates to the entire course of Sawyerr's work. While Sawyerr took it for granted that the gospel is about a particular and specific individual in the person of Jesus of Nazareth, the gospel *message* – that is, the point about telling the good news about Jesus – if it is to be believed, must be subject to the kind of reconfiguration that only context can determine. The theology that the Church had developed to express the gospel at all times and everywhere needs to be localized, particularized and made amenable to the 'thought forms' of the African people. In other words, just as the Word became incarnate, so too should the word about the Word.

Sawyerr's Relevance

Harry Sawyerr's legacy is threefold. Firstly, he demonstrated in his writings and teaching that local African 'tribal' religions deserve to be considered among other 'world religions'. Much of his work was in identifying the axiological and continental nature of the central concepts inherent in the religio-cultural practices he described. He therefore successfully *dislodged* the Hebrew experience from a place of monopoly as the experience or prism through which God can be understood. Sawyerr acknowledged the normative place of the Hebrew experience in theology, but he also held that one does not have to live through the culture of the Hebrews to be able to interpret well the meaning, value or significance of the incarnation. Sawyerr freed up our theological language from being captive to Western concepts used to interpret the Christian revelation. The gospel message could also be expressed using legitimate religio-cultural insights to great effect on the African continent.[21]

In indigenizing and enculturating theology in this way, Sawyerr was radical in his theological method. In a major endeavour of the colonial enterprise (the spread of Christianity), he succeeded in erecting a checkpoint, in service to the enterprise! His theology was not so much anti-Western as it was simply African. He attempted to elevate the latter to the status of the former.

Secondly, Sawyerr *popularized* the value of thinking theologically as readily in non-Western (specifically, African) concepts as in Western ones. He employed the (philosophical and theological) insights of central axioms in African religious practices to understand and better explain – or articulate more appropriately – Christian faith. He did this by showing how no less legitimate and adequate African cultural values are when compared to semitic or Western values, and how they possess significantly within themselves the seed of the gospel values Christianity preaches. Sawyerr's attempts at indigenizing theological reflection by using African concepts to interpret the gospel won him great praise. For him, this too was a matter of identity. He was African, and resisted the dominant ideology that placed 'African' peoples, values, cultures and religion outside the fray of intellectual reflection. He brought it back and lifted it high, consistently highlighting its value and significance to the theological enterprise.[22]

Thirdly, Sawyerr resisted the thought of leaving these insights solely in the hands of those who study religions as phenomena. He laboured instead to see these African insights holding sway over how theology was done on the continent, how the theological craft might be plied, or practised, by Africans. To centralize African religious practices and intrinsic insights and concepts is to make the theologian self-aware of acquiring a *perspective* hitherto unacknowledged, unarticulated and unprofessed. But with the employment of different (from Western) analytical tools, the theologian begins to discern differing truths in the same Christian revelation, and comes thereby to a fuller appreciation of the Christian revelation as it really is. The maturing of differing perspectives,[23] differing truths, in theological reflection is an enduring legacy of Henry Sawyerr.

So we see that, in Sawyerr's company, Christian revelation gives licence to holding multiple perspectives on gospel truth. When in the New Testament we see four differing accounts of the one life of Jesus Christ, we are already provided with differing perspectives of the one true event. The inclusion of four accounts ('according to' Mark, Matthew, Luke and John), as in the mythical four corners of the universe, speaks of the universality as well as the diversity of the gospel.

It is for no less than these reasons that Sawyerr is regarded as the father of the theological inculturation or indigenization in West Africa.

He fought to achieve in the religious sphere what his compatriots had achieved in the political sphere, a kind of freedom and space that allowed one's collective identity to be affirmed, and to flourish.

Notes

1 Sawyerr was loved and respected for his 'quick mind and gentle loving spirit'. Friends considered Edith, whom he married in 1935, 'an equal and amiable wife' who together with Harry 'radiated happiness among a wide circle of friends'. He died in Freetown, Sierra Leone in August of 1986 at the age of 76. See Michael Ramsey, 'An Appreciation', in *New Testament Christianity for Africa and the World: Essays in Honour of Harry Sawyerr*, eds M. E. Glasswell and E. W. Fasholé-Luke (London: SPCK, 1974), 1.

2 Sawyerr admits as much, and confesses reading Danquah's work more than 20 times in three years. See Andrew F. Walls, 'The Significance of Harry Sawyerr', in *The Cross-Cultural Process in Christian History* (Maryknoll: Orbis Books, 2002), 165–73.

3 Mark E. Glasswell and E. W. Fasholé-Luke, 'Introduction', in *New Testament Christianity for Africa and the World*, 3–7.

4 John S. Pobee, 'Sawyerr, Harry Alphonso Ebun', in *Religion, Past and Present*, http://dx.doi.org/10.1163/1877-5888-rpp_SIM_025233 (accessed 19.5.2022).

5 Walls, 'The Significance of Harry Sawyerr', 16.

6 Sawyerr promoted academic excellence for Africans. He insisted on the necessity of education in his young country in order for Africa to take its proper place in the world at large. He was president of Milton Margai Teacher Training College (1960–9), a member of the Public Service Commission of Sierra Leone (1968–9), chair of Sierra Leone Board of Education (1969–74), and awarded the Grand Commander, Order of the Star of Africa (Liberia) in 1971. He was also a member of the Commission on Faith and Order of the World Council of Churches (1962–75), and after retirement continued to serve the Church and left Sierra Leone only for Codrington College, Barbados.

7 So much so, that Sawyerr began to respond directly to these aspersions in his writings. See his 'Do Africans Believe in God?', *Sierra Leone Studies* (1961): 148–67; 'Science and Superstition', *Sierra Leone Science Association Bulletin*, 1.2 (1963): 17–26; 'Traditional Sacrificial Rituals and Christian Worship', *Sierra Leone Bulletin of Religion*, 2.1 (1960): 18–27; 'Sacrifice', in *Biblical Revelation and Traditional Beliefs*, eds Kwesi A. Dickson and Paul Ellingworth (London: Lutterworth Press, 1969), 57–82.

8 See T. Cullen Young, 'How Far Can African Ceremonial Be Incorporated in the Christian System?', *Africa*, 8.2 (1935): 210–17. This was a paper originally delivered at the International Congress of Anthropological and Ethnological Sciences, in London 1934.

9 On the African continent, much seminal work had already been done by *non-African* cultural anthropologists.

10 These were the West African theological pioneers of the 1960s identifying the theological (ideological) similarities between traditional religions and Christianity, establishing their fundamental value to doing theology in Africa as well as

evangelizing on the continent. The generation that succeeded them, while building on this, would often take a different trajectory. While retaining the importance of evangelism, they would tend to speak more of ministry in the African context, which required a greater attention to the lived realities of injustice and liberation. And while they have moved the debate on from Sawyerr's day, critical questions remain as to whether African religions have been subjected to the kind of analytical rigour that Sawyerr hoped to see. See Herman Browne, *Theological Anthropology: A Dialectic Study of the African and Liberation Traditions* (London: Avon Books, 1996), 187.

11 Each strand of African, 'indigenized' and 'liberation' theology needs the other in order to define critically and adequately its problems, aims and approaches. What Stephen Munga hopes we will remember is that 'the unity of African theology cannot be engineered by any emotional zeal to end the opposition'. See Stephen Munga, 'Abstract', in *Beyond the Controversy: A Study of African Theologies of Inculturation and Liberation* (Lund: Lund University Press, 1998).

12 Harry Sawyerr, 'What Is African Theology?', in *A Reader in African Christian Theology*, ed. John Parratt (London: SPCK, 1987), 22.

13 This is what Sawyerr calls 'integrative offerings, chiefly by blood'. See his 'Sacrifice', 69.

14 The logic of sacrifice in both its associative and dis-associative dimensions is discussed more lengthily elsewhere. See Browne, *Theological Anthropology*, 47–9.

15 Sawyerr, 'Sacrifice', 77.

16 One of Sawyerr's pupils makes an interesting observation about sacrifice, somewhat overlooked by Sawyerr, that finds no counterpart in the Old Testament. While the 'African rites seem to have a forward-looking reference in so far as they are designed to influence the course of events in the future (secure benefits in the future), those that are mentioned in the OT seem to be retrospective in their main inspiration ... They all seem to have reference to an immediate past that is either being acknowledged in thanksgiving or in repentance'. See P. E. S. Thompson, 'The Anatomy of Sacrifice', in *New Testament Christianity for Africa and the World*, 20.

17 John Baillie, *The Sense of the Presence of God* (London: Lutterworth Press, 1962), 33: 'Reality is what I come up against, what takes me by surprise, the other than myself that pulls me up and obliges me to reckon with it and adjust myself to it, because it will not consent simply to adjust itself to me.'

18 See 'The Practice of Presence', in *The Practice of Presence: Shorter Writings of Harry Sawyerr*, ed. John Parratt (Grand Rapids: Eerdmans, 1996), 5.

19 See Harry Sawyerr, 'Jesus Christ – Universal Brother', in *African Christian Spirituality*, ed. Aylward Shorter (New York: Orbis Books, 1980), 65.

20 See 'Soteriology Viewed from the African Situation', in Parratt, *The Practice of Presence: Shorter Writings of Harry Sawyerr*, 124.

21 This dislodging constitutes a freedom from an ideological domination. It is not just people that need liberation, but the ideology (itself) that oppresses them. This point is made incisively by Juan L. Segundo in *The Liberation of Theology* (Maryknoll: Orbis Books, 1976) and more illustratively by R. H. S. Boyd, *India and the Latin Captivity of the Church: The cultural Context of the Gospel* (Cambridge: Cambridge University Press, 1974).

22 See Acts 17 in which Paul's message to the Athenians is not to deny the value of worshipping their God, but to reveal to them more of the character of that God.

23 With the emergence of liberation theology in Latin America and black

theology in North America, Sawyerr was soon proven right in his insistence all along on differing perspectives. Beginning with James H. Cone, *A Black Theology of Liberation* (1970) and Gustavo Guttiérrez, *A Theology of Liberation*, first published in Peru 1971, it is now common wisdom in theological reflection to be conscious of plural perspectives emerging from differing situatedness.

15

Jenny Te Paa-Daniel

ESTHER MOMBO

When I think of Jenny Te Paa-Daniel, a song from my mother's community comes to mind. This song is entitled '*omwana we imbere*' (the first-born). The song is in praise for the first-born child and the joys and the challenges that come with the first-born. I would sing the song for Jenny because to me she is a first on all fronts. A Māori woman from Aotearoa New Zealand, she is a trailblazer, a leader, a mentor – a visionary theologian for the Anglican Communion. In her contribution to the book *Vulnerability and Resilience: Body and Liberating Theologies*, Jenny Te Paa observes that

> as self-respecting twenty-first century postcolonial Christians and theological educators we ought to be capable of articulating with Gospel confidence our understanding of how all elaborations of knowledge including theological knowledge always reflect dominant power interests ... we ought also to have been the first to adopt scholarly practices committed to equitable and mutually beneficial forms of collaboration with subaltern individuals and communities. How else would the long-standing Eurocentric hegemonies so deeply entrenched in theological curricula, pedagogy, assessment and accrediting ever be disrupted, exposed, and transformed?[1]

These words encapsulate the ministry Jenny has had in theological education. In this chapter I discuss her role in theological education as it is exhibited in her ministry, and the gift she offers both to the Church at large and the Anglican Communion in particular. Rooted in her tradition she was the first indigenous woman to be recognized and mandated to take on leadership in the field of theological education in the Anglican family of churches. This is a field that over the years she creatively transformed by naming the structural systems that were not affirming either to individuals or to their churches. She has constantly interrogated all the forces and factors perpetuating inequalities, and at all levels. So be they race, gender or tribe, Jenny has had something to say. She has offered a critique of how the voices of women, and of indigenous people, have been stifled by those who purport to speak on their behalf, but actually may mute them from speaking for themselves. Jenny's commitment to creating space for all to access theological education and be empowered to serve has been an exemplary way of mentorship. She has opened doors for women and also for many young people to drink from the wells of their traditions, understanding how to navigate the systems and gain a place. And as well as opening doors for those who were excluded, Jenny has provided mentorship in different ways, so creating spaces for others to access more rooms in the institutional Church and other places.

Yet as a dean in a college of an Anglican church that was born out of colonialism, Jenny would contend that the end of colonialism and the ushering in of independence, in varied ways, did not change the status of so many marginalized groups in her society, especially in religious spaces.

As the First Woman in Theological Leadership Among Her People

Jenny's exemplary leadership imbues the qualities of listening, collaborating and co-creating, breaking rules and working for justice for all. I first met her in a theological consultation of women deans and leaders in theological education at a conference in June 2001. The meeting was organized by the World Council of Churches (WCC) programme Ecumenical Theological Education (ETE) and organized by Dr Nyambura Njoroge, a Kenyan who was herself the first woman ordained by the Presbyterian Church of East Africa as well as the first ordained woman in Africa to earn a PhD in theology and ethics. Nyambura Njoroge brought together a consultation of 50 women deans and presidents of theological seminaries and colleges that relate to World Council of Churches member churches and we gathered at the Bossey Ecumenical Institute, in Celigny, Switzerland. The title of the conference was 'Transforming Theological Education: Women and Leadership'. Areas of focus at the conference included the relationship between churches and theological institutions, ecumenical learning at the institutions, and the financial stability in our institutions. But the key focus was on forms of leadership and the mentoring of younger women.

As chair of Ecumenical Theological Education (ETE) at the time, Jenny led the consultation for two days and then returned to New Zealand to attend to other urgent matters. The consultation affirmed much of the leadership work the women were doing in theological education while also being a forum for networking across the globe.

From this consultation, we began a journey in theological education leadership and mentorship. Through Jenny's work women from the majority world were guided to opportunities to study theology at the highest levels. It happened through monetary and mentorship roles that had been led publicly and remotely by Jenny. Among those who were assisted in this way are my Kenyan compatriots the Revd Dorcas Ndoro and the Revd Irene Ayallo.

Between 1999 and 2006 Jenny's name was held as precious in circles of the WCC and its work on theological education. Being both creative and steady, she chaired the working group on theological education. Through her wise leadership, grounded in listening, she heard spoken voices and was alert to the unspoken. Through that ETE platform she journeyed with those on the margins by offering to share her platform so that others were able to name their needs and identify intervention and actions most suitable to their own circumstances. It is Jenny's active and intentional care in listening that has helped many to access theological education.

Jenny's Tradition

Jenny was born into a *whanau* (family) steeped in the faith and cultural traditions of her tribal people. The life in a small rural village pivoted around twin organizing pillars of the *Marae* traditional meeting house where all the major life and death events and ceremonies pertaining to the people of the village were conducted and the Church. As a Māori woman, she is surrounded by a circle of people with whom she is deeply connected and who have provided her with the strength and courage to be. Her indigeneity is rooted in a strong family tradition of aunts and uncles, elders on whom she drew her strength for her ministry in theological education. Jenny's elders have supported her growth academically and in her ministry in the church.

The First to Graduate

Jenny was the first Māori to obtain an academic degree in Theology from the University of Auckland; this was in 1992. She proceeded to enrol for a MA in Education in the same university; she completed that in 1995. After a few years Jenny chose to proceed to enrol for a PhD and did so this time not in Aotearoa New Zealand, but at the Graduate Theological Union in Berkeley, California, emerging with her PhD in 2001. Jenny's thesis was on race politics and theological education, and its insights have pervaded the rest of her work. Theological education became her 'trade-mark' as it were, and is an area to which she has so deeply committed herself. Jenny was the first out of a missionary and colonial context to study at such depth the colonial roots of race, of politics, and of clerical-ism. Growing up in a missionary and colonial context, Jenny had her own life experience of these issues and was alert to them from very early on.

The First Dean

After her BA in Theological Studies Jenny was given a teaching job and soon in 1995 she was appointed the first Ahorangi (or dean) of Te Rau Kahikatea, a newly created indigenous leadership position that was intended to reflect equality of status and responsibility alongside a non-indigenous dean at St John's College, Auckland. The Te Rau Kahikatea was the first of a kind in the Anglican Communion. As a Māori lay-woman, Jenny was appointed into a pioneering leadership role. She was noticed by her elders who found in her someone able to shape a college true to the needs of the First People and whose theology also served the needs of the ministry students and local churches. Jenny's vision for the college and its theological education was rooted in her belief about the purpose of theology, and with her guidance the Te Rau Kahikatea was transformed into a distinctive place for training.

The vision for the college was threefold. Firstly, it was to be a place of hospitality and cultural safety for Māori students. Secondly, it was to be a place to generate Māori theological scholarship. Thirdly, it was to be a place where critical issues affecting life chances and opportunities for Māori could be opened up to theological scrutiny. The elders who had noticed Jenny as one with leadership qualities to oversee the college and to be their 'face' within the institution affirmed Jenny's vision, and they wanted to ensure that she was part and parcel of this place of theological education as it was being newly imagined.

As dean, Jenny wanted the college to become a place of radically theo-logically expansive teaching and learning committed to raising up, and now constantly retraining, men and women who are first and foremost truly exemplary Christ-like servant leaders. She saw her role as one of encouraging and enabling the development of Christ-like disciples, willing and competent to be witnesses in the world to the teachings and example of Jesus. Because the college itself was still home to students from the various Tikanga of the Church of Aotearoa New Zealand and Polynesia, not just Māori, Jenny figured it was important to develop a new theo-logical educational paradigm characterized by inclusivity, mutuality and cultural enrichment. In her service Jenny was aware of the extraordinary privilege and the demanding professional role that she was undertaking, and she was well aware of the challenges of staffing.[2] She worked hard to bring about an authentically inclusive environment that would work towards qualified Māori theologians.

In an article on being Anglican in the twenty-first century, Jenny narrates the development of her church from the perspectives of the Māori people. It is full of struggle with colonial leadership and authority. But three things clearly helped the indigenous people to claim a space in the church they 'loved and served'. This included their knowledge of what was going on in different parts of the world, in places also influenced by the Church Missionary Society (CMS). For example, in Africa, Adjai Crowther had been consecrated as the first 'Negro' Anglican bishop in 1864.

As well as their knowledge of developments in other parts of the world, the Māori were aware about their siblings in political and economic spheres in leadership in their own land.[3] It was time for such leadership in the church. And so in 1981 Whakahuihui Vercoe was consecrated as the first Māori Bishop of Aotearoa. Also in 1981, Te Pihopa Aotearoa (the Māori Tikanga) met for the first time at Houmaitawhiti *Marae* in Rotorua.[4]

Jenny's narrative of the story of her church is important in many ways but two are especially worth mentioning. Firstly, Jenny juxtaposes two great historical moments of decolonization. Then, as is her style, a story is an interrogation as much as it is a narrative. Jenny makes plain the pain and struggle of the people as they seek their own identity and come to own a multiple identity. For them, owning their identity and accepting other identities is about belonging to the wider Church in communion.

The politics of identity are imbued in Jenny's life and study. While acknowledging the struggles of the people to participate fully in the Anglican Church, Jenny is always keen to show the agency of the elders not only to prove that they can take on leadership, but also to show that they have the numbers in the Church. This dual emphasis is often a feature of Jenny's writing and also characteristic of how she approaches her own role in leadership to co-create and collaborate with others in the Anglican Communion in the shared search for a transformative Anglicanism. To do this, she has collaborated with many people but has always been especially willing to work alongside those who, as a result of colonial and decolonial dynamics, are marginalized. In serving different commissions of the Anglican Communion, the call to hear both the dominant and marginal voices is important. Jenny has brought ways to know the agency of the marginalized as articulated in their words and voices.

Theological Paradigm and Influence

In her younger years Jenny pursued a series of professional careers in social work, social policy, development, and education. These laid a foundation for her later theological education and have shaped the perspectives she brought to it. Jenny's background in these various fields has influenced the way she sees Jesus, just as her lived reality as Māori does. She came to see that the Jesus she was taught about in church did not tally well with what she understood of Jesus as a radical activist who stood against injustice, who advocated for the least in society, and who insisted on unconditional inclusion for all in God's creation. What she understood Jesus to stand for became her theological mantra in her own studies, in her teaching, and in her personal practice of faith. Hence, the motifs of justice and liberation are deeply embedded in her theological enquiry. They shape how she sees identity and they determine how she contests tribalism. For insight, take her 'advice' as she

> urge[s] each one of you to continue to gain deep and comprehensive understanding of the root causes of the ... two phenomena of race and of religious hatred, for it is indeed their underlying politics of humanly constructed difference, framed as 'identity', which is at the heart of virtually every major global conflict in our world today.[5]

Tribalism has arms in all spaces including our ecclesial family. It is rooted in histories of colonialism that were based on faulty constructs of race. In theological education tribalism is also expressed in exclusion and discrimination relating to gender and sexual violence.

So theological education is important for several reasons. Firstly, to empower those on the margins so that they have more resources to resist systems and structures of oppression and violence. Secondly, to affirm the full humanity of all members of the human community. Thirdly, to create a space for women's voices to be heard amid male-dominated organizations like churches. It may also encourage a broader dialogue among the different groups in the Church. In discussing tribalism within the Church, Jenny calls for change.

Dialogue on Decolonization

Jenny notes that decolonization is being applied in various disciplines, although little attention had been paid to it in Anglican theological academies and seminaries. She contends that unless

Anglicans first hold up a mirror, and commit to examining the ways in which the colonial shackles of imperialism, elitism, racism and sexism, continue to inform and influence our ways of being Anglican in the world we will both knowingly and unwittingly continue to act to exclude, we will both knowingly and unwittingly continue to falter in our pastoral reach and certainly we will both knowingly and unwittingly continue to delimit the effectiveness, indeed the integrity of our witness in the world.[6]

Jenny further calls for a 're-examination of the irrefutable participation in aiding both intentionally and unwittingly, the imperialist practice of mission driven by the unholy alliances between the Cross and the Crown'. Thus, Jenny notes that 'Anglican Studies sits within a predominantly Eurocentric Anglican theological educational framework which is a behemoth system outdated, outmoded and unjust'. It is therefore important that a decolonizing process should begin from an acknowledgement of the power of empire that continues to have much influence in the context of the Anglican Communion. This may require asking questions about '*decolonizing from what and why*' before there is a possibility of 'the healing balm that is desperately needed'.

Jenny proposes a *transcendent imagination* that can inculcate a critical determination to refuse to see history as simply an experience but as something that continues to impact societies today. There is also need for '*transcendent praxis*' oriented towards the transformation of those societies. For any of this to occur what is needed is education that begins from a commitment to liberation. Other problems to be considered include 'declericalizing and demystifying and contextualization of theological education'. One result of decolonization is to do with undermining existing hierarchies of institutionally legitimated expertise. Jenny knew this well in her own work as dean of a theological institution.

Radical Inclusion

The undermining of hierarchies is a theme that links to another emphasis in Jenny's work, that on radical inclusion.

Multiple forms of colonialism, especially European colonialism, have created a virulent context for contemporary racism and tribalism, including in the Church. In its first iteration, European colonialism left its mark in the former colonies and, in the aftermath of historical decolonization, domestic forms of discrimination have solidified against minority groups in African, Asian and Latin American contexts. Such racism and tribalism are not only subtly concealed in everyday life but also overt systemic race- and tribal-based violence.

Radical inclusion can only happen through confronting social power imbalances and turning towards God's goodness. This allows people to claim a moral authority to lead change rather than following the local powers that be. Scripture and theology ought not to be used as weapons to reinforce social hierarchies of any kind. At the heart of Jesus' message is the proclamation of the reversal of hierarchies he encountered, in his announcement that the last will be first (Matthew 20.16). In confronting the persistence of exclusion and discrimination in our ecclesial spaces, underlying asymmetries of power that allow such marginalization to continue must be challenged. Crucial to this is a recognition of the full humanity of all people including women, persons of colour, LGBTIQIA+ persons, those living with disabilities, and other marginalized groups.

For radical inclusion to be realized there is a need to constantly revisit the patriarchy that is embedded in our theologies, texts and ecclesial traditions. Nyambura Njoroge has described patriarchy as a destructive powerhouse, with systematic and normative inequalities as its hallmark. It needs to be brought to its knees.[7] Instead of the prevailing patriarchy that thrives in dichotomizing people, partnerships and symmetries need to appear. Dichotomization is a mechanism that accompanies objectification. By splitting phenomena into conflicting parts, it facilitates the pursuit of 'power over' – which justifies abuse of all sorts. 'Power over' is a hierarchical system that is dysfunctional but continues to be supported. Patriarchy is a source of all sorts of violence including theological abuse and violence carried within Christian sources and doctrines. But less so when Jenny Te Paa-Daniel has been at work.

The Bible portrays the means of salvation as free from sacred violence through the prophetic and Gospel narratives. Among the prophets, violence against all is roundly condemned as in opposition to the divine plan – 'violence shall no more be heard in your land, devastation or destruction within your borders; you shall call your walls Salvation, and your gates, praise' (Isaiah 60.18). 'Act with justice and righteousness and deliver from the hand of the oppressor anyone who has been robbed. And do no wrong or violence to the alien, the orphan, and the widow, or shed innocent blood in this place' (Jeremiah 22.3). The New Testament also makes a clear pronouncement against violence – from the days of John the Baptist until now the kingdom of heaven has suffered violence, and the violent take it by force (Matthew 11.12). 'The Spirit of the Lord is upon me, because he has anointed me to bring good news to the poor. He has sent me to proclaim release to the captives and recovery of sight to the blind, to let the oppressed go free, to proclaim the year of the Lord's favour' (Luke 4.18–19). This is the manifesto that has guided those who chose to opt for radical inclusion and a liberation motif. Throughout the scriptures, we learn and acknowledge that salvation is liberation:

> Liberation theologies take an analysis of their concrete socio-political situation as their starting point. Their analysis seeks to uncover oppression, exploitation, alienation, and discrimination. The interpretation of experience as an experience of oppression is common to all liberation theologies.[8]

Liberation is an integral theological task for gender inclusion. Liberation takes on board experience, especially of those who are on the margins. Inclusion of gender should be able to expose the abuse of scripture evident in our theologies shown by scholars like Musa Dube and other postcolonial theorists. With a liberation theological approach we can interrogate the ways in which scriptures have been used to exclude, stigmatize and ostracize those that have been othered in society.

Radical inclusion calls for a redefinition of power to move from power over to power with, which continues to be of concern in our society today. To effect radical inclusion in this case, we need to view dismantling patriarchy as a matter of our own salvation. This is more than using the politically correct language that has been used this far. We have got to create new stories that become part of an urgent Christian message of an ethical life after patriarchy. God did not create us as victims and victimizers; God created us in God's own image.

Theological Education

Theological education in many paradigms is made from the crucible of colonial and missionary orientation, rather than the pots of African lived realities. Theological education is within the four traditional strands of systematic theology: biblical theology, history of Christianity, pastoral/practical, and mission theologies. The intersectionality of these different strands is still an alien concept in Africa even with the emergence of the discipline of 'World Christianity'. Further, theological education still perpetuates different forms of exclusion of women, and other gender and sexual minority groups. Theological education that is expected to be an empowering space appears not to be. Decolonization of Anglican studies can be compared to the need to move away from what is captured in the epigram of Frantz Fanon, 'black skin, white face', even after many years of postcolonization.

Theological education seeks to assist the people of God to, firstly, discern what God is saying and doing through the life of all God's peoples, in community and as individuals; secondly, to relate what we discover of God's self-disclosure in Jesus Christ as witnessed in scripture, sacred tradition and the ministries of the Church; thirdly, to do so in the confidence that God continues to lead us into the fullness of truth through the guidance of the Holy Spirit in a changing world whose cultural and social diversities evidence both the surpassing richness of God's grace and the immediacy of God's judgement of our failures of faithfulness. But for several years now within the Anglican fraternity there have been issues around theological education as it has been a place of contestation as a result of the subject of sexuality. Some visible features of these 'discourses and acts' include the public defence of the authority of scripture, historic orthodoxy (i.e. the faith once delivered to the saints), the faithful marginalized on account of their 'orthodoxy'.[9] Orthodoxy that has been a contention should not be pegged on sexuality alone but should be inclusive of all the issues that have been used to deny the humanity of others.

The divisions in theological education and interpretation lead to an exclusive theological education. But theological education is not for an exclusive club, but it is for the people of God. Thus the engagement of Jenny in the development of Theological Education in Anglican Communion (TEAC) to provide curricula for all. Other aspects of theological education for all have been in the process of engendering theological education, looking at issues of the philosophy and theoretical framework of the curriculum. This also looks at the methods of delivery and the nature of the student's environment. The process of engendering theological gives room for 'demystifying' theology and moving it away from being studied for ordination. In promoting inclusive and life-affirming theological education the life and work of Jenny is to partner with God, by participating in contesting all forms of discrimination, domination, and going against the rules that justify domination and muting of other voices. The aim of theological education in empowering the Church is to listen to the voices of victims of multiple forms of violence, to legitimize the victims' lived experiences theologically, and to uncover redemptive meanings from the Bible.

Conclusion

This chapter highlights one of the many facets of the work, both in print and in person, of Jenny Te Paa-Daniel, as a first in Anglican theological education. It celebrates her insight into and practice of justice and liberation. Jenny has shown us the importance of theological education and its importance in empowering the people of God in the Anglican Communion.

Notes

1 Jenny Te Paa-Daniel, 'Esse Quam Videri … *to Be and Not to Seem*', in *Vulnerability and Resilience. Body and Liberating Theologies*, ed. Jione Havea (Lanham: Lexington Books, 2020), 199–212 (200).

2 In 1995 there were no Māori with postgraduate qualifications in Theology. At the time of writing (2023) the known Māori (Anglican) graduates with higher degrees in theology are as follows: one PhD, one DMin, two MTh. All graduates have been either faculty or students of Te Rau Kahikatea.

3 Jenny Te Paa-Daniel, 'Indigenous Peoples: A Case Study on Being a Twenty-first Century Maori Anglican', in *The Oxford Handbook of Anglican Studies*, eds Mark Chapman, Sathinathan Clarke and Martyn Percy (Oxford: Oxford University Press, 2015), 326–40.

4 See Te Paa-Daniel, 'Indigenous'.

5 This quote is from Jenny Te Paa's Commencement Speech at Church Divinity School of the Pacific in Berkeley, California, on 23 May 2014.

6 This quotation is from an unpublished paper Jenny Te Paa gave at the Anglican seminar of the American Academy of Religion.

7 Nyambura Njoroge, 'The Missing Voice of African Women Doing Theology', *Journal of Theology for Southern Africa*, 99 (November 1997): 81.

8 Francis Schüssler Fiorenza, 'Systematic Theology: Task and Methods', in *Systematic Theology: Roman Catholic Perspectives Volume 1*, eds Francis Schüssler Fiorenza and John P. Galvin (Minneapolis: Fortress Press, 1991), 62.

9 Joseph Galgalo and Esther Mombo, 'Theological Education in Africa in the Post-1998 Lambeth Conference', *Journal of Anglican Studies*, 6.1 (2008): 31–40.

16

Miroslav Volf

GEORGE SUMNER

While biography may not be destiny, it is always informative about an author, and this is especially true in the broadly evangelical tradition, where the 'conversion narrative' came to prominence. This is particularly true of Miroslav Volf. He grew up in a Christian home, in what was then Yugoslavia, but is now Croatia. As Pentecostal Christians, his family were, when he was young, a minority within a minority. For this reason, the theme of identity runs like a golden thread through all his writing. To be sure, one's distinctively Christian baptismal identity is primary, but the word 'identity' has additional resonances. Ethnically, in the Balkans, it involved questions of trauma, anger and survival. There, it also implied inter-religious tension especially with Islam. For Volf as a scholar, it intersected with postmodern philosophical concerns, especially in the face of questions of secularity and globalization. Put most simply, how can one protect selfhood and at the same time fend off fanaticism? These questions are as old as Constantine and the Crusades, as modern as an Enlightenment figure like Gotthold Ephraim Lessing, hoping for religious competition only in charity (in the play *Nathan the Wise*), and also especially pertinent to the harsh nationalism of our own time, a generation after Volf's first writings. Seen from another perspective, he is a scholar with evangelical presuppositions pursuing in an ad hoc manner the equivalent of a project in natural theology, the pursuit of overlap with globalized culture, the secular common good, with trauma therapy, with Islam, etc.

Before proceeding, we should present some more biographical specifics. The son of a pastor, and influenced in early life by the missiologist Peter Kuzmic, Miroslav Volf studied at the Zagreb Evangelical Seminary and Fuller Seminary, Pasadena, before completing a doctorate at Tubingen under Jurgen Moltmann. His Habilitationsschrift became his book *After Our Likeness.*[1] He has taught theology at Fuller Seminary and Yale Divinity School. In his time at the latter, he had a noted collaboration with former British Prime Minister Tony Blair around the subject of globalization and the common good as well as a controversial hand in the conversation with imams around 'A Common Word Between Us and You'.

We do well to preface our consideration of his work with affirmation of his continuing traditional doctrinal and kerygmatic commitments (though these are sometimes implied, not stated, in his writings). A good testament to these is a short treatment of Christian discipleship (for a Lenten book at the request of Archbishop Rowan Williams) called *Free of Charge*.[2] It could serve well as an introduction to discipleship in contemporary life for a new Christian, treating as it does the Trinity, grace and the atonement. Before wading into his own constructions and possible critiques, his profound faith and his gift as catechist, by virtue of his experience as well as his mind, should precede. Here we see Volf in the 'faith seeking understanding' tradition which permeates all his works of dialogue and public engagement. In that book, divine giving and forgiving precede, and only then can our lives be defined by human giving and forgiving as the two fitting responses to grace. Here is found the heart of the Reformation witness to the gospel, of Luther's *Heidelberg Disputation*, at its simplest and most profound.[3] Volf takes up many of these same basic themes of our faith and applies them to wider issues such as the grounding of morality, theodicy and national optimism and guilt in his *Against the Tide*.[4]

Themes/Dialogues

In what follows we will consider Miroslav Volf's contribution by focusing on four dialogues, four loci, and four calls to *koinonia* in our embattled world.

Christianity and Islam

In recent years, with the same larger goal of parsing identity and charity before him, Volf took a prominent role in the Muslim–Christian initiative, and subsequent controversy, around 'A Common Word Between Us and You' in 2004. The initiative sought to build a more friendly relationship on the shared commitment to the 'Golden Rule' of these two 'religions of the book'. This was undergirded by the claim to worship the same God, along with the removal of the straw man of a distinction between a Christian God of reason and a Muslim God of will. Interestingly, in support of this line of reasoning, in his book *Allah* Volf appealed to the great fifteenth-century bishop and conciliarist Nicholas of Cusa and his irenic 'The Peace of the Faith'.[5] There Volf finds precedent for understanding Muslim objections to the Trinity to be denials of claims to tritheism to which Christians also should object. Volf then cites Nicholas's argument that if one thinks through what it means to believe in the one God who speaks, creates a world, etc., one by implication believes also in his Word, which is none other than he. In other words, Muslims with their confession of the one God ought by reason to understand that one God as triune. What Volf leaves unsaid is that they believe no such thing, and that furthermore this triunity is none other than what we see in the divine economy in the incarnation. But Volf is right in Nicholas's pursuit of conversation in the place of warfare.

What are we to make of Volf's argument in *Allah* in the service of this project? The strategy of marking out a zone of charity is familiar in Volf, and its intent admirable. Furthermore, the specific claim that Muslims and Christians both worship the true God is defensible; one can find as much in Thomas Aquinas, for example. Likewise, the Christian use of 'Allah' for God is consistent with the translation of the local name in different contexts (as the missiologist Lamin Sanneh has taught us). And yet Volf himself, citing Luther, is aware that one could equally well say that Christians and Muslims differ over who is the 'right' God. On this score, it is worth noting that the Muslim condemnation of *shirk*, the attribution of 'association' to God, is aimed, whether accurately or not, at the claim that 'Father' and 'Son' could be attributed to the one God. Secondly, the claim that religious understanding must be built on 'worship of the same God' has a curiously premodern *cuius regio huius religio* (whosesoever region, their religion) sound to it. Wouldn't this doom Muslim–Hindu relations in south Asia? And what of the bloodshed in sixteenth-century England or twentieth-century Ireland? Why are resources for charity found within each tradition not enough? On another front, isn't the heart of Christian–Muslim dialogue the apprehension that the relationship entails both the greatest proximity and the sharpest difference of identity at one and the same time, and that this argument within agreement must for resolution await the Last Day?

Globalization and the religions

Nowhere is religion a more thorough proxy for ethnic and political strife than in the Balkans. In the heyday of optimism about globalization, Volf asked what is the relation of the transcendence it evokes to human flourishing in such an age. With globalization in the West has come an 'age of authenticity' also characterized by an emphasis on 'ordinary life'. The phrase is Charles Taylor's, who is the interlocutor on this topic, whether acknowledged or assumed.

We might most boldly ask if religion is, on the widest stage, good for us. The question might most readily come from outside the realm of faith, whether asked from a secular or more revisionist theological perspective. And of course the question is not about religion as a concept on its own, but the religions themselves. Nor does the question whether the religions conduce to human flourishing imply an answer to the truth question. How does Volf address these issues?

The underpinning for the argument in his book *Flourishing* is the ongoing historic connection between global religions and globalization itself though, in the present instance of the latter, technological inter-connectivity and secularity render globalization potent and put the religions on the defensive (though Volf challenges the notion that they are shrinking).[6] Volf seeks to see globalization 'from within' the gospel's per-spective, and as a result he gives an optimist's account of it. His first and main point is that humans were simply not made to live 'by bread alone', and will be frustrated so long as they strive to do so. We must recognize that left to our own devices we are of insatiable desires, anxious in the face of death, and prone to treat one another as means only and not as ends. Only by virtue of faith (Christian in Volf's case, but he is willing to hazard an extrapolation) can we reach a deeper kind of flourishing which acknowledges transcendence. Here he is answering a basic ques-tion posed, for example, by Charles Taylor, whether transcendence is a threat to that flourishing in ordinary life which characterizes the secular age.

This witness of religion to a deeper flourishing cannot stop at the indi-vidual's angst, and must also offer its witness in the political realm, for the common good, as it offers warrants from its own tradition's resources, for political pluralism, tolerance and the charity of listening. This ought not to be taken to mean the extinction of theological exclusivism, as religions can still contend, until the eschaton, that they offer the final truth – so long as, in the meantime, they contend by means of charity. And what are we to make of this case? All we can say (in Spanish by the inter-religious way of the Andalus and its medieval *Convivencia*) is 'ojala' – that is, 'may it be God's choice'! In other words, Volf offers in a sense the best case scenario. But are there not times when our witness to the crucified one will not coincide with secularity's flourishing? Will there not be moments when we cannot but note, it is to be hoped humbly, our profound dif-ferences of belief? And will there not be times when religions, themselves marred by sin, will fall far short of charity and listening? Still, we cannot fault Volf for accentuating in our riven time the possible, the 'angels of our better nature'.

'Truth and Reconciliation': Exclusion and Embrace

Exclusion and Embrace is Volf's single most significant work, one that is at once deeply personal, engaged with the widest circle of other scholars, and the most ambitious theologically.[7] He responds to postmodern philosophers, feminists, critical historians, and more 'communitarian' and traditional Christian voices, but throughout the work his own experience of being under threat of exclusion and violence is never very far away. And in each section of the work, Volf returns to the central affirmations of the gospel: the theology of the cross, the preceding confrontation of Jesus and Pilate, the consequent radical doctrine of forgiveness, the image of the Father welcoming the prodigal that it illustrates, and the final surrender of judgement and resolution to God at the end of things. His insistence that mutual repentance and forgiveness is consistent with striving for justice has the same structure as justification and sanctification in Christian theology. In this sense, the book, humble, dialogical and so open-ended throughout, is a deeply evangelical work.

Let us consider the contemporary issues he deals with along the way. First, in what sense can one maintain identity without falling into the exclusion that war-torn Yugoslavia evinced? Volf circles around a description of a different, specifically Christian kind of identity, one that is consistent with relation, 'binding'. He encourages a 'contrapuntal reading' (after Edward Said) and an enlarged thinking (after Hannah Arendt) which are consistent with making one's own claims. Secondly, he offers a phenomenology of embrace. What kind of space between does it require? What kind of letting go? And how does it require a 'step toward the other' (after Emmanuel Levinas)? The general description he undertakes makes specifically Christian themes more generally available. Behind his treatment Volf is acknowledging and dissenting from Hegel's famous treatment of Master and Slave as foundational to the self defined in relation to the other.

While Volf engages a number of other conversation-partners, the following three are worthy of note. He considers the question of whether forgiving involves forgetting, and returns to the question later in the work. The interlocutor here is specifically Elie Wiesel, and his imperative to remember, and the trauma of the Holocaust he endured (here Volf is once again in the tradition of his teacher Moltmann). He wrestles with the question, worried as he is that retaining the memory may imply retaining the attendant desire for vengeance. He finally consigns the question to God's forgetting in Isaiah (God who of course remembers all!). Once again, the question reaches its limit in the encompassing nature of God in the divine justice and mercy.

Secondly, Part II of *Exclusion and Embrace* involves an extended conversation with Alasdair MacIntyre, and with MacIntyre's key question 'whose justice, which rationality?' Volf agrees with his analysis of the need for a distinctively Christian tradition in which each is conceived, though it stands alongside other traditions that it must be challenged by and strive to make sense. At the same time, he pushes back at what he sees as MacIntyre's excessive concern for coherence. But it may be that Volf is not so much criticizing MacIntyre as pointing out the complexity of his vision. (Overarching all these specific debates is a more general question about the Christian mission in postmodernity.) Going back to the biographical starting-point, the identity of Volf's faith had no lack of particularity, nor of sociological separateness, whatever the costs these entailed. So in this engagement with MacIntyre we can see an answer he could give to the vision of a 'new Benedict'. We can also see what his attitude might be to recent emphases on radical difference as a starting-point for inter-religious dialogue – for example, Joseph Dinoia. There too Volf's beginning point with particularity proceeds to a concerted effort to emphasize overlaps in the Venn diagram.

In this world, we can at best witness to the truth before the powers, in obedience to Christ's witness before Pilate. But what we witness to is final and comprehensive, 'God's being true to Himself', to echo Thomas Torrance. Likewise, doctrine itself may seek coherence, but its espousal in the world by the Church must acknowledge areas of overlap (natural theology, apologetics, missional engagement, dialogue) and admit that it cannot offer truth from 'everywhere', as it were, but at best be our truth 'here' in appreciation of the other's truth 'there'.

Thirdly, Volf deals directly with the question of violence in the pursuit of justice. How could we help but spark another round of violence? Here Volf engages with René Girard and his vision of 'violence and the sacred'. The problem cannot be answered sufficiently by the modern appeal to reason alone, nor via the reduction of everything to power relations. What is required is one who can break the cycle, and for Christians that one is the crucified and risen one. While Volf acknowledges that for those who face the real threat of violence, the judgement of God must be affirmed, though it is a judgement on those who themselves ultimately refuse God's forgiveness. At the same time this judgement is not ours, and so we have no appeal to, or easy identification with, the 'white rider' in Revelation. God's judgement is God's alone, and he is none other than

Christ who forgives his own tormentors and surrenders himself to death on the cross.

The identity of the Church

At the outset we perceived issues of identity running through Volf's work, and one can see this in his first major work, on the Trinity and ecclesiology. Volf is concerned specifically with the Free Church tradition from which he later came to Anglicanism, and he brings Free Church emphasis on the local church into conversation with the Roman Catholic and Orthodox traditions, making, as they do, what would seem a more direct appeal to catholicity. He makes the simple but compelling point that the rejection of the former tradition calls into question the real catholicity of the latter. Volf seeks what one might call the underlying 'grammar' of catholicity as he identifies the features of congregational sufficiency, openness and faithfulness to the apostolic as crucial, though various traditions may emphasize them differently and to different degrees. Volf complements his discussion of the catholicity of the churches with what John Zizioulas calls 'the catholic person', whereby our relations to others in the body of Christ are themselves taken into our own being, while including our differentiated individuality.[8]

Volf has received criticism for his argument from divine triunity to human diversity-in-unity in the human realm in the Church, though, and in the revised conclusion of *Exclusion and Embrace* he acknowledges the risk of such projection, and he emphasizes the limits of the analogy. It is worth noting that he also relates the debate over communion and catholicity to the perennial and more general problem of the One and the Many. Of equal theological interest is the way he puts the question against an eschatological horizon. What has each tradition to contribute to that fullness towards which we head and of which we have an anticipation in our relation to Jesus Christ? This eschatological move implies an ecclesiological fullness of which the churches are a part and towards which they are pilgrims.

We may then from this early and formative work draw another conclusion helpful in understanding the theology that follows later, which we may see as other examples of the same kind, by analogy with Trinitarian plurality in unity. Each question has an interlocutor, and in each case the common ground, the place around which each has something complementary to offer, must be determined by the question and the speakers themselves. Volf does not have a single method predetermined, though the paradigm of the doctrine of God presents consistently throughout as his template.

Conclusion

Perhaps the most pressing question of our time has to do with the shape of a postmodernity missiology – one that takes account of the dangerous and centrifugal social forces so prevalent in our time, as well as the challenges of a commodified secularity. It cannot revert to a cultural apologetic in the sense of a twentieth-century 'correlationism'. A response that 'gives a reason for the hope in us' (1 Peter 3.15) must be grounded in the Church's identity in its worship of the triune God even as the Church has a care to the ecumenically ecclesiological, inter-religious and political and theological dimensions of its calling. In short, it must be evangelically *dialogical*, seeking 'as far as it lies within us, to be a peace with all' (Romans 12.18). It must confess its own identity in a manner that allays the hostilities which identity in the worldly sense can enflame. Because this aptly describes the research agenda of Miroslav Volf, he continues to be a compelling voice for our time.

Notes

1 Miroslav Volf, *After Our Likeness: The Church as an Image of the Triune God* (Grand Rapids: Eerdmans, 1998).

2 Miroslav Volf, *Free of Charge: Giving and Forgiving in a Culture Stripped of Grace* (Grand Rapids: Zondervan, 2005).

3 Volf, *Free of Charge*, 37.

4 Miroslav Volf, *Against the Tide: Love in a Time of Petty Dreams and Persistent Emnities* (Grand Rapids: Eerdmans, 2009).

5 Miroslav Volf, *Allah: A Christian Response* (New York: HarperOne, 2011). It might, however, be noted that the Platonist Nicholas had a very strong doctrine of ineffability, and that he imagines an inclusive kind of Church making room for an Islamic kind of Christianity, which provided no attraction for the Sultan.

6 Miroslav Volf, *Flourishing: Why We Need Religion in a Globalized World* (New Haven: Yale University Press, 2016).

7 Miroslav Volf, *Exclusion and Embrace: A Theological Exploration of Identity, Otherness, and Reconciliation* (Nashville: Abingdon Press, 1995).

8 This argument preoccupies the final section of *After Our Likeness*.

17

Gerald O. West

CYNTHIA BRIGGS KITTREDGE

Gerald West (1956–) is a socially engaged white South African biblical scholar and Anglican theologian whose work in hermeneutics of the Bible has changed the field of academic biblical studies, advanced the struggle for justice for the poor and marginalized in South Africa, and introduced novel, but arguably 'Anglican', ways of reading scripture as a church in the wider Anglican Communion. A pastor in an Assemblies of God church in the 1980s during the anti-apartheid struggle in South Africa, in which the Anglican Church had a visible and prominent role, West came of age as a biblical scholar in a political context where interpretation of the Bible mattered. A particular reading of scripture had undergirded the system of apartheid, and a liberative reading and proclamation played a significant role in the struggle to overturn it. West's prolific and influential work has been forged within these dynamics of biblical interpretation and political rhetoric and action. West made the deliberate choice to become an Anglican, choosing 'to relocate my Christian walk within a church that was actively engaged in the liberation struggle'. He describes his Anglican identity as 'above all a political identity'.[1] The University of Kwazulu-Natal where he was Professor in the School of Theology and the Ujamaa Centre for Biblical and Theological Community Development and Research which he founded and directed in Pietermaritzburg, South Africa, are the institutional contexts for his work. West has lectured around the world, holding visiting lectureships in Norway, Scotland, England, the USA, Italy, India, New Zealand, and Australia. As a biblical scholar and theologian, West is known for his work in reading the Bible with, and for, the poor and marginalized and for amplifying the voices and perspectives of those readers for the wider interpretive conversation. As a scholar, teacher and practical theologian, he has contributed to renewed attention to reading the Bible in the Anglican Communion through his leadership in the design and process of Bible studies at the 2008 and 2020 Lambeth Conferences and the Bible in the life of the Church.

West developed a deep love for the Bible while an undergraduate at Rhodes University studying linguistics. He quickly learned to apply the tools of linguistics to the reading of the Bible, learning Greek and Hebrew to assist in this work. After graduation he began work as a pastor in the Assemblies of God tradition, but because of his active engagement with the South African anti-apartheid struggle and his use of the Bible in this work, he was asked by the denomination to leave his role as pastor in 1983. He then became a full-time instructor of English and linguistics at Rhodes. In the early 1980s, as political repression increased in the Eastern Cape, West was encouraged to find refuge in graduate studies abroad, and he enrolled at Sheffield University in England where he attained MA and PhD degrees.

At Sheffield University, West was profoundly shaped by professors, mentors and colleagues such as Anthony Thiselton, David Clines, David Gunn, John Rogerson, Philip Davies, David Jobling, Norman Gottwald, Mark Brett, Daniel Carroll, Stephen Fowl and Matt Wiebe. He was also influenced by the camaraderie formed with other South Africans in exile throughout England, especially the black South African priest Barney Pityana. Here, West solidified his conviction that his work would be done in and for the black struggle.

After returning to South Africa in the late 1980s at the Department of Theological Studies at the University of Natal, West formed friendships and partnerships with black scholars and theologians such as Allan Boesak, Frank Chikane, and especially Itumeleng Mosala, further grounding his work in a commitment to contextual and black theology. The early emphasis of his work was primarily an anti-apartheid context, but with the shift to majority rule in the early 1990s, the scope of his work broadened to include related issues of oppression, especially race, gender, sexuality, economic injustice and HIV/AIDS issues.[2]

In the late 1980s West founded the Ujamaa Centre, 'a non-partisan, non-denominational, Centre for Community Development and Research which supports capacity building on development, good governance on church and civil society levels through theological education to ensure rigorous participation of all citizens in social transformation'.[3] The Ujamaa Centre convenes contextual Bible study within community-based organizations to use their faith resources, including the Bible, for the transformation of their communities. West is the author of 12 books, including *Biblical Hermeneutics of Liberation* (1995), *The Academy of the Poor* (1999), *The Bible in Africa* (2000), *Reading the Bible in the Global Village* (2002), 'Genesis' in the *People's Bible Commentary* (2006), *Reading Other-wise* (2007) and *The Stolen Bible* (2016). His work appears in many journal articles, book chapters, and conference papers.

Three Major Themes: The Sites of Struggle

Three major themes stretch across West's work: (1) the conviction that biblical interpretation is a theological, political and rhetorical activity; (2) the practice of reading the Bible for and with 'ordinary readers' among the poor and marginalized; and (3) the concept of the Bible and of Anglicanism itself as a 'site of struggle' in which pastors, teachers, preachers and clergy, and lay readers, choose to intervene and participate on the basis of their theological and ethical convictions.

Emerging from the crucible of the liberation struggle in South Africa, Gerald West's hermeneutics display the close interrelationship between the Bible, politics and power. West often quotes Desmond Tutu's reiteration of a common anecdote which he typically recounted in a humorous tone, 'When the white missionaries came to us, they had the Bible and we had the land. They said to us, "Let us pray." When we opened our eyes, we had the Bible and they had our land!'[4] This quip encapsulates the interrelationship between imperial conquest, missionary activity, contextual reception of Christianity in South Africa, and the ambiguous and complex role of the Bible in that dynamic. West explores the political dimension of biblical interpretation in his early work as he develops the model of 'reading with' and 'reading other-wise' in contextual Bible study. In his work on the reception of the Bible in South Africa in the *Stolen Bible* he describes and gives voice to the way that the Bible was 'stolen' from the missionaries and 'used' in diverse ways.[5]

Liberation and feminist hermeneutics brought to the field of critical biblical studies and to communities for whom the Bible is authoritative the insight that reading the Bible is always shaped by theological and political commitments. Readings of the Bible throughout history have had practical political consequences – literally promoting life or death for the poor, for women, and for the enslaved. Biblical interpretation is not simply accepting the traditional teaching of the Church about what the text 'means' nor is it applying 'neutral' or 'objective' or scientific historical criticism of the academy. Rather, it is perspectival, practised in and for a community. Therefore, one must name explicitly one's hermeneutical principles, the community with whom and for whom one reads, and one's theological commitments. As feminist biblical scholars, aware of the deployment of the Bible in the subordinating and silencing of women, argued that commitment to the liberation of all wo/men was their hermeneutical lens, so West names liberation from oppression and justice, as the goal towards which his biblical interpretation points. Because of the intensity and urgency of the struggle over the Bible in the South African context, South African biblical scholars were among the earliest to attempt to persuade the academy of the non-neutrality and the political dimension of biblical interpretation.

As do Latin American liberation theologians and those doing black theology, West understands that the primary interlocutors for theology are the poor, and they are the community to whom he is responsible. The relationship of a socially engaged biblical scholar and ordinary poor and marginalized 'readers' of the Bible is at the heart of liberation hermeneutics.[6] In a reflection on his vocation, West summarizes four aspects of his South African biblical hermeneutics: (1) reading the Bible with local marginalized and oppressed communities, in the tradition of 'reading from below' in black and contextual theology; (2) reading the Bible for the objective of personal and social transformation, as contrasted with a desire for objective or critical 'knowledge'; (3) reading the Bible with the academy to bring the tools of biblical scholarship to local communities and bring the questions of local communities to the realm of academic research; and (4) reading the Bible in the classroom with a threefold pedagogical cord of 'engagement with the Bible, critical distance, contextualization'. In a dialogical process 'ordinary readers' ask questions about how power and privilege function in the text, issues overlooked by academic biblical scholarship, and biblical scholars offer critical perspectives on the composition, history or social context that can resource contextual Bible study. In all these aspects of his vocation, West's teaching does critical reading of the Bible with people in community and classroom.

The 'See, Judge, Act' Model

The Contextual Bible Study model, developed in Brazil by Carlos Dreher, uses the image of Jesus on the Emmaus road in Luke 24.13–35 as the paradigm for teaching. Here, Jesus is the 'popular educator' who walks along 'with' the disciples, listens, establishes trust, and guides them into new ways of seeing, so they are prepared to continue the work of Jesus. West describes the process of Contextual Bible Study with 'ordinary readers' at the Ujamaa Centre, where community-oriented groups come to work with the facilitators for social transformation. In an exploration of the story of the poor widow making her offering in the temple in Mark 12.41–44, West displays the steps and hermeneutical rationale for the process.[7] The method broadly follows the 'See, Judge, Act' model developed by Father Joseph Cardijn in Belgium and propagated in South Africa.[8] First, contextual Bible is defined as an act of faith, one that always begins with an expression of community.[9] Liturgical expression, like singing and dancing, accompany and punctuate the teaching and learning. Facilitators create a community of trust and collaboration that honours the expertise of the readers and hearers of the text. Questions and responses from everyone in the group are elicited, shared, recorded and reviewed during the process. Playful responses like drawing and acting engage the imagination. The 'familiar' text, the poor widow making her offering in the temple, is read and heard together, and the group gathers the initial reactions of the readers. Then in a sequence of presentation and exploration, the facilitators introduce the wider literary context of this episode, focusing on the relationship with the passages that precede and follow, and tracing the characterization of the role of the scribes and the theme of the temple that extends from Jesus' entry into the temple in Mark 11.27 to his departure in Mark 13.2. West demonstrates how this method is 'slowing down' the 'seeing' process. Facilitators then share social and historical context about the role of the temple in religious observance and its relationship with the political system of Roman occupation. As the facilitators provide resources of critical biblical study, here the basic elements of literary and social context, the traditional 'familiar' reading in which the poor widow is an example of individual self-giving, becomes more complex and challenging as the critique of the scribes and the temple that characterize Mark's story of Jesus is highlighted. The act of 'judging' involves evaluation of that pattern of critique in the Gospel and then the attempt to discover analogies and comparisons with contemporary social and political life in South Africa. As the process unfolds, the prophetic dimension of Jesus' teaching appears in vivid relief, and the participants are motivated to concrete action in society grounded in their faith. The final step, 'act', is provoked by the final question, 'How does this text speak to our respective contexts? What action will you plan in response to this Bible study?'[10] West's account of the process of contextual Bible study at the Ujamaa Centre demonstrates the effects of the practical deployment of critical biblical studies in the setting of faith.

Contextual, perspectival, socially located

West's contextual Bible study makes use of the structure of authority within Anglicanism that was articulated by the Anglican divines in the formative period of the Church and which has shifted as Anglicanism has moved from an imperial to a postcolonial church.[11] While holding scripture as the primary authority for theology, Anglicans recognize multiple sources of authority alongside scripture. With scripture, they name 'tradition', the teaching of the Church, articulated in the creeds, the liturgical tradition, and the prayer book. The third strand, 'reason', includes critical reasoning, the willingness to ask questions of the sacred text, and includes now in the Anglican Communion other 'indigenous knowledge systems'. In practice, there has also been a fourth strand, named by Rowan Greer as 'experience'.[12] Experience, of course, is not a universal category, but is contextual, perspectival and socially located. One can see how these elements are present as West reads the Bible with ordinary readers. Contextual Bible study begins with the centrality of scripture as the subject of study and source for spiritual and social transformation. The singing and dancing surrounding the process may be understood in a general way as representing tradition. The use of the resources of critical biblical study function as a dimension of reason. Attention to the socio-political setting of the biblical passage itself and to analogies with the contemporary context points to the particularity of experience. As these sources work together, in the community of the interpreters, 'meaning' of the authoritative is both discovered and made.

As Anglicanism has become a postcolonial church, reading scripture in context has become more diverse and complex:

> For the very same Bible that was pivotal and the primary source for the imperial British project and the colonial Anglican Church was appropriated by African Anglicans, after a long struggle for recognition and a place in the colonial church ... Ever since, post-colonial Anglican Christians from around the world have been reading the Bible for themselves and bringing their contexts to bear on what it means to be 'Anglican'.[13]

West has devoted his academic and organizational energies to attending to and describing that diversity in the South African context throughout his work, culminating in the publication of *The Stolen Bible: From Tool of Imperialism to African Icon* in 2016. As a scholar and theologian, he has advocated for, and explored, the theological and practical potential of reading scripture in context as Anglicans.

The context of postcolonial Anglicanism has brought to the fore a third theme of West's work – understanding both scripture and Anglicanism as a 'site of struggle' that is constantly negotiated and contested. The concept of a 'site of struggle' in scripture acknowledges that reading is not neutral, nor is the Bible itself. Scripture can be and has been harnessed for both domination and liberation and contains diverse traditions within it. 'Christianity' and 'Anglicanism' as well are neither totally innocent nor completely guilty in their social and political effects. Rather, it is the responsibility of the carriers of tradition and readers of the Bible to find there, and deploy, resources for healing/salvation/liberation in light of their faith. When taking on the role of biblical interpreter or Anglican theologian, one confronts choices about what strands of 'tradition' one will develop and what biblical visions to amplify and build upon. For example, one might stress the biblical injunctions for Christians to submit to worldly authorities or the encouragement to resist the powers and principalities. In an article that explores the task of Anglican biblical interpretation in the South African context, West argues that biblical interpretation must closely attend to its social location in the postcolonial context. In contrast to most of the Anglican Church's history in South Africa which ignored its 'earthly location', South African Anglican biblical interpretation must engage reality as a postcolonial project. With that goal, Anglican biblical interpretation has both a descriptive and an interventionist task. The first task is to describe both 'an analysis of how the Bible's own colonial contours have contributed to imperialism, colonialism, and mission, and an analysis of how the Bible has been read by colonial and postcolonial subjects'.[14] Such a two-pronged description addresses the complexity of the Bible as a site of struggle, and it focuses the agency of indigenous biblical readers in remaking the Christianity they 'received' from the missionaries. West's 2016 volume *The Stolen Bible* offers a significant contribution to the descriptive task. Here he explores the readings of the Bible by Jan Van Riebeeck, the founder of the Cape Colony in the seventeenth century; those of Robert Moffat, the Scottish missionary to the Tswana on the colony's northern frontier; also those of Isaiah Shembe, the Zulu prophet, and Thabo Mbeki, the second post-apartheid South African president.

The second task for Anglican South African biblical hermeneutics is what West calls 'the interventionist' task. Here West argues that scholars involved in this project must develop a voice from their precise location within and for the Anglican Communion. Such an intervention names its own theological and ethical priorities, its 'political' stance, and draws on the rich resources of South African biblical scholarship including the methodological resources of inculturation, liberation, feminist and postcolonial biblical hermeneutics and the variety of ecclesio-theologies from the missionary history of South Africa including Anglo-Catholic, evangelical, Pentecostal and charismatic. By naming the ecclesial perspectives in addition to the academic ones, West recognizes the status of 'ordinary readers' in faith communities that contribute to the interpretive conversation. Finally, West identifies critical political issues in the South African context for biblical hermeneutics to address, particularly gender issues and HIV/AIDS.

Many Hands and Many Voices

Growing awareness of the diversity of postcolonial Anglicanism came to a point of crisis in the period following the Lambeth Conference of 1998 in which the bishops voted to reaffirm the Church's traditional teaching on marriage and sexuality and passed a resolution that stated: 'in view of the teaching of scripture, upholds faithfulness in marriage between a man and a woman in lifelong union' and that it could not 'advise the legitimising or blessing of same sex unions nor ordaining those involved in same gender unions'.[15] While it was the Church's judgement about homosexuality that was the presenting issue of dispute, it became clear that the key theological issue was the different approaches to interpreting the Bible. The belief that the Bible had a self-evident, 'literal' meaning that existed outside of culture and context and theological orientation lay beneath the Lambeth Statement.[16] Biblical scholars and theologians from the Communion recognized that the breadth of interpretive strategies of scripture by Anglicans was far wider than the Lambeth Statement suggested. The role of reason and of experience in the dynamic of interpretation required more exploration and elaboration.

The crisis of biblical interpretation intensified in the dispute that followed the consecration in the Episcopal Church of Gene Robinson as Bishop of New Hampshire. Commissioned by the Lambeth Consultation on Communion, the Windsor Report in 2004 reaffirmed the authority of scripture and its need for interpretation and asserted that 'our shared reading of scripture, across the boundaries of culture, region and tradition ought to be the central feature of our common life ...' From these conflicted discussions it became more evident that how we read scripture is intimately connected with how we are Anglican.

In this time of contested interpretations of the Bible, Gerald West was invited by the then Archbishop of Canterbury Rowan Williams to design and lead the Bible studies for Lambeth 2008. The design reflected the principles/practices of contextual Bible study. The Bible study groups were made up of bishops from around the Communion and their spouses who read the Gospel of John together with an attitude of faith and a commitment to listening to one another. Participants were encouraged to speak from their social location, ecclesial context and personal experience. It was significant that the bishops' spouses, the majority of whom were wives, participated in the Bible study. For many, the pressure of the conflicts in the Church around sexuality had been a weight upon them as well as their husbands.[17] Their participation in the Bible study reflected their important role as ministers in the community of faith. The publication of the conference, *In the Beginning was the Word*, describes the communal nature of the work:

> So we offer you here Bible studies that have been used and shaped by many hands and many voices. We trust that you will add your hands and voices to these Bible studies in making them your own.[18]

As in contextual Bible study with 'ordinary readers', critical scholarly perspectives on the Gospel of John that stress the 'logic' and 'voice' of John are central in the group. The questions asked by the facilitators are designed to connect the text to the lives and social reality of the participants:

> We have tried 'to hear' John's Gospel, and to follow its internal logic and structure. But we also constantly bring biblical text and context into dialogue through the questions we offer to you. How you enter into the dialogue between biblical text and your context is up to you.[19]

Bible study members are encouraged to allow 'sufficient time for engaging with the questions and the input'. This is the 'slowing down' of the reading process and attending to lengthened 'seeing'. The Reflections Group 2008 reported that the Bible studies were the most enriching part of the conference:

> It is here that we have experienced a death to self-interest and the possibility of God's Spirit bringing new life. It is here that 'the stone is being rolled away'. The Bible studies offered to the Lambeth Conference sought to place every participant under the authority of scripture and to enable them to journey with John's Gospel, by following a particular feature of the Gospel itself, the 'I am' sayings, by drawing attention to the detail of the text, whether historical, literary, or thematic detail, by offering opportunities for participants to place their contexts and personal concerns alongside scripture, by locating John's Gospel within the wider context of the biblical canon, and by placing the process of the Bible study in the hands of a bishop who would serve the group by facilitating the formation of a sacred and safe site for a reverent and respectful engagement among the participants.[20]

By bringing his hermeneutical perspectives to the design of the Bible studies for Lambeth 2008 and by modelling contextual Bible study in a situation of diversity, Gerald West demonstrated how an academic theologian and biblical scholar can make a practical contribution to the ongoing life of Anglicanism in a postcolonial context.

In the wake of Lambeth 2008 the Anglican Consultative Council established 'The Bible in the Life of the Church' project that brought together clergy, scholars and lay people 'to wrestle seriously with Scripture and how it is understood in our ecclesial life'.[21] Rather than gathering statements about how the Bible 'should' be read, the intent was to observe and to learn from how the Bible 'is' read in different parts of the Anglican communion.[22] Thus it was descriptive, rather than prescriptive, like West describes the first part of the South African Anglican biblical scholar's task. The project, coordinated by Stephen Lyon, reflected many of the interpretive emphases of Gerald West: the focus on the reception of scripture by 'ordinary readers', its remaking by indigenous readers in specific contexts, and its engaging scripture reading with ethical issues, the care of creation and issues of social justice. As the controversy over sexuality in the Communion led to awareness of the diversity of approaches to reading the Bible, it also led to renewed and sustained attention to the Bible in the life of the Church, and to the role of the Bible as scripture. Gerald West has played a major role in this movement in the Anglican Communion.

In the planning for the most recent Lambeth Conference, Bible study was again at the centre of the design, this time with the First Letter of Peter as the chosen text. The First Letter of Peter has a powerful and ambiguous reception history, because of its general prescription to 'accept the authority of every human institution including the emperor as supreme' (2.13) and its specific instruction to slaves to 'accept the authority of your masters with all deference, not only those who are kind and gentle but also those who are harsh' (2.18) and to wives to accept the authority of their husbands (3.1). Under the leadership of Jennifer Strawbridge, a group of international scholars were gathered to prepare the Bible studies on 1 Peter. The style and method of the gathering reflects awareness that different contexts shape responses to scripture and that faith and scholarship can coexist:

> Over the course of five days and two meetings in London as well as countless emails and correspondence, faithful scholars from around the world gathered for the St Augustine Seminar to spend time with 1 Peter and to seek the guidance of the Holy Spirit in their engagement with Scripture. This commentary draws on the stories, struggles and prayers of scholars from six continents and represents a range of Christian traditions and experiences. The work from these gatherings is drawn together in what follows, where different approaches to Scripture are

brought together in such a way that difference is not hidden, and the conversation continues.[23]

Gerald West again serves as a member of the team of scholars for this Lambeth Conference. West's outlook that the Bible is a site of struggle and can be read for liberation or domination is reflected in how the Bible study frames the interpretive issue in 1 Peter 3. He describes that a response to 1 Peter lies along a continuum ranging from conformity, to resilience, to resistance. His conviction that social context and position with respect to power must be considered in one's interpretation is articulated in the form of challenging questions put to faithful readers of 1 Peter:

> Thus 3.8–17 requires hard interpretive work from the reader of this letter. How are we to understand the relationship between 'the Lord' and the many other claims to lordship of that time, including the lordship of 'human institutions' (2.13), 'masters' (2.18) and 'husbands' (3.1)? And how is sanctifying Christ as Lord in our hearts an act both of resilience and of resistance in a world of lord-less powers? Framing the argument with respect to the three forms of human authority using 3.15 provides a way of understanding an important tension or continuum that Peter is grappling with. Given the demands of competing claims of 'lordship', how should Christians behave, particularly when, as in the case of Peter's community, Christians are a marginalized and vulnerable community? Furthermore, how are contemporary Christians in very different contexts, especially those in which Christianity is or has been a dominant religious tradition, to understand the message of 1 Peter?

The writers of the Bible study make explicit that the text presents choices for readers to negotiate from their own social locations, and they convey a confidence in the ability of faithful conversation about this canonical scripture to encompass a range of interpretations from different places.

Negotiating Difference, Encompassing Struggle

As a scholar, Gerald West has not only shaped the field of biblical studies but through his research, writing and participation in the structure of gatherings of the Anglican Communion has contributed to a more conscious and explicit engagement by people of faith with the Bible, as a significant authority for theology and the formation of community. As he has stressed, the Bible as a 'site of struggle' that can offer support for both domination and liberation, West has also displayed a kind of confidence that, when gathered in assemblies of faith, Anglicans can negotiate differences so that the community can encompass the struggle. Receivers and interpreters have the critical role of handling that ambiguity and, out of their faithful reading, proclaiming good news.

Gerald West's work has shown that the white South African biblical scholar's 'descriptive task' – to describe how the Bible has been received – can perform a constructive function by displaying the role that theological, ethical and political commitments play in how scripture is interpreted in Christian community. Attentive and careful description also highlights the role of diverse culture and history in reading the Bible and in living out Christian faith in a postcolonial context. The simple contrast between those who accept biblical authority and those who do not cannot be sustained when scripture is brought back into the centre of prayer, conversation and relationship by faithful Anglicans from different social contexts.

As he has taken up the 'interventionist' task in his scholarship and in contextual Bible study with a wide range of communities, Gerald West has powerfully raised up Jesus' prophetic critique of society's injustices and the ways 'religion' has perpetuated them. He has argued that the Anglican Church has moved away from a theology of liberation and retreated into conventional 'Church Theology'.[24] West has been a major force in gathering Anglicans around the Bible. Future theological work will reveal how reading the Bible together as Anglicans will realize its potential to recover the prophetic voice of Jesus in scripture and in the Church, as the world faces ever more urgent ethical and political challenges.

Notes

1 Conversation with Gerald O. West, 16 June 2021. I am grateful to Derek M. Larson for his research assistance with this chapter.

2 Gerald O. West, 'The Vocation of an African Biblical Scholar on the Margins of Biblical Scholarship', *Old Testament Essays*, 19.1 (2006): 307–36.

3 http://ujamaa.ukzn.ac.za/history.aspx (accessed 28.2.2024).

4 Gerald O. West, 'The Bible', *The Oxford Handbook of Anglican Studies*, eds Mark D. Chapman, Sathianathan Clarke, and Martyn Percy (New York: Oxford, 2015), 363.

5 Gerald O. West, *The Stolen Bible: From Tool of Imperialism to African Icon* (Leiden: Brill, 2016).

6 Gerald O. West, *Academy of the Poor: Towards a Dialogical Reading of the Bible* (Sheffield: Sheffield Academic Press, 1999), 12.

7 Gerald O. West, 'Do Two Walk Together? Walking with the Other through Contextual Bible Study', *Anglican Theological Review*, 93.3 (2011): 431–49 (431).

8 West, 'Do Two Walk Together?': 445

9 West, 'Do Two Walk Together?': 434.

10 West, 'Do Two Walk Together?': 444.

11 West, 'The Bible'.

12 Rowan A. Greer, *Anglican Approaches to Scripture: From the Reformation to the Present* (New York: Herder & Herder, 2006).

13 West, 'The Bible', 363.

14 Gerald O. West, '(Southern) African Anglican Biblical Interpretation: A Post-colonial Project', *Journal of Anglican Studies*, 8.2 (2010): 140–64 (141).

15 https://www.anglicancommunion.org/media/76650/1998.pdf (accessed 1.3.2024).

16 Njogonkulu Ndugabe, 'Scripture: What is at Issue in Anglicanism Today?', *Anglican Theological Review*, 83.1 (2001): 12–23.

17 Conversation with Gerald O. West, 16 June 2021.

18 Gerald O. West, ed., *In the Beginning was the Word: Group Bible Studies from the Gospel of John* (London: SPCK: 2009), 8.

19 West, *In the Beginning*, 8.

20 https://www.anglicancommunion.org/media/72554/reflections_document_-final-.pdf (accessed 1.3.2024).

21 *The Bible in the Life of the Church*, ed. Clare Amos (Norwich: Canterbury Press, 2013), p. xii.

22 Stephen Lyon, 'Mind the Gap! "The Bible in the Life of the Church" Project', *Anglican Theological Review*, 93.3 (2014): 451–64.

23 *The First Letter of Peter: A Global Commentary*, ed. Jennifer Strawbridge (London: SPCK, 2020).

24 West, '(Southern) African Anglican Biblical Interpretation'.

18

Gale A. Yee

STEPHEN BURNS

When Gale A. Yee became the first Asian American and first woman of colour to become president of the Society of Biblical Literature (SBL), that esteemed and elite academy was well over a century old. She became president in 2019, and the guild had existed for 139 years. Yee's milestone was 32 years after the election of the first woman to the role of president (Elisabeth Schüssler Fiorenza in 1987) and nine years after the first person of colour in that role (Vincent Wimbush in 2010).[1] No doubt, the weight of history (read: racism, sexism …) leaning on the guild would mean that it would take someone of 'tenacity, brilliance, collegiality, political savvy, and prolific scholarly production'[2] to step up, push back, and lead forward as the figurehead, as the first woman of colour. In Gale Yee those gifts are found in abundance. Yee seized the opportunity to make the 'whiteness' of her academy visible – and problematic – focusing on whiteness as she had done in an earlier foray to negotiate 'a white hegemonic guild',[3] her 'Yin/Yang is Not Me'.[4] She stepped into the role of SBL president with an impressive trajectory of writing that was far from shy of naming racism and sexism.

I should say that Yee's biblical guild is not one to which I belong (though my own disciplines – liturgy, practical theology – are as surely mired in like-kind problems as biblical studies). And while many of the chapters in this collection are written by those who know the persons who comprise their subject-matter through (mainly if not only through) their theological writing, that is not the case here. I write primarily as someone who has been Gale's colleague, as well as her next-door neighbour. This means that while I must confess that I may miss the nuances of her brilliance with, say, the books of Judges or Hosea in her hands, I can attest to experience of having listened to her preach the scriptures she also teaches; I have shared with her in worship in the seminary community we served;[5] and I can attest to the vivacity of her person, her humour, her kindness and more. Mind pictures of Gale's face laughing (so common!) or (occasionally, and justifiably) seething with anger, and memory of things like the reading that passed from desk to desk, or titbits of food that went from table to table in our homes, are able to shape my understanding of Gale in this chapter in her honour even though such things are mostly under the surface in my best attempt to do justice to the heft of her scholarly contribution. Personal insights, which so often have *not* made their way into merely 'academic' presentations, seem especially apt in Gale Yee's case, however, as no small part of her daring and brilliance is her willingness to make known and scrutinize aspects of her life as they are inextricably entangled with her professional finesse, as they have come to be harnessed by and for her leadership of scholarship. This makes for much focus on the 'triad of gender, race, and class': 'my Chinese American ethnicity, my lower-class origins, and my female gender', factors that have 'made deep marks on my interpretation of the biblical text, whether I consciously knew it or not'.[6] The sparkling 'intersectional anthology' Yee published just after her SBL presidency allows for the force of her thinking about this 'triad' – or 'troika' , or 'tripych' or even 'holy Trinity'[7] – to be quite apparent, and is made accessible for a wider audience than some of her other studies delving deeply into Hebrew Bible texts. The triad is central to her 'ampersand' approach,[8] focusing her attention not simply through one lens, but several together, all at once, as this allows for sharpened analysis.

Gale Yee suggests in *Towards an Asian-American Biblical Hermeneutics* that the 'towards' in the title of her anthology signals a 'modesty'. But if modesty is apt to her achievement, it also needs to be asserted that the collection itself, for all its punchiness, collects only some – a small sum – of the thinking that runs through her very 'prolific scholarly contribution'. Moreover, however modest it may be, it sets out an agenda that evidently the SBL at large and over time (and as one among other 'white hegemonic guilds') had not engaged as it might and should have learned to, and Yee throws down the gauntlet that the time has come.

Formation as a Scholar

Early factors

Gale Yee grew up 'on the southside of Chicago', in a suburb that was largely comprised of African American and Puerto Rican neighbours.[9] She is a third-generation Chinese American, her forebears having moved from the Hoy San district in the Kuantung province in China to Butte, Montana, USA. Yee conveys a deep sense of the trials of their migration and recognizes that her own scholarly explorations of the Hebrew Bible have been shaped deeply by her family history – for example, she has a certain preoccupation with the book of Ruth.[10]

First of all, Yee's maternal grandfather came to rural Montana, with his wife arriving 15 years later. At some point in Butte, she left him and took off west to Seattle. Between handing over her children to guardians and being pursued by the 'Chinese mafia', that grandmother escaped much further to the east, to Chicago, out of the reach of the gangs sent after her, and only when she was safely away did she send for her daughter, Gale's mother, to join her. Grandmother opened a restaurant, as it happened across the road from Holy Name Roman Catholic cathedral – a point that would have some significance in Gale Yee's religious upbringing. As a young adult, Gale's mother met and married a Chinese American man who became Gale's father. He was a seafarer in the navy, raised in Cincinnati and stationed in Chicago through World War Two. On leaving the navy her father became a cook in the family restaurant, and her mother ran the home. Gale was the first of 12 children. She was named after Gale Storm, an American singer[11] whose music was liked by her parents.[12]

The home in which Gale grew up through her first decade was memorably also inhabited by cockroaches.[13] However, it wasn't until she was 11, when her family moved to a 'white' neighbourhood elsewhere in the city, that she became aware of meeting racists face to face among other school kids.[14] In her childhood homes, Gale did not speak a Chinese language – her mother 'deliberately not teaching' one so as 'to help us inculturate'[15] – and in fact Gale has never learned either Mandarin or Cantonese, even though she learned multiple languages as part of her doctoral studies. Her lack of a Chinese language proved to be of major significance to her only much later in her life, on sabbatical in Hong Kong, as she squared up, as it were, to her 'Americanness'. Early on, though, despite speaking only English, her location amid Puerto Rican and African American friends and neighbours meant that 'assimilation' to 'dominant' white American society was marginal, even if the point of not speaking Chinese at home was in order to encourage inculturation. Very importantly for what she was to learn and represent throughout her life, Gale Yee reflects that she had to become 'American' long before she became aware of being 'Asian American'.

The Roman Catholic Church provided another identity-marker for the young Gale as she gradually became aware that her involvement in it made her marginal among Asian Americans who were then (if not now?), if Christian, largely Protestant in affiliation. It was as a young Roman Catholic that Gale became the first member of her family to go to college (two generations previously, her grandmother had been illiterate),[16] and she did so at first in her home town, as an English major and then New Testament postgraduate student at Loyola University (1975), before moving on to a relatively nearby city, though across the border into Canada. St Michael's is a Roman Catholic member college of the prestigious Toronto School of Theology, and it is there that she earned her doctorate in Hebrew Bible (1985), supervised by an Old Testament scholar of the Oblates of St Francis de Sales, who did his own studies at the Pontifical Biblical Institute (Rome). Although her education was in Catholic contexts, a factor that may have placed her on a certain kind of edge was that she was immersed both in the first wave of the ecumenical Taizé Community's incursions on youth culture (going there as early as 1971) and in charismatic renewal expressed in Roman Catholic mode. She was likely far from alone in at least that latter adventure – given that someone like Amos Yong reckons that something like 30 per cent of the Roman Catholic Church is charismatic[17] – but her being part of it, as well as pioneering the way across the North Atlantic to Taizé (which is in France), perhaps made for some kind of tension with at least aspects of her then tradition's 'official' positions and with its concerns with hierarchy. Consider, for example, the General Instruction on the Roman Missal's obsession with 'hierarchically arrayed' orders, its 'high culture' versions of liturgy (with Latin being lost from wider culture, never mind church, inevitably therefore becoming 'high'), and how what Vatican Council II calls a 'richer share' at the table of the word is presented in assembly.[18] These factors, in so far as they were present, may be relevant to Gale Yee's later claim that she was never bound to the Roman Church's doctrines of biblical authority, as what she was gripped by was the sense of the Bible's 'beauty and spirituality'.[19] No doubt her undergraduate love of English was also at play, as she describes her time doing doctoral work as one in which she was 'engrossed' by the turn from historical to literary criticism of the Bible. One way or another Gale also had a growing consciousness that her own affections were somehow different from that of Protestant colleagues in their particular struggles with texts of scripture and their authority. In any case, whatever made for her sense of freedom from whomsoever's immobilizing takes on biblical authority, she found her way to the 'hermeneutics of suspicion' which would prevail in distinctive ways through her work. Very interestingly, Yee doesn't seem to have much – or any? – direct dependence on her predecessor in the SBL president's chair, Elisabeth Schüssler Fiorenza, and her take on the hermeneutics of suspicion in *In Memory of Her*; *Bread Not Stone*, etc.[20] At the same time, something that her spirituality was giving her was an ethics that conspired with the hermeneutics of suspicion such that she was able to foreground ethical questions about biblical interpretation.

This ethical dimension has clearly always mattered to her and, importantly, she has been capable and self-critical enough to turn its questions
on herself: 'Whom does my interpretation help, whom does it hurt, and
whose interests does it serve?'[21]

Later factors

After college in Toronto, Gale Yee took up her first teaching post. It
was at another Roman Catholic institution back in her own country: the
College of St Thomas (latterly a university) in St Paul, in Minnesota, a
midwestern state almost adjacent to her own. While this is another city
relatively near Chicago, aspects of her life there were by this time quite
removed from the impoverished circumstances of her childhood – she
had a doctorate 'in the bag' and her teaching post opened up to her a very
different kind of 'class' identity. It is all the more notable, then, that class
has ever remained a central lens in Yee's work. For when at this time of
her life she got her doctoral work published – her first book, on Hosea[22]
– she might have gone on to write more commentaries in genres and with
optics well-established in the guild which she was qualified to join, and
for which the SBL has been a key avenue of distribution. While many
more books have followed – some on specific books of the Hebrew Bible
(Judges and Joshua most notably), and she has presided over a massive
commentary on the whole of the 'Old Testament' – her work has tended
to foreground hermeneutical and ethical concerns. Interestingly, it was
from her time at St Thomas that her major cross-over to the New Testament, with *Jewish Feasts in the Gospel of John*, came.[23] Most notably,
though, all of her publications after this time are marked by concerns that
came into focus for her during the late 1980s when she was in St Paul in
Minnesota. That is, she became a feminist.

Yee's Feminist Turn – Among Other Commitments

Two factors were important in Yee's feminist turn: teaching a unit on
'Women in Religion' in that first teaching post and then taking on the
co-chair of a section of the SBL, which she'd by now joined, on 'women
in the biblical world'. Before long, the SBL was also the setting of another
important group for Gale as in 1992 (so five years after Fiorenza was the
first woman president) SBL launched a section for women and 'racial ethnic
minorities' (known as CUREMP: the Committee on Underrepresented
Racial and Ethnic Minority in the Profession). A founding member, Yee

was chair by 1995. However, it was yet another setting that would provide what Gale Yee has called her 'official "coming out" as an Asian American',[24] and this was a presentation she made in 1994 at the sibling guild to the SBL, the American Academy of Religion. This came at the invitation of Kwok Pui-lan, herself on the cusp of publishing her own *Discovering the Bible in the Non-Biblical World*.[25] As it would turn out, Kwok and Yee would become colleagues as well as close friends.

Clearly, this sequence of events made for a time of some tumult for Gale Yee, as she poured great energy into groups that marked herself and others out in the guild, including those to do with Asian American as well as feminist identification. SBL was not the only setting for such energies, and the Pacific Asian and North American Asian Women in Theology and Ministry (PANAAWTM) became another important forum, as of 1998. Having become a feminist, she also needed more language to voice what she wanted to do and be. She was becoming, to project backwards later nomenclature, 'feminist and intersectional' as she was later to identify her terms,[26] but at the time she was conscious of finding herself with 'no models' for the kind of analysis that her particular intersectional perspective would involve.[27] Something of which she was evidently aware was the deficiency of certain forms of feminism that were at that time becoming prevalent: Yee notes that versions of feminism – 'second wave', 'liberal', and other descriptors – have 'primarily advanced the concerns of white, heterosexual, middle class, educated women and neglected the concerns of poor women of colour'.[28] So they were not to be for her. At the same time, in relation to her 'Asian Americanness' she became alert to her own unease with the term 'Asian American' being used as a kind of catch-all that covered all kinds of difference. The label runs the risk of women from diverse countries and cultures being lumped together, their diversity therefore being erased. For her own part, Yee has remained sensitive to the ways some women within the constructed grouping have long remained, as it were, unseen and voiceless and are still in search of self-determining terms.[29] We can, I think, expect Yee to delight in the like of the sounds of female Filipino feminist theologians adopting for themselves the descriptor 'babayi', especially in response to their own feelings of having being 'Deleted. Disgarded. Dismissed. Lost.'[30]

In her own case, the first PANAAWTM forum would also be decisive for Yee, and again with Kwok's involvement. Kwok gave Yee information about a post open at the seminary she had joined, the Episcopal Divinity School (EDS) in Cambridge, Massachusetts. The post was in 'feminist liberation theologies', and Yee later learnt that the seminary hoped that the job might be snapped up by a student fresh from study. Remarkably, Yee, by then a tenured professor elsewhere, applied and was given the job. She remained at EDS – 'one of the most anti-racist and anti-oppression seminaries in the US' – until her retirement. Her intersectional anthology is dedicated to EDS's faculty, staff and students, and includes a chapter dedicated to Kwok among other references to 'my good friend Kwok Pui Lan'.[31] While the anthology appeared after her retirement, it scoops up both early, formative papers from the fledgling Asian-American perspective, like 'Yin/Yang is Not Me', as well as quite recent developments, like Yee's advocacy in print for persons who are part of the LGBTQIA+ rainbow.[32]

Provocative Discussions

Within several years of her appointment at EDS, Yee published a major book which represents so much of what she would consistently champion: *Poor Banished Children of Eve: Women as Evil in the Hebrew Bible* (2003).[33] Started at St Thomas and completed at EDS its main title is an allusion to the Salve Regina, a devotion to Mary used in the Roman Catholic tradition – not least as a post-compline canticle, a kind of 'goodnight' – and apt in a way to the leave-taking Yee was making of that tradition as she began to belong in the Episcopal Church. All of her work from this point on is therefore fittingly regarded as 'Anglican', with the emphases in biblical interpretation in which she was flourishing making a very distinctive contribution to Anglican biblical scholarship at that time – and also since then.

Poor Banished Daughters of Eve, while focused in turn on Eve in Genesis, Hosea's lambast at Israel as 'faithless wife' of the Eternal, the lewd and promiscuous supposedly nymphomaniac sisters portrayed in Ezekiel, and 'the other woman' – a foreigner – castigated in Proverbs, is relentless in its application of Yee's 'ideological criticism'. Furthermore, hers is specifically 'materialist-feminist' in its vigilance, correlating sexist and racist ideologies with 'the modes of production that construct them'.[34] This involves an 'intrinsic' analysis of her selected biblical texts and how they receive, rework, and/or reinscribe the ideologies of the contexts from which they come. It then turns to 'extrinsic' analysis that reconstructs gender relationships, kinship arrangements, and other aspects of those contexts. Dense and detailed beyond my capacities to summarize its richness, the essential conviction that courses through and is demonstrated in this book is that 'gender-centred study' also demands alertness to 'the broader context of class, race, and colonialism'. Put another way, 'sexism interlocks'.[35] Moreover, sexism embedded in the symbol of 'evil women' in the Hebrew Bible is related to other pernicious operations of 'a hegemony of domination'. And while the book primarily tracks that in 'ancient Israel', it is because the Hebrew Bible is 'foundational in more ways than one' that its symbol-making disturbingly 'permeates Western consciousness'.[36]

Astonishingly, and akin to the 'modesty' Yee wants to suggest by 'towards' in her later *Towards an Asian-American Biblical Hermeneutics*, she also suggests that her 'provocative discussion'[37] in *Poor Banished Children of Eve* is 'a modest contribution' towards a critique of 'oppressive structures in our time' as these are able to be critiqued and resisted having been alerted to oppressions encoded in biblical writ.[38] In the moving conclusion of the book, she speaks of being 'overwhelmed by the urgency for an ethics of reading the biblical text that confronts injustice' (note: 'ethics' here being a reiteration of a well-embedded lens), and of her convictions about 'insidiously complex interconnections among religion – based on the biblical text – and the "-isms": sexism, racism, classism, colonialism, heterosexism, fundamentalism, and so forth'.[39] She could later assert quite plainly that 'isms in the text' are '*not* the Word of God'.[40]

It must be said that Yee's provocative discussions in *Poor Banished Children of Eve*, as they lever at various 'complex interconnections', do not readily make for 'popular' reading. The book is not geared at a mass market and nor was it likely to be met with a wide welcome given its acuity about problems afflicting not just guilds but contemporary societies, Western consciousness even, not to mention the Bible itself. The later more accessible anthology makes good of this, but even so at least two key distillations can be drawn from the earlier more technically demanding book. The distillation might still do at least some justice to the extraordinary power of Yee's analysis. The first thing to emphasize is her unflinching recognition that 'the Bible continues to be used to legitimate sinful realities'.[41] Then, 'the need to resist gender as the fundamental category of analysis'[42] because gender is only one form of oppression colluding with others. Wide swathes of the Anglican tradition Yee has made her own, both more 'conservative' and supposedly 'liberal' (consider: 'liberal feminism' again here) traditions have a long way to go in catching up with her, to put it mildly.

At least for the time being – because Yee remains highly energetic with her writing – *Poor Banished Children of Eve* and *Towards an Asian-American Biblical Hermeneutics* sit as kinds of 'book ends' of the robust approach to biblical study she has pioneered. The themes of the former continue to be deepened and developed by the latter, even as they opened out for a wider readership. And one pivotal point of connection between the two books perhaps starts with the back cover commendation of the earlier book by Norman Gottwald.[43] Gottwald praises *Poor Banished Children of Eve* as 'a high-water mark' for feminist entry into 'mainstream biblical studies' (the guild as was, of old) and then the first page of the later anthology relates how Gale Yee's classes at EDS typically began with Gottwald's 'self-inventory' in which students would be asked to identify factors at play when they interpret the Bible. Gender, ethnicity and social class are among a longer list of 18 factors; and whereas numerous times *Poor Banished Children of Eve* draws on technical points in Gottwald's scholarship, the intersectional anthology demonstrates Yee's command of clues from him which she has made completely her own.[44] She takes these up in an 'autobiographical approach' from which she has not shied, whatever the conventions of the academy.[45]

Portals into Questions

Key to that autobiographical approach are 'vignettes' that yield insight into Yee's own troika'd identity.[46] Two are especially striking.

The first is from a round of job interviews at the time between completing her thesis and her initial post. She remembers mainly male interviewers wanting to hear from her about the difference between her 'women's way' of reading the Bible and 'traditional' ways of reading.[47] She then notes that a decade later the question had shifted, to difference to do with ethnicity. Yee relates that on one occasion her retort to such a question was, 'What does a white German male interpretation of the biblical text look like?' She adds sagely, 'I did not get that job.'[48] But these experiences would be a key portal into her resistance to 'racial/ethnic pigeonholing',[49] and via reading Rey Chow's work on *The Protestant Ethnic and the Spirit of Capitalism* (2002) she become attuned to different kinds of pressure to mimic and imitate the dominant culture: *having* to imitate white norms, *wanting* to imitate them, and *being expected* by white culture to conform to suffocating constructs in a 'racial display' – what Chow significantly called 'coercive mimeticism'.[50]

The second key portal was alluded to earlier, arising during Yee's sabbatical in Hong Kong. Her application for an identity card disallowed her own answer to its question about her 'nationality': 'Chinese American'. It forced her to choose either one or the other, Chinese *or* American. She reflects, 'I had to choose, and I choose "American".'[51] Consequently, she could see herself to be 'an oddity in both contexts', a strange juxtaposition: an 'ethnic foreigner'.[52]

These two anecdotes, which Yee first presents in 'Yin/Yang is Not Me', she keeps talking about, drilling down into, in different terms, notably 'model minority' and 'perpetual foreigner'.[53] Among other things these terms enable Yee to articulate a poignant expression of what she terms 'racial melancholia' – that is, the inability to 'get over' certain kinds of loss that rear up in the space where the terms overlap. As she says, 'Asian Americans become almost, but not quite, "white" in US society: the model minority but also the perpetual foreigner', caught in the struggle between.[54] All of this gives clues as to what she looks for – and finds – in the Bible. Ruth, to give just one example.

Woman Warrior

I have charted above some of how Gale Yee came to discover the insight she has brought to biblical studies, and the experiences and methods she has fused to energize her own approach. Over time she has come to use the language of 'intersectionality' to consider and critique dynamics at play in both her own life and the biblical text. The language is found, for example, in the title of her SBL presidential address and the subtitle of her anthology in its shadow, among numerous other examples. Yee adopts the nomenclature from Kimberlé Crenshaw, an African American political theorist. But although the language was 'popularized' by Crenshaw, as Monica Jyotsna Melanchthon notes – for example, in Melanchthon's Indian context – others had long studied and spoken of 'dual marginalities', 'simultaneous oppressions' and such like, and in some instances had done so as far back in the past as the SBL's beginnings.[55] Yee's opting for a term coined and current in US-ian contexts is itself a reflection of Yee's own 'choice' to be American, a choice that her experience in Hong Kong forced on to her. However, although events and contexts forced her into certain choices, it would be a profound mistake to be given the impression that Gale Yee is one to be pushed around. This point can be related to a key image in Yee's work, the 'warrior woman'.

Notably, the image of a woman-warrior is one Yee first drew from popular culture – perhaps in the shadow of her finding no role models for herself in the guild? She describes then coming across a book by Maxine Hong Kingston, *The Warrior Woman*, a decade or more after its publication in 1976–7.[56] Kingston's book includes a focus on a figure from ancient Chinese culture, Fa Mulan. Yee started to make connections with her own experience of cinema, thinking of Fa Mulan as a sort of Wonder Woman (at least a *non-American* female counterpart for Superman).[57] Yee also came to realize that it was also from cinema, as well as radio, comics and other popular media, that she had absorbed her own earliest contact with Asian cultures, through films with Charlie

Chan and similar and television characters like the 'Flash Gordon' figure Ming the Merciless – which were in fact products of 'pushers of white American culture'.[58] Yee reveals that, while unwittingly engaging white culture's pushing of Asian stereotypes, she had adopted for herself the nickname of 'Dragon Lady', and even named her first car – a Plymouth Duster – 'Dusty Dragon'.[59] But she had also grown up with an interest in popular culture's females in the martial arts, crack karate and kung fu fighters.[60] So on reading Kingston's book certain thoughts were able to come together. On the one hand, Yee was equipped to recognize 'the American Orientalism that plays a significant part in the mass-marketed Disney production' *Mulan*,[61] and such like, but on the other hand that the Chinese Fa Mulan was 'a compelling, indomitable woman, who knew the martial arts and who, like me, was Chinese!'[62] Sorting through these images she was able to appraise herself as a kind of 'woman warrior', someone who – like Fa Mulan ('my avatar') – 'mightily fought against the evils that inflicted society and threatened her kinship community'.[63]

Although Yee has written about her car Dusty Dragon, one thing that I haven't been able to find in her writing is any explicit connection between the horse-riding woman-warrior figures she came to so appreciate and her own love of horse-riding. When I was her next-door neighbour, riding was Gale's main hobby; the way she took time out from the demands of her scholarly production and work in the seminary. I remember vividly a decoration on her front door that proclaimed 'I'd rather be riding!' Gale would go riding every opportunity she had, and in one notable story she related to her British-Australian neighbours (my family), she once took some kind of group riding holiday where, she later learned, other members of the group had included Princess Beatrice from the British royal family, whom Gale had not recognized, but found 'charming' – much to our mutual amusement.

Conclusion

My chapter has done no more – in fact it has done considerably less – than Gale Yee's own introductions to her work in her own words. But I hope it invites others to find out more about how she interprets the Bible to make room in the text for herself and for others who have been and are oppressed by the unholy trinity[64] of race, class and gender. What this chapter can also do is convey my great respect and affection for Gale, congratulate and thank her, and commend her fearless scholarship to others who yearn for more of the ethic of justice for which she struggles.

As a biblical scholar and in keeping with at least some conventions in her discipline, Gale does not always draw explicit theological conclusions from her textual interpretation. But in concluding I would like to briefly suggest two theological points of focus that I carry from Gale's work. Firstly, I am struck by how her explorations sometimes draw attention to names and faces: for example, 'Except for my face and name, none of the usual ethnic markers of being Asian fit me', 'What reminds me every day of my Asian identity are my name and my face. Something you hear, my name Yee, and something you see, my Chinese face.'[65] In certain work, she turns that focus on faces and names to search for glimpses of a womb-goddess good at midwifery in texts both intrinsic and extrinsic to the Hebrew Bible and mediated by oppressed women – women whose names (Shiphrah, Puah, in Exodus 1.15–21) mean 'beauty' and 'splendour'.[66] Gale Yee's attention to faces and names, harnessed by the power of her intersectional analysis, is an exciting and vital avenue for reflection on whose faces and names 'image' God. Not least the faces and names of othered, overlooked foreigners who midwife the work and praise of God (see Psalm 22.9; 71.6, texts to which Gale herself points).[67]

Secondly, while the Salve Regina, from which Gale Yee drew the title of her book *Poor Banished Children of Eve*, depicts Mary as 'clement, devoted, and sweet', these cloying descriptors are by no means the only way to understand Mary. The mother of Jesus is also depicted as a woman of immense courage, and of her 'courageous choice, a woman who proclaims God's vindication of those who need it, who survived poverty, flight and exile'.[68] Moreover, Luke's Gospel depicts Mary as a woman of courage with a strong song of justice in her lungs, whose Magnificat (Luke 1.46–55) 'insistently reminds us of her courage as she allies herself with the divine defeat of evil'.[69] We can see Gale Yee in the tradition of *this* kind of Mary when she writes that she 'will continue to "become" a "woman warrior" for the rest of my life'![70]

Notes

1 Vincent Wimbush was African American; in 2018 another African American, Brian Blount, was elected. Before that, the Latinx Fernando F. Segovia was elected in 2014. Yee was the first Asian American as well as the first woman of colour in 2019.

2 Gregory L. Cuéllar, 'Reading Yee's Intersectionality as an Intervening Counterdiscourse to Whiteness', *The Bible and Critical Theory*, 17.1 (2021): 4.

3 Gale A. Yee, *Towards an Asian American Biblical Hermeneutics: An Intersectional Anthology* (Eugene: Cascade, 2021), 81.

4 Yee, *Intersectional Anthology*, 65–84; Gale A. Yee, 'Thinking Intersectionally: Gender, Race, Class, and the Etceteras of Our Discipline', *Journal of Biblical Literature*, 139. 1 (2020): 7–26.

5 For some of her own perspectives on at least psalms in preaching and worship, see Gale A. Yee, 'Cast Your Burden on the Lord: Praying the Psalms', in *A Biblical Study Guide for Equal Pulpits* (Eugene: Cascade, 2022), 27–39.

6 Yee, *Intersectional Anthology*, 7.

7 Yee, *Intersectional Anthology*, 5, 56, and Gale A. Yee, 'The Process of Becoming a Woman Warrior from the Slums', in *Asian and Asian-American Women in Theology and Religion: Embodying Knowledge*, ed. Kwok Pui-lan (New York: Palgrave, 2020), 15–29 (26). I note that Yee's long-time colleague Carter Heyward refers to the same triad as an 'unholy trinity'. See Carter Heyward, *She Flies On: A White Southern Christian Debutante Wakes Up* (New York: Seabury Press, 2017), 29.

8 Yee, *Intersectional Anthology*, 122.

9 See Yee, *Intersectional Anthology*, 54–9.

10 For example, Yee, *Intersectional Anthology*, 85, cf. 96.

11 https://en.wikipedia.org/wiki/Gale_Storm (accessed 29.1.2024).

12 The first time I wrote to her, I did so to 'Gail', never having heard of a Gale. This is how I learned about her name.

13 Yee, 'Process of Becoming', 16.

14 Yee, 'Process of Becoming', 16.

15 Yee, *Intersectional Anthology*, 56, cf. 66.

16 Yee, *Intersectional Anthology*, 55.

17 See Amos Yong, *Renewing Christian Theology: Systematics for a Global Christianity* (Waco: Baylor University Press, 2014), 5.

18 See, for example, *The Liturgy Documents, Vol. 1*, ed. David Lysik (Chicago: Literary Training Publications, 2004), 14 (for *Sacrosanctum Concilium* no. 51), 40 (for the entrance of the fetish with 'hierarchical array' in the General Instruction of the Roman Missal, notable not least for its massive amplification of what are only found in smaller traces in *Sacrosanctum concilium*).

19 Yee, *Intersectional Anthology*, 3.

20 Elisabeth Schüssler Fiorenza, *In Memory of Her: A Feminist Theological Reconstruction of Christian Origins* (New York: Crossroad/Herder & Herder, reprint edn, 1994), and *Bread Not Stone: The Challenge of Feminist Biblical Interpretation* (Boston: Beacon Press, anniversary edn, 1995).

21 Yee, *Intersectional Anthology*, 3.

22 Gale A. Yee, *Composition and Tradition in the Book of Hosea: A Redaction Critical Investigation* (Atlanta: Scholars Press, 1987).

23 Gale A. Yee, *Jewish Feasts in the Gospel of John* (Collegeville: Michael Glazier, 1989). Although understandable enough for one who became a primarily Hebrew Bible scholar, it is interesting to note that Yee's intersectional anthology includes just one reference to Jesus: 133.

24 Yee, *Intersectional Anthology*, 4.

25 Kwok Pui-lan, *Discovering the Bible in the Non-biblical World* (Maryknoll: Orbis Books, 1995).

26 Yee, *Intersectional Anthology*, 4.

27 Yee, *Intersectional Anthology*, 5.

28 Yee, *Intersectional Anthology*, 16.

29 Yee, *Intersectional Anthology*, 57, cf. 63; Yee, 'Process of Becoming', 18.

30 See Cristina Lledo Gomez, 'Deleted and Reclaimed Borders: Embracing My Native Self', in *Bordered Bodies, Bothered Voices: Native and Migrant Theologies*,

ed. Jione Havea (Eugene: Pickwick, 2022), 119–38. Notably Jione Havea is also the guest editor of the special issue of *The Bible and Critical Theory* referred to in other footnotes.

31 Yee, *Intersectional Anthology*, x, 1, 180.

32 The intersectional approach discussed in this chapter is key in the focus Yee enlarges to advocate for queer siblings, taking Isaiah 56.1–8 as a key to 'biblical affirmation' (Yee, *Intersectional Anthology*, 165) and 'biblical support' (175) for acceptance of queer folk and which she turns to stand up against a few 'scare texts' that are too commonly summoned to condemn queer people. The 'stunning reversal' (166) she tracks in the passage engages her common theme of 'foreigners' but places the 'eunuchs' of Isaiah adjacent to them. Notably, in the shadow of comments later in this chapter about other foci in Yee's work, she emphasizes how eunuchs are given the divine promise of a 'name' (166, 176) as, contrary to what 'racist bullies and gay bashers' may spit at them, they may 'hear the alternate voice of Third Isaiah who proclaims a newness in God's work of salvation' and welcomes them into the 'house of prayer for *all* peoples' (175, emphasis in original).

33 Gale A. Yee, *Poor Banished Children of Eve: Women as Evil in the Hebrew Bible* (Minneapolis: Fortress Press, 2003).

34 Yee, *Children of Eve*, 4.

35 Yee, *Children of Eve*, 7.

36 Yee, *Children of Eve*, 4.

37 Yee, *Children of Eve*, back cover.

38 Yee, *Children of Eve*, 7.

39 Yee, *Children of Eve*, 164–5.

40 Yee, *Intersectional Anthology*, 3.

41 Yee, *Children of Eve*, 165.

42 Yee, *Children of Eve*, 166.

43 Yee, *Children of Eve*, back cover, and see also index, at 286, and then 245–6.

44 Yee, *Intersectional Anthology*, 1, 11.

45 It would seem that across the guild's long history not many presidents had made their autobiographies key to their own methods. Notably it was not until 2019 that the society published a collection to which Yee was one of the seven contributors: *Women and the Society of Biblical Literature, Biblical Scholarship in North America*, ed. Nicole L. Tilford (Atlanta: SBL Press, 2019). Biographies – notably of women – feature in that book.

46 Yee, *Intersectional Anthology*, 5.

47 Yee, *Intersectional Anthology*, 65–6.

48 Yee, *Intersectional Anthology*, 66.

49 Yee, *Intersectional Anthology*, 67.

50 Yee, *Intersectional Anthology*, 67.

51 Yee, *Intersectional Anthology*, 69.

52 Yee, *Intersectional Anthology*, 70.

53 Yee, *Intersectional Anthology*, 87–94.

54 Yee, *Intersectional Anthology*, 112, with the 'almost' revealed by constant microaggressions, like the question 'Where are you really from?' (e.g. 7).

55 Monica Jyotsna Melancththon, 'Widows: Tamar (Gen 38), Judith, Etcetera', *The Bible and Critical Theory*, 17.1 (2021): 55–73 (56).

56 Yee, *Intersectional Anthology*, 79, 123.

57 Yee, *Intersectional Anthology*, 123; Yee, 'Process of Becoming', 15.

58 Yee, *Intersectional Anthology*, 76.

59 Yee, *Intersectional Anthology*, 75.

60 Yee, *Intersectional Anthology*, 76.

61 Yee, *Intersectional Anthology*, 124.

62 Yee, 'Process of Becoming', 15.

63 Yee, 'Process of Becoming', 16, 15.

64 Here I follow Heyward. See note 6 above.

65 Yee, *Intersectional Anthology*, 66, 77.

66 Yee, 'Midwives in Egypt, Mesopotamia, and Ancient Israel: An Intersectional Investigation', *Biblical Theology Bulletin*, 52.3 (2022): 152.

67 Yee, 'Midwives in Egypt': 157.

68 Ann Loades, *Grace is Not Faceless: Reflections on Mary*, ed. Stephen Burns (London: Darton, Longman and Todd, 2021), 49.

69 Loades, *Grace is Not Faceless*, 90.

70 Yee, 'Process of Becoming', 23.

Afterword

PENIEL RAJKUMAR

'Now that you know us theologically ...'

As early as in 1974 the inspirational John S. Mbiti drew our attention to the shift in the gravity of World Christianity towards new centres in Africa, Asia and Latin America and raised an important point about the theological implications of this shift:

> Theologians from the New (or younger) churches [of the South] have made their pilgrimages to the theological learning of the older churches [of the North]. We had no alternative. We have eaten theology with you; we have drunk theology with you; we have dreamed theology with you ... We know you theologically. The question is. Do you know us theologically? Would you like to know us theologically?[1]

Anglican Theology: Postcolonial Perspectives, through its eclectic assemblage of essays, can be understood as offering answers for all those who might be inclined to positively respond to the question Mbiti raised almost 50 years ago – 'Would you like to know us theologically?' Bearing witness to the insistently postcolonial character of Anglican theology in a context now often described in terms of 'World Christianities', the book in many ways eschews the classic postcolonial question of Gayatri Chakravorty Spivak, 'Can the subaltern speak?'[2] Instead, what seems implicit throughout this volume is the question – 'Can we listen to the voices of the subalterns?' – if we understand the broad term 'subalterns' in the context of this book as those 'Anglican theologians little-known or neglected in the north and west', to use the editors' own words from the Introduction. It is not that these theologians have not 'spoken'. They have indeed been some of the most erudite and prophetic voices of our time. However, whether they have been accepted as representing the voice of contemporary Anglicanism is the deeper concern that foregrounds this volume. The unspoken invitation at the heart of this book is to listen – to hear both the words captured in this volume and beyond, especially paying attention to the loud silence that surrounds the acceptance of tri-continental theologians as representatives of contemporary Anglicanism.

In my opinion, the book accomplishes two important things.

Reweaving the Theological Mat of Anglicanism

Firstly, the book reweaves the theological mat of Anglican theology today by pulling together diverse strands of theologizing from across the Anglican Communion, thereby co-creating a space that can draw us together for renewed dialogue and debates on the scope, style and substance of Anglican theology(ies) in a postcolonial world.

This reweaving of the theological mat of Anglican theology is also in some ways a cartographical exercise because it simultaneously involves redrawing the theological map of Anglican theologies by highlighting and celebrating the polycentric nature of Anglicanism. The idea of cartography or map-making that I have in mind is not necessarily the politically expedient, imperial geo-political fabrications forcefully foisted 'by the arbitrariness of a colonial mapmaker's pen',[3] which continue to divide people and distort futures on the basis of colonial legacies. The idea of cartography that I have in mind is more akin to decolonial mapping practices of indigenous communities who offer a more dynamic mapping of the world we inhabit, rather than a static one. This provides us with new methods of relating to our worlds with a focus on relationality and the recovery of what has been erased and forgotten – all of which are quintessential to a reimagination of Anglican theological landscapes vis-à-vis the witness, words and writings of the people whom they shaped.

Through this reweaving of the theological mat and the redrawing of the theological map of Anglicanism, the various contributions in this book help us to address a persistent impasse in Anglican theology. Anyone attentive to the changing dynamics of global Anglicanism will recognize that though global Anglicanism has now found home and host in the tricontinental countries (particularly Africa and Asia, without failing to remember Latin America and Oceania), this demographic shift has not necessarily led to a renewed understanding of Anglican theology. There seems to be a rather dispassionate contentment with rehearsing Eurocentric and monologic ways of conflating Anglicanism with England and Englishness. This impasse is now long recognized as 'a deficiency that needs to be addressed'.[4]

Overcoming this impasse needs passionate, (im)patient and perseverant chipping away at the grand wall of epistemic imperialism that still continues to divide Christian theologies emerging from the West and

North as 'mainstream' and the tricontinental world as 'contextual'. This epistemic imperialism that is predicated by the claims to universality and normativity of these 'mainstream theologies' stems from, and has in turn sustained, historical injustices. It has created a theological divide that has privileged the 'objective' over the experiential. In contexts of such epistemic imperialism the acts of reweaving the mat and redrawing the maps of our theologies can be significant steps towards creating and inhabiting a renewed Anglican theological world – which, not only recognizes, but also seeks to reverse, the presence, pervasiveness and persistence of colonialism (both in the past and the present) as not just a political reality but also an epistemological and theological one.

All this focus on reweaving the mat and redrawing the map of Anglican theologies so that it corresponds more coherently to the demographic shift of global Anglicanism, should not distract us into thinking of this thrust towards the postcolonial reimagination of Anglican theologies as something dictated by numerical considerations alone. Rather, the thrust here is on breaking the monologic around Anglican theologies and affirming their pluriform nature by holding together both the polycentric (multi-centred) as well as the polysemic (multi-layered) nature of global Anglicanism, which should lead us to my next point.

Diversifying the Menu of Anglican Theology

Spreading out the rewoven mat of Anglican theologies is also an invitation for a feast. In many ways, *Anglican Theology: Postcolonial Perspectives* is undoubtedly a feast, to put it in clichéd terms. In several cultures, including my own, a mat also provides the ritual and communal space for common celebration, on which rural communities bring together their various gifts in the context of a community meal and collaborate in its preparation.

In line with this image of the mat and feast, the second important thing about this volume is that it calls us to diversify the menu of the feast of Anglican theology by interrupting its ongoing 'whiteness'. Kehinde Andrews, in his book *The New Age of Empire: How Racism and Colonialism Still Rule the World*, reminds us that in a neocolonial world 'diversifying those dining on the spoils of the empire does not change the menu'.[5] This likely also holds true for Anglican theology. As I mentioned earlier, one of the important challenges that global theologies have to address today is the question of epistemic imperialism. Doing theology amid a context identified as that of the empire is in some ways about de-mythologizing the persistent 'Eurocentric normativity' of our theological churning – which has been sustained in some ways by the empires of our times.

In many places around the world theology continues to serve as the surrogate space for the rehabilitation of colonialism, even after the departure of colonial regimes and imperial missions. It does so by being caught in a 'first in Europe and then elsewhere'[6] frame of thinking, which reinstates the West as the theological world's centre of gravity. In this theological cosmos, Christian theologies from Asia, Africa, Latin America and Oceania are rendered as perpetual latecomers and constant learners in doing theology, because their ways of thinking and doing theology do not mimic the logic of the empire. The price of participation in this theological economy is therefore self-erasure, and coerced unlearning of diverse methods and modes of thinking about God and the world. In such contexts, the challenge that emerges from the various prophetic voices that have been featured in this volume is what the South African theologian Vuyani Vellem felicitously calls 'unthinking the west',[7] where we seek to free all forms of theologizing from the stranglehold of epistemic imperialism. This task necessitates moving beyond our current failure and fatigue – both in terms of our imagination and action – to cultivate more global understandings of the Anglican theological tradition.

Where Next?

Thus far, having learnt a bit more of some of the leading theologians of our times, and (to use Mbiti's phrase) having come to 'know them theologically', how do we sit with them on the rewoven mat of Anglican theology and dine with them from a diversified theological menu, so that together we may dream of a reimagined Anglican theological future?

Dreaming of a reimagined Anglican theological future in our times necessitates a new Pentecost experience. Very often the theological framework from which Christians reflect on diversity is that of the Pentecost, using the language of speaking in many tongues. However, the Pentecost experience that I am alluding to is a different one. This Pentecost experience will be marked not by the gift of 'speaking in many tongues', but by the gift of 'listening with many ears'. It is an invitation to listen – to hear both the words and beyond – the sighs, smiles, struggles and the silences that punctuate the lives of those who continue to be undermined and sidelined by the political economy of global theologies.

The Pentecost experience of listening can be part of a redemptive politics of transforming our theologizing. Public theologian Luke Bretherton interprets listening as 'a way for churches to practice humility in their negotiation of political life'.[8] According to Bretherton, listening serves as an 'antidote to self-glorification, idolatry, and regimes of control' and can serve as a therapy for the self-love or pride that attempts to 'pursue illusions of self-sufficiency both in relation to God and neighbour'.[9] As a constitutive element of hospitality, listening 'trusts and gives space and time to those who are excluded from the determination of space and time by the existing hegemony'.[10] If the sacred and shared space of Anglican theological articulation has to address the issue of division and discrimination we may need to embrace the challenge of becoming a listening space which is not 'over-dominated' and over-determined by the voices of the dominant and powerful, that drown out all other voices, or predetermine how one can speak or what one may say.[11] The imminent challenge may be to become this community of the new Pentecost – and learn the gift of many ears – and let ourselves be re-signified by the voices and visions of the 'others'.

Dreaming of a reimagined Anglican theological future may also require an intentional politics of decentring the West from the centre of Anglican theological imagination. This requires moving beyond the preferred framework of difference – a domesticating discourse that creates space for other theologies while still recentring the West. The framework of difference often manages to recentre the West as being generously tolerant of theologies that are different. The result is a neo-orientalism marked by the romanticization of these theologies, while not letting the methods and motivations of these theologies to critique and challenge Eurocentric and Anglicized ways of doing theology. In this logic, theologies from Asia, Africa, Latin America and the Pacific become artefacts and exhibits which are included in the showcases of postcolonial generosity. The inclusion of such theologies has little more use than to serve as the waters that the Pilates of today use to wash their hands from their complicity in the empire. What we need today is a robust understanding of how the construction of difference by Christianity in different historical epochs is done, 'taking into consideration the contestation of meaning, the shaping of the imagination, and the changing power relations'.[12] As Kwok Pui-lan reminds us, understandings of difference are often 'constituted and produced in concrete situations, often with significant power differentials'.[13] This should prompt us to question whether the appreciation of difference in our Christian theological enterprise is embedded in a matrix of power which has usurped the language of difference only to tolerate 'other' theologies, and not necessarily to decentre Europe and the West from the epistemic core of Christian theology.

If this is the case we need a politics of decentring that is much more radical. Decolonizing and unthinking the West in Anglican theological imagination and production need to be rooted in a genuine kenosis and metanoia – resulting in the giving up of power, space and privilege by those in positions of domination. Otherwise, Anglican theological processes become rehearsal grounds for what has been called the original sin of imperial Christianity – namely 'Host-ility' – the perpetual will to host always.

As I conclude this Afterword, the time for one group of Anglicans to play hosts of Anglican theology is now over. The challenge today is to learn to be mutual guests on the rewoven mats of Anglican theologies and feast on the diversified menus of Anglican theologies. On the one hand, this can be risky because it entails losing ourselves fully to the gift that the 'other' is and brings. But, on the other hand, it can also be redemptive because in this process of losing ourselves to the other also lies the possibility for us to fully find ourselves and free ourselves to live into the bonds of affection that bind us as Anglicans. It is to these bonds, which can serve as the umbilical paths towards new identities and beginnings, that all Anglican theologies in our postcolonial context should point and lead to. As such, this book is a step along this path.

Notes

1 John Mbiti, 'Theological Impotence and the Universality of the Church', *Mission Trends 3: Third World Theologies*, eds Gerald Anderson and Thomas Stransky (New York: Paulist, 1976), 16–17. This article first appeared in *Lutheran World*, 21, no. 3, 1974.

2 This is the title of Spivak's essay, which appeared in *Marxism and the Interpretation of Culture*, eds Cary Nelson and Lawrence Grossberg (London: Macmillan, 1988).

3 Shashi Tharoor, *Inglorious Empire: What The British Did To India* (New Delhi: Penguin Books, 2016), 248.

4 Mark Chapman, *Anglican Theology* (Edinburgh: T&T Clark, 2012), 172.

5 Kehinde Andrews, *The New Age of Empire: How Racism and Colonialism Still Rule the World* (London: Penguin, 2021), xix.

6 Dipesh Chakrabarthy, *Provincialising Europe: Postcolonial Thought and Historical Difference* (Princeton: Princeton University Press, new edn, 2009), 3.

7 Vuyani Vellem, 'Un-thinking the West: The Spirit of Doing Black Theology of Liberation in Decolonial Times', *HTS Teologiese Studies*, 73.3 (2017): 1–9 (2).

8 Luke Bretherton, *Church and Contemporary Politics: The Conditions and Possibilities of Faithful Witness* (Oxford: Wiley-Blackwell, 2009), 214.

9 Bretherton, *Church and Contemporary Politics*, 214.

10 Bretherton, *Church and Contemporary Politics*, 215.

11 Bretherton, *Church and Contemporary Politics*, 215.

12 Kwok Pui-lan, *Postcolonial Imagination and Feminist Theology* (London: SCM Press, 2005), 198, 199. Kwok is referring here to the work of Rey Chow, *The Protestant Ethnic and the Spirit of Capitalism* (New York: Columbia University Press, 2002).

13 Kwok, *Postcolonial Imagination and Feminist Theology*, 205.

Appendix

Suggested Further Reading

The Anglican theologians who are subjects of this book used different media to do their theology and they have had different kinds of opportunities to publish. All bar one have made numerous contributions to academic publishing in their own and wider contexts. So some classes and groups using this book may go in search of primary readings by the subjects themselves, or more about them by others. The following list of suggested Further Reading points to just some of the subjects' work. In the most part the suggestions are short chapters and articles suitable for reading alongside the chapters in this book. Inevitably, depending on readers' access to theological libraries and online publication of journals, some readings may be easier to find than others. Other possibilities may be found. Unless stated, the author of the selection is the subject.

Denise Ackermann

'"Take Up a Taunt Song": Women, Lament and Healing in South Africa', in *Reconstruction: The WCC Assembly Harare 1998 and the Churches in Southern Africa*, ed. Leny Lagerwerf (Meinema: Zoetermeer, 1998), pp. 133–50.

'Lamenting Tragedy From "The Other Side"', in *Sameness and Difference: Problems and Potentials in South African Civil Society*, eds James R. Cochrane and Bastienne Klein (Washington, DC Council for Research in Values and Philosophy, 2000), pp. 213–42.

Naim Ateek

'The Future of Palestinian Christianity', in *The Forgotten Faithful: A Window into the Lives and Witness of Christians in the Holy Land*, eds Naim Ateek, Cedar Duaybis and Maurine Tobin (Jerusalem: Sabeel Ecumenical Liberation Theology Center, 2007), pp. 136–50.

'Christ is the Key', in *A Palestinean Theology of Liberation: The Bible, Justice and the Palestine-Israel Conflict* (Maryknoll: Orbis Books, 2017), pp. 83–104.

Mukti Barton

'I am Black and Beautiful', *Black Theology: An International Journal*, 2.2 (2004): 167–87.

'Wrestling with Imperial Patriarchy', *Feminist Theology*, 21.1 (2012): 7–25.

Burgess Carr

'The Mission of the Moratorium', *Occasional Bulletin of the Missionary Research Library*, 25.2 (1975).
'African Churches in Conflict', *The Harvard Crimson* (18 April 1978). At https://www.thecrimson.com/article/1978/4/18/african-churches-in-conflict-pchurch-state-relations/ (accessed 29.1.2024).

Verna J. Dozier

Richard H. Schmidt, 'Verna Dozier (b. 1929): Re-envisioning the Laity', in *Glorious Companions: Five Centuries of Anglican Spirituality* (Grand Rapids: Eerdmans, 2002), pp. 287–97.
Cynthia L. Shattuck and Fredrica Harris Thompsett, 'Called to be Saints', in *Confronted by God: The Essential Verna Dozier* (New York: Seabury Books, 2006), pp. 133–60.

Julius Gathogo

'Afro-Pentecostalism as the Dominant Ecclesiastical Paradigm in the Twenty-first Century', in *The Postcolonial Church: Bible, Theology, and Mission*, eds R. S. Wufula, Esther Mombo and Joseph Wandera (Alameda: Borderless Press, 2016), pp. 77–92.
'Theology and Reconstruction in Africa', in *Routledge Handbook of African Theology*, ed. Elias Kifon Bongmba (Abingdon: Routledge, 2020), pp. 194–209.

Winston Halapua

'Moana Waves, Oceania and Homosexuality', in *Other Voices, Other Worlds: The Global Church Speaks Out on Homosexuality*, ed. Terry Brown (New York: Church Publishing, 2006), pp. 26–39.
'Theomoana: Towards a Tinkanga Theology', in *Talanoa Rhythmns: Voices from Oceania*, ed. Nasili Vaka'uta (Wellington: Massey University Press, 2010), 69–101.

Kwok Pui-lan

'Woman, Dogs and Crumbs: Constructing a Postcolonial Discourse', in *Discovering the Bible in the Non-biblical World* (Maryknoll: Orbis Books, 1995), pp. 71–83.
'Engendering Christ', in *Postcolonial Imagination and Feminist Theology* (London: SCM Press, 2005), pp. 168–85.

Jaci Maraschin

'Culture, Spirit and Worship', in *Beyond Colonial Anglicanism: The Anglican Communion in the Twenty-first Century*, eds Ian T. Douglas and Kwok Pui-lan (New York: Church Publishing, 2000), pp. 318–37.
'Worship and the Excluded', in *Liberation Theology and Sexuality*, ed. Marcella Althaus-Reid (London: SCM Press, 2009), pp. 163–78.

John S. Mbiti

'Some African Concepts of Christology', in *Christ and the Younger Churches: Theological Contributions from Asia, Africa and Latin America* (London: SPCK, 1972), pp. 51–62.
'Christianity and Traditional Religions in Africa', *International Review of Mission*, 59 (1970): 430–40.

Jesse Mugambi

'Christological Paradigms in African Christianity', in *Jesus in African Christianity: Experimentation and Diversity in African Christology*, eds Jesse Mugambi and Laurenti Magesa (Nairobi: Acton, 1998), pp. 137–61.
'Theological Method in African Christianity', in *Theological Method and Aspects of Worship in African Christianity*, ed. Mary Getui (Nairobi: Acton, 2000), pp. 5–40.

Nyameko Barney Pityana

'Towards a Black Theology for Britain', in *Theology in the City: A Theological Response to 'Faith in the City'*, ed. Anthony Harvey (London: SPCK, 1989), pp. 98–113.
'Culture and the Church: The Quest for a New Ecclesiology', in *Being Church in South Africa Today*, eds Barney Pityana and Charles Villa-Vincencio (Cape Town: South African Council of Churches, 1995), pp. 87–99.

Harry Sawyerr

'What is African Theology?', in *The Practice of Presence: Shorter Writings of Harry Sawyerr*, ed. John Parratt (Grand Rapids: Eerdmans, 1996), pp. 85–99.
Andrew F. Walls, 'The Significance of Harry Sawyerr', in *The Cross-Cultural Process in Christian History: Studies in the Transmission and Appropriation of Faith* (Maryknoll: Orbis Books, 2002), pp. 165–73.

Jenny Te Paa-Daniel

'Women's Leadership Development for the Anglican Communion: Oh Lord, How Long Must We Wait …?', in *Anglican Women on Church and Mission*, eds Kwok Pui-lan et al. (Norwich: Canterbury Press, 2012), pp. 77–96.
'*Esse Quam Videri* … to Be and Not to Seem', in *Vulnerability and Resilience: Body and Liberating Theologies*, ed. Jione Havea (Lanham: Lexington Books, 2020), pp. 199–212.

Miroslav Volf

'Exclusion', in *Exclusion and Embrace: A Theological Exploration of Identity, Otherness, and Reconciliation* (Nashville: Abingdon, 1996), pp. 57–98.
'The One God and the Holy Trinity', in *Allah: A Christian Response* (San Francisco: HarperCollins, 2011), pp. 127–48.

Gerald West

'The Difference It Makes with Whom we Read', in *The Academy of the Poor: Toward a Dialogical Reading of the Bible* (Sheffield: Sheffield Academic Press, 1999), pp. 21–34.

'(Southern) African Anglican Biblical Interpretation: A Postcolonial Project', *Journal of Anglican Studies*, 8.2 (2010): 140–64.

'The Bible', in *The Oxford Handbook of Anglican Studies*, ed. Mark D. Chapman, Sathianathan Clarke and Martyn Percy (New York: Oxford, 2015), pp. 359–71.

Gale Yee

'Thinking Intersectionally: Gender, Race, Class and the Etceteras of Our Discipline', *Journal of Biblical Literature*, 139.1 (2020): 7–26.

'The Process of Becoming a Woman Warrior from the Slums', in *Asian and Asian American Women in Theology and Religion*, ed. Kwok Pui-lan (New York: Palgrave Macmillan, 2020), pp. 15–29.

Index of Names and Subjects

www.ingramcontent.com/pod-product-compliance
Lightning Source LLC
Chambersburg PA
CBHW032013040325
22965CB00007B/33